Cyber Bullying

Cyber Bullying

Bullying in the Digital Age

Robin M. Kowalski, Ph.D.,
Susan P. Limber, Ph.D., and
Patricia W. Agatston, Ph.D.

Blackwell
Publishing

BLACKWELL PUBLISHING
350 Main Street, Malden, MA 02148–5020, USA
9600 Garsington Road, Oxford OX4 2DQ, UK
550 Swanston Street, Carlton, Victoria 3053, Australia

First published 2008 by Blackwell Publishing Ltd

1   2008

Library of Congress Cataloging-in-Publication Data

Kowalski, Robin M.
   Cyber bullying : bullying in the digital age / Robin M. Kowalski,
Susan P. Limber, and Patricia W. Agatston.
      p. cm.
   Includes bibliographical references and index.
   ISBN 978-1-4051-5991-3 (hardcover : alk. paper) — ISBN 978-1-4051-5992-0
(pbk. : alk. paper)   1. Cyberbullying.   2. Bullying.   I. Limber, Sue.
   II. Agatston, Patricia W.   III. Title.
   HV6773.K69 2008
   302.3′4—dc22

                                                                      2007019835

A catalogue record for this title is available from the British Library.

Set in 10.5 on 12.5pt Minion
by SNP Best-set Typesetter Ltd., Hong Kong
Printed and bound in Singapore
by Markono Print Media Pte Ltd

The publisher's policy is to use permanent paper from mills that operate a
sustainable forestry policy, and which has been manufactured from pulp processed
using acid-free and elementary chlorine-free practices. Furthermore, the publisher
ensures that the text paper and cover board used have met acceptable environmental
accreditation standards.

For further information on
Blackwell Publishing, visit our website at
www.blackwellpublishing.com

This book is dedicated to the children who we believe deserve to feel safe from bullying, in both the real and the virtual worlds.

Contents

〜

Foreword

～

October 7, 2003, will always be the day that divides my life. Before that day, my son Ryan was alive. A sweet, gentle, and lanky 13-year-old fumbling his way through early adolescence and trying to establish his place in the often confusing and difficult social world of middle school. After that day, my son would be gone forever. A death by suicide. Some would call it bullycide or even cyber bullycide. I just call it a huge hole in my heart that will never heal.

Ryan's young teen life included swimming, camping, skateboarding, biking, snowboarding, playing computer games and instant messaging. A typical array of "healthy" and "normal" teen activities . . . or so it seemed. My son loved being online, staying connected with his friends after the school day and throughout the summer. But, during the summer of 2003, significantly more time was spent online, mainly instant messaging. I was concerned and felt compelled to remind him of our internet safety rules.

No IMing/chatting with strangers
No giving any personal information (name/address/phone) to strangers
No sending pictures to strangers
No secret passwords

Our last rule was a safety one. I told my two older children that they had to use the password I gave them for any accounts they signed up. I promised I would not read personal messages or spy on them but, "God forbid you don't follow the first few rules and you just disappear one day. I will want instant access to all of your activities online." Never in a million years did I imagine this rule would someday end up becoming the key to unlocking the mystery of why my son took his own life.

A few days after his funeral, I logged on to his AOL IM account because that was the one place he spent most of his time during the last few months. I logged on to see if there were any clues to his final action. It was in that safe world of being somewhat anonymous that several of his classmates told me of the bullying and cyber bullying that took place during the months leading up to his suicide. One boy had bullied Ryan since 5th grade, and briefly befriended him after Ryan stood up to him in an afterschool brawl. My son the comedian shared an embarrassing and humorous moment with his new friend. The "friend" twisted this information into a rumor that Ryan had something done to him and, therefore, Ryan must be gay. The rumor and taunting continued beyond that school day . . . well into the night and throughout the summer of 2003. My son approached a pretty, "popular" girl from his school online and worked on establishing a relationship with her, I'm sure as a surefire way to squash the "gay" rumor.

When the 8th grade school year started up again, Ryan approached his new girlfriend in person. I'm sure he was never prepared to handle what happened next. In front of her friends, she told him he was just a loser and that she did not want anything to do with him. She said she had been only joking online. He found out that she and her friends thought it would be funny to make him think she liked him and to get him to say a lot of personal, embarrassing things. She copied and pasted their private IM exchanges into ones with her friends. They all had a good laugh at Ryan's expense.

Now certainly my son was not the first boy in history to be bullied and have his heart crushed by a pretty girl's rejection. But when I discovered a folder filled with IM exchanges and further interviewed his classmates, I realized that technology was being utilized as a weapon far more effective and far reaching than the simple tools we had as kids.

It's one thing to be bullied and humiliated in front of a few kids. It's one thing to feel rejection and have your heart crushed by a girl. But it must be a totally different experience, compared to a generation ago, to have these hurts and humiliation witnessed by a far larger, online adolescent audience. I believe my son would have survived these incidents of bullying and humiliation if they had taken place before the advent of computers and the internet. But I believe there are few of us who would have had the resiliency and stamina to sustain such a nuclear level attack on our feelings and reputation as a young teen in the midst of rapid physical and emotional changes and raging hormones. I believe bullying through technology has the effect of accelerating and amplifying the hurt to levels that will probably result in a rise in teen suicide rates. Recent statistics indicate that, indeed, teen suicide is on the rise again after many years of declining rates.

My son was an early casualty and his death an early warning to our society that we'd better pay close attention to how our children use technology. We need to study this new societal problem with a sense of urgency and great diligence. We must also be swift and deliberate in our lawmaking and social policy development when it comes to protecting our youth from the misuse of technology against them and amongst them.

This book will prove to be an invaluable resource. It will level set the reader about what bullying is and its harmful effects. Then it will explore the increasing ways technology is utilized to extend bullying behavior well into cyberspace. It brings us up to speed on the latest research findings and maps out very concrete preventative and responsive actions for both parents and educators.

John Halligan, Ryan's Dad
http://www.RyanPatrickHalligan.org

Preface

〰

We decided to write about cyber bullying after working together on various bullying prevention efforts and conducting preliminary research on cyber bullying over the past several years. One day we came face to face with an extreme example of cyber bullying that occurred in a suburban school district. Patti Agatston can still remember calling Sue Limber two years ago and saying, "You need to look at this Web site targeting a student. The mother has asked me to help her find out who did it and get it removed, and I cannot believe what I am seeing!" From that initial conversation, we began carving out the steps necessary to intervene in an actual severe cyber bullying episode, with much help from the Center for Safe and Responsible Internet Use's online documents authored by Nancy Willard. After that trial-by-fire experience, we met and discussed how useful it would be to personally interview students and parents, via focus groups and individual interviews, to better understand their experiences and perspectives. We noted that the paper and pencil surveys were insufficient to capture the emotional impact of this new form of bullying on parents and children. A broader idea emerged: writing a book describing our findings that would include actual interviews from students and parents.

One purpose of this book is to educate parents, educators, and community organizations about the growing problem of cyber bullying. But another is to empower the adults in the community to prevent this new form of bullying from becoming a regular experience for youth navigating the internet and other technological tools. Many adults and educators have found themselves in our position, learning more about cyber bullying at the moment when intervention is necessary. We hope that this book will help adults gain the knowledge and tools necessary to be true resources to young people in preventing and addressing cyber bullying episodes, rather than being viewed as hindrances, which unfortunately is frequently a perception of young people, as we will discuss.

Robin Kowalski and Sue Limber, psychologists and faculty members at Clemson University in South Carolina, have been researching cyber bullying through a variety of methods for several years, and some of their innovative research is published for the first time in this book. In addition, Patti Agatston, a psychologist and counselor, collaborated with Robin and Sue to develop individual and group questionnaires to use while interviewing parents and students regarding cyber bullying. Patti teamed up with her colleague Michael Carpenter to conduct focus groups during the spring and fall of 2006. Michael Carpenter was one of the first nationally certified trainers for the Olweus Bullying Prevention Program and one of the founders of the Prevention/Intervention Center, the Cobb County Georgia School District's nationally recognized student assistance program, where Patti Agatston also works. Patti conducted the female focus groups on cyber bullying, while Michael led the male focus groups. In addition, Patti conducted a variety of individual interviews with parents and students from various middle and high schools in the district who were willing to be interviewed regarding their experiences with cyber bullying. The reader will have an opportunity to hear first hand from some of the parents and students who were interviewed for this book.

We will share some suggestions and recommendations as a result of the research and interviews that we have conducted. We hope that the reader will find it more meaningful to know that these recommendations are being made based on research that has involved parents and youth in actual dialogue, in addition to survey methods. We also realize that new technologies with new potentials for bullying will emerge that require continued dialogue with parents and youth to understand the experiences they are having. The challenge is to incorporate these new technologies in a way that enhances rather than detracts from our daily life.

There are many people who contributed to the writing of this book, and the conducting of the research, to whom we offer our heartfelt gratitude. First, we want to thank a number of principals of the Cobb County School District who made it possible to conduct focus groups and individual interviews, including Linda Clark, William D. Griggers, Susan Gunderman, Denise Magee, Janet Peeler, Geraldine Ray, Ivia Redmond, Grant Rivera, and James Snell. Special thanks are given to the following school counselors for going above and beyond the call of duty to facilitate our work: Yvonne Young, Colleen Brown, and Susan Strickland, as well as health teacher Eric Homansky. Thanks also go to the staff of the Prevention/Intervention

Center – Jeff Inman, Jeff Dess, Luisa Resendiz, Joyce Hutchings, Janice Mosher, and Michael Carpenter – who provided encouragement, support, and a place to lock up sensitive data. Rebecca Alley at Clemson University provided invaluable assistance with legal research and analysis. Many students at Clemson University invested considerable time and energy collecting, inputting, and analyzing data: Lindsey Sporrer, Erin Hunter, Richard Reams, Karissa Chorbajian, Kristy Kelso, Natalie Irby, Angela Gorney, Amy Scheck, Ryan Cook, Melissa Redfearn, Jessica Allen, Ann-Mac Calloway, Melinda Keith, Stephanie Kerr, Laura Singer, Jana Spearman, Lance Tripp, Jessica Farris, Kelly Finnegan, and Laura Vernon. We are grateful for their help.

We would also like to thank Christine Cardone and Sarah Coleman at Wiley-Blackwell for their support of this project and for their encouragement throughout the process. We are indebted to them and the staff at Wiley-Blackwell for their support.

Thanks to the many work colleagues, friends, and relatives who supported us by offering encouragement, suggestions, and by reading and responding to our work, including Andrew Agatston, Robert Agatston, Teresa Hubbard, Rachel Galli, Frank and Kathy Walton, and Randolph and Frances Kowalski.

Finally, we thank our children, Austin, Jack, Mary, Noah, and Jordan, who inspire us to believe that all children have the right to feel safe from bullying, in both the real and the virtual worlds.

1

Introduction

∽

What makes cyber bullying so dangerous . . . is that anyone can practice it without having to confront the victim. You don't have to be strong or fast, simply equipped with a cell phone or computer and a willingness to terrorize.

(King, 2006)

Bullying creates memories that often last a lifetime. Simply hearing the name of a person who bullied them, even years or decades after the bullying occurred, may be enough to send chills up the backs of many people. When most think of bullying, they conjure up the image of a big thug who terrorized kids on the playground at school. Usually a male, he was someone to be feared. As horrible as encounters with this bully[1] may have been, though, the end of the school day often brought a reprieve as the victim left school and went home.

Cyber bullying: many people are not familiar with the term. But, for those who are and who have experienced it, the memories, like those of traditional bullying, can last a lifetime. Cyber bullying, also known as electronic bullying or online social cruelty, is defined as bullying through e-mail, instant messaging (IM), in a chat room, on a Web site, or through digital messages or images sent to a cellular phone. Although sharing certain features in common with traditional bullying (see Chapter 3 for a more detailed discussion of this), cyber bullying represents a somewhat unique phenomenon that has only recently begun to receive attention in both the popular press and in academic circles. Cyber bullying not only looks and feels a bit different than traditional bullying, but, as will be discussed later in this book, it presents some unique challenges in dealing with it, especially for parents, educators, and other adults who interact with children. In discussing the relationship between traditional bullying and cyber bullying, a reporter for MSNBC stated: "Kids can be cruel. And kids with technology can be cruel on a world-wide scale" (Sullivan, 2006). As is clear from its definition, cyber bullying is a relatively recent method of bullying made possible because of technological advances over the past 10–15 years. Two of the most notable of these advances are the Internet and the cellular phone.

One of the interesting questions that is often raised in connection with the Internet is: To what degree has it changed the lives of the adolescents who are using it? We believe that this is really the wrong question. Although the Internet may have changed the lives of the parents of these adolescents, for the adolescents themselves the existence of the Internet is all they have ever known. It simply *is* part of their life. The fact that parents of these children did not grow up with cellular phones and in-room computers, whereas these technologies are prevalent in the lives of the adolescents, accounts, in part, for the gap between parents and children in understanding both the uses and dangers of the Internet.

Parents, at least initially, tend to view the Internet as a helpful tool to aid their children with homework. Similarly, in parents' eyes, cellular phones are a means for kids to call home in emergencies. Children and youth, on the other hand, perceive the Internet, cellular phones, and related technologies as critical tools for their social life. For most parents, this technology is new and somewhat foreign and, therefore, something about which their children need to be cautious. For children and youth, on the other hand, these communication technologies have always existed, so they have a comfort level with technology that is foreign to many of their parents. Many parents candidly admit that their children are the ones who have taught them most of what they know about the Internet and related technologies. For example, in a focus group interview about cyber bullying, one teenager stated that she had taught her father how to access her brother's computer search history.

Importantly, though, what children are doing today isn't all that different from what their parents did when they were growing up – it is just that the vehicle through which they are doing it differs. For example, Lindsay Notwell referred to text messaging as "the note-passing of the new millennium . . . the Game Boy of wireless communications, for people who think with their thumbs" (Carpenter, 2003). Researchers with the Media Awareness Network (Wing, 2005), in discussing the extent to which the Internet affords adolescents the opportunity to try on new roles and identities, pointed out that kids have been playing "dress up" for centuries. The technological mediums used today, however, present some unique challenges that didn't confront children two or three decades ago. Traditionally, notes were passed between two individuals, often in class, and hidden from the view of the teacher and most other students in the class. Today, "notes" are passed via instant messaging and e-mail for a much wider audience to see. Hand-held Game Boys that might, only a few years ago, have been played while a child watched television in the living room have been replaced by X-Box Live that is played with multiple other people on a computer that most likely resides in the child's room.

For better or for worse, technology is here to stay, and it is a staple in the lives of adolescents today. *Time* magazine's recent selection of "You" as the person of the year attests to this (Grossman, 2006). In trying to select a person who helped to shape the course of history, writers at *Time* realized that the story of 2006 was "a story about community and collaboration . . . It's about the cosmic compendium of knowledge Wikipedia and the million-channel people's network YouTube and the online metropolis MySpace" (Grossman, 2006). In focus groups conducted with Canadian children in Grades 4 through 11, researchers found that children and adolescents view the Internet as "an opportunity to explore the adult world without supervision" (Wing, 2005). This preference is in keeping with their need to test their wings outside the family. A majority of children (57%) also use the Net to explore topics that interest them on an average school day, and a significant proportion use it to express themselves on their own Web sites (28%) or in online diaries and Web logs (15%; Wing, 2005).

Children and the Internet

Although many adults are unsure how to surf the Net, children and youth are only too savvy in doing so. So many kids use the Internet and its many communication venues that it has been referred to as the "digital communication backbone of teens' daily lives" (Lenhart, Madden, & Hitlin, 2005, p. iii). Want to punish a teenager? Simply threaten to take their computer away. To a teenager, that may seem to be a punishment worse than death (or, at least, a punishment that is the equivalent of a social death).

Several large-scale surveys have given us a picture of the prevalence of the use of technology among teenagers today and some of the potential dangers faced by teens. According to *The 2005 Digital Future Report* (Center for the Digital Future, 2005), released annually over the past five years, Internet use among Americans has continued to increase, as has overall time spent online. In 2005, 79% of Americans spent time online, averaging 13.3 hours a week, a significant increase over the previous four years (see Figures 1.1 and 1.2). In the 2005 report, among all Americans e-mail was the most frequent online activity, with instant messaging appearing ninth in the list. Contributing to the higher percentage of individuals online are adolescents, with over 97% of adolescents aged 12–18 using the Internet. This high rate of Internet activity among children and young adults has led people such as Bill Belsey, President of Bullying.org Canada, to refer to teenagers today as the "always on generation." In Canada, 94% of respondents indicated that they had access to the Internet in their home; 61% of these had high-speed access. Kids who had their own personal computer as opposed to using a family computer spent twice as much time online (Wing, 2005).

The Pew Internet & American Life Project report indicated that 21 million adolescents (87%) between the ages of 12 and 17 spend time online. Over half of the teens surveyed report that they spent time each day online (Lenhart et al., 2005). Almost half (45%) of the adolescents had their own cell phones; 33% communicated via text messaging. Seventy-five percent of the online teenagers surveyed reported using instant messaging, with 48% of these saying they used it daily. The biggest leap in online activity occurs between the 6th and 7th grades, according to the Pew report (Lenhart et al., 2005). Whereas only 60% of 6th graders indicated that they used the

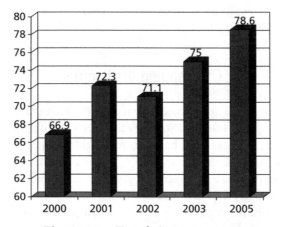

Figure 1.1 Trends in Internet use
Source: Center for the Digital Future at the Annenburg USC School (2005), *The 2005 Digital Future Report.* (http://www.digitalcenter.org)

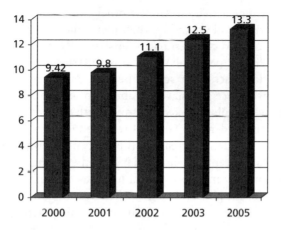

Figure 1.2 Hours per week spent online
Source: Center for the Digital Future at the
Annenburg USC School (2005), *The 2005 Digital
Future Report.* (http://www.digitalcenter.org)

Internet, 82% of 7th graders reported online activity. The report further noted that boys (particularly 6th grade boys) are much less active in their use of the Internet than girls. Whereas only 44% of the 6th grade boys reported going online, 79% of 6th grade girls reported using the Internet. Girls also are more likely than boys to use instant messaging. Seventy-eight percent of girls and 71% of boys said that they had tried instant messaging. Girls also try instant messaging at an earlier age than boys. Whereas girls may once have spent more time than boys talking on a land line with their friends, the Internet has now provided them with new avenues for communicating with those friends.

An even more recent report connected with the Pew Internet Project (Lenhart & Madden, 2007) showed that 55% of teens between the ages of 12 and 17 use social network sites, with over half of these teens (55%) having created their own online profiles. Girls, particularly those between the ages of 15 and 17, reported being more likely to use social network sites than boys in the same age range.

In 2000 and again in 2003, the Media Awareness Network (Wing, 2005) launched a series of research studies examining the online behavior of Canadian children and adolescents. In 2003, the organization conducted a series of focus groups with both parents and adolescents. Two years later, they administered a survey to 5,272 children in grades four to eleven to examine their online activities. Among other things, the study found that 23% of the children and youth had their own cellular phone. Twenty-two percent of school-aged children had Web cams. By the time they reached 11th grade, 31% had personal Web cams. Internet use tends to decline slightly once kids reach high school because most are driving or have friends who drive. Once they have the ability to see one another in person, they rely less on technology to keep in touch with one another. Eighty-nine percent of the respondents in Grade 4 reported playing games online. As the ages of the children increased, the percentage who played games decreased and the percentage who used instant messaging increased. Across all age groups, instant messaging was ranked as the first choice of online activity by 62% of the girls and 43% of the boys. Of concern, only 16% of the respondents reported talking about their online activities with their parents.

The Canadian survey revealed some disturbing information about the kinds of sites that adolescents like to visit. Of the 50 favorite Web sites listed, nearly one-third included violent or sexual information. In Quebec, the most popular site among girls in Grades 8 to 11 is Doyoulookgood. com. "On this Montreal-based site, users post photos, videos and information about themselves so others can vote on their looks. Members can search for people by age, starting as young as 13" (Wing, 2005).

The use of social networking sites, such as MySpace, Xanga, LiveJournal, and Nexopia has increased markedly in the past couple of years. MySpace first appeared in January of 2004. Since that time, it has acquired 87 million accounts, and is adding approximately 270,000 new accounts every day (Granneman, 2006). By September of 2006, MySpace was the most visited Web site on the Internet, having recently replaced Yahoo. Nexopia, the Canadian equivalent of MySpace, has a user base of approximately 899,000 users, with 229,000 accessing the site on average each day. Bebo, similar to MySpace except affiliated more with schools and universities, has seen similar rates of growth. Within its first year, Bebo acquired 25 million users ("Focus: Brave new world," 2006). One-quarter of the accounts on MySpace belong to minors. Ernie Allen, President of the National Center for Missing and Exploited Children, said, in reference to adolescents posting personal information on social networking sites: "What they're doing [when they post information about themselves online] is opening a window to people who may not have the best intentions" (Olsen, 2006b).

A recent survey of 1,160 children between the ages of 13 and 17, conducted in March, 2006, by the National Center for Missing and Exploited Children in conjunction with Cox Communication's Take Charge program, found that 61% of 13–17-year-old children have a personal profile on a social network site ("Take charge," 2006). Half of these had included a picture with their profile. Ninety-five percent listed a personal e-mail address, and 84% had a screen name that they used for instant messaging. Fourteen percent of the respondents had had a face-to-face interaction with someone they had met over the Internet, including 9% of these in the 13–15-year-old age range, and 22% in the 16–17-year-old age range. Thirty percent indicated that they were considering a face-to-face meeting with someone they had met online. Seventy-one percent of the kids stated that they had received messages via the Internet from someone they didn't know. Of those, almost half (40%) admitted to carrying on an online conversation with the unknown individual.

Not surprisingly, given that children and adolescents communicate with all sorts of people on the Internet, some of whom are friends and others of whom are strangers, experiences with the Internet and related technologies may be positive or negative. Profiles of kids on the Internet, and data on the types of information to which children are exposed while surfing the Internet, change rapidly. For example, in 2006 the findings from the second Youth Internet Safety Survey (YISS-2) were released (Wolak, Mitchell, & Finkelhor, 2006). The first Youth Internet Safety Survey (YISS-1) had been conducted approximately five years earlier (Ybarra & Mitchell, 2004). A comparison of the data from the two surveys showed that, whereas the percentage of children and youth who reported receiving online sexual solicitations had decreased from YISS-1 to YISS-2, the proportion who reported online harassment and unsolicited exposure to sexual images increased. (See Chapter 4 for a more detailed discussion of these studies.) A disturbing note to this reported increase in the number of children experiencing online exposure to sexual material is the fact that an increased number of parents (55%) in YISS-2 reported the use of computer blockers, filters, and keystroke software programs, compared to YISS-1 (33%). So, despite these increased parental controls, the number of children and youth who reported unwanted exposure to sexual material continued to increase. Also disturbing, according to YISS-2 (Wolak et al., 2006) an increasing number of perpetrators of online harassment are friends or acquaintances of the victim: 46% in the YISS-2 survey compared to 28% in YISS-1. Furthermore, the proportion of respondents in YISS-2 (14%) who said that the individuals making online sexual solicitations were offline friends or acquaintances increased from YISS-1, by 3%.

Effects of Internet Use on Children and Youth

There is debate regarding the extent to which high levels of Internet use interfere with psychological functioning, particularly among children and adolescents. On the one hand, Internet use allows for the possible development of new relationships, and for the easy maintenance of existing friendships and relationships. Russell and his colleagues (2003) found that frequent Internet use broadened people's social networks, particularly for people who were shy and socially anxious (see also, Gross, Juvonen, & Gable, 2002; McKenna & Bargh, 2000). Related research by Roberts, Smith, and Pollock (2000) found that socially anxious individuals were more confident communicating electronically than face-to-face. With time, however, this confidence carried over into face-to-face interactions. Socially anxious individuals are also more likely than nonsocially anxious people to communicate electronically with strangers or acquaintances (Gross et al., 2002). Using Thibaut and Kelley's (1959) analogy, Bargh and his colleagues (2002) compared the Internet to talking to "strangers on a train": people often freely disclose to strangers sitting next to them on a train aspects of themselves that they would not reveal to others. The Internet affords people the opportunity to disclose aspects of their "true self" that they would not reveal in face-to-face interactions.

Thus, the Internet has the potential to increase students' social interaction and enhance collaborative learning experiences (Beran & Li, 2005). At the same time, however, Robert Mahaffey, a criminal investigator for the Mississippi Attorney General's cyber crime unit, stated that: "The Internet is the wild, wild West of the 21st century, and it should be viewed that way" ("FBI: Blogging can be dangerous," 2005). Just like the wild, wild West, the Internet is full of excitement and adventure, but it is also full of danger and often unknown "bandits." Using a similar analogy, Franek (2005/2006) stated that "we need to be vigilant sheriffs in this new Wild West – a cyber-world buzzing with kids just a few keystrokes away from harming other people, often for no other reason than that the sheriffs are sleeping. As anyone who has ever been the victim of bullying and harassment will tell you, the bullets may not be real, but they can hurt" (p. 40).

On the positive side, the anonymity afforded by the Internet allows people to try on multiple roles and experiment with different "selves" without fear of negative evaluation or social sanctions that might follow such experimentation in face-to-face encounters. Significant numbers of adolescents (24%) in the Pew Internet & American Life survey admitted to pretending to be different people online (Lenhart et al., 2005). Fifty-six percent had more than one e-mail address or screen name. Users can pretend to be older or younger, male or female, African American or Caucasian, liberal or conservative, homosexual or heterosexual. The list of possible roles they can play and identities they can assume is endless. On the one hand, this can be beneficial to a teenager who is searching to discover who he or she is.

On the other hand, pretending to be someone they are not may lead children and adolescents to "meet" people online and, perhaps, subsequently in the real world, who also are not who they say they are. Indeed, 39% of the respondents in the 2001 Pew report (Lenhart, Rainie, & Lewis, 2001) admitted to playing a trick on someone or pretending to be somebody different when using instant messaging. Sixty percent of the teens reported that they had received e-mails or IMs from a stranger and 50% exchanged e-mails or IMs with a stranger. Seventeen percent of respondents in the Young Canadians in a Wired World Survey (Wing, 2005) reported that they "had pretended to be someone else so 'I can act mean to people and not get into trouble'." In addition, 59% of the respondents admitted to pretending to be someone that they weren't online. Of these, 52% pretended to be a different age, 26% assumed different personality characteristics, 24% pretended to have abilities they didn't have, and 23% claimed an appearance that was different from their actual appearance. Over 60% of the respondents to the NCMEC/COX Communications Survey ("Take charge," 2006) indicated that they had friends who had lied about their age over the Internet; another third stated that they had friends who had discovered that the person with whom they were communicating online was a different gender or age than they had originally claimed.

Opportunities for self-affirmation and self-expression provided by the Internet can quickly become vehicles for denigration and cyber bullying. For example, as noted earlier one site, doyoulookgood.com, rated as the most popular site among Canadian girls in grades 8 to 11 (Wing, 2005), allows users to set up personal accounts whereby they post pictures of and personal information about themselves. Site visitors can then pull up a person's profile and vote on the individual's attractiveness as well as send messages to the person. At the time of writing, there were 1,376,249 registered members to doyoulookgood.com, 661,535 photos on the site, and 4,429 members currently online. In addition, 1,615 new members had been added in the previous 24 hours, split approximately equally between men and women. Although the individual who receives positive ratings has the potential to have his or her self-esteem raised, the opposite scenario is probably more likely – negative ratings or negative comments that serve to denigrate the individual whose photo is posted on the Web site. Such negative postings represent only the tip of the iceberg of cyber bullying.

Perhaps not surprisingly, some evidence suggests that increased Internet use is associated with adverse psychological effects. In one of the first large-scale studies examining the psychological effects of Internet use, Kraut et al. (1998) found higher levels of Internet use to be associated with higher levels of depression and loneliness.

In a nationwide survey of more than 63,000 children in 5th through 8th grade conducted by i-SAFE America, 30% said they had said mean or hurtful things to another person online, with 3% saying they did so often. Conversely, from a pool of approximately 20,700 students 37% of the respondents said that someone had said mean hurtful things to them online. Four percent reported that it happened quite often. Nine percent had felt worried or threatened in the past year because someone was bothering or harassing them online (i-SAFE, 2006–2007). Thirty-four percent of the respondents in the Young Canadians in a Wired World survey reported having been bullied, with 74% of these being bullied at school and 27% being bullied over the Internet (Wing, 2005). Another 12% reported having been sexually harassed, with 70% of these being sexually harassed over the Internet.

How prevalent has cyber bullying become? Pretty prevalent. It used to be that kids could go off to summer camp to make new friends, gain some independence, learn new skills, and quite simply have an enjoyable way to spend part of their summer.[2] Long before the days of cellular phones, palm pilots, and laptops, campers might take a camera with them so that they could remember some of the cool things they saw at camp and so that they could have pictures of their new friends. Now, however, summer camp is a bit of a different experience. Kids might walk around camp listening to their iPod or talking on their cellular phone or Blackberry. Back at the lodge, they might be found tied to a computer, IMing their friends or posting information on their own or another person's MySpace site – until recently, anyway. Cyber bullying has become so worrisome for some adults that some summer camps have decided to ban digital cameras from the camp premises (Belluck, 2006). Of course, that also means that, in some cases, cellular phones with cameras have to be confiscated as well. The fear? That not-so-well-meaning campers will take inappropriate pictures of other campers or doctor "normal" pictures and then post these images on the Web, such as on social networking sites, like MySpace or Xanga (Belluck, 2006). In some instances, camps are trademarking their names and logos so that they have legal recourse if such images are posted (Belluck, 2006). Of course, cellular phones that include cameras have already been banned from many athletic clubs and gyms for the same reason (Charny, 2003).

Prototypes of Cyber Bullying

In recent months, countless examples of cyber bullying have been reported in the media, a few of which will be briefly recounted here as prototypes of cyber bullying. As will become apparent, cyber bullying includes a range of experiences, some legal, some illegal.

In perhaps one of the first and best-known illustrations of cyber bullying, Ghyslain Raza created a video of himself on November 4, 2002, acting out a scene from the movie *Star Wars*, using a golf-ball retriever as his light saber. Unfortunately, classmates then posted the video online without his permission or knowledge, where it was seen by millions. Eventually, in 2004, a Web site was created that contained original and modified clips from the video, along with special effects, and music from the *Star Wars* movie. The site received over 76 million hits (Lampert, 2006). In addition, other Web sites contained clips from the video spliced into action movies. Some speculated that Ghyslain's image was the most downloaded image of 2004. Labeled the "Star Wars Kid," Ghyslain was forced to change schools and received psychiatric help. On April 7, 2006, Raza's parents, who had filed a lawsuit against the classmates who had placed the video on the Internet, settled out of court with the families of these students.

A young man, angry over the fact that his girlfriend broke up with him, used photo-editing tools to paste her head onto a pornographic picture and sent it to everyone in his e-mail address book (Paulson, 2003).

15-year-old Jodi Plumb discovered a Web site devoted entirely to insulting her. Included on the Web site were comments about her weight as well as a date for her death. She discovered the Web site when a classmate used a digital camera to take a picture of Jodi for the Web site. Jodi said "I was really hurt because I did not know who'd done it" ("Cyber bullies target girl," 2006).

Phoebe Pluckrose-Oliver, 10 years old, received abusive text messages and phone calls from girls at her school. According to Phoebe, "They started phoning me and saying that I was in the cow club and that I should phone the loser line and stuff" ("Girl tormented by phone bullies," 2001).

Kylie Kenney was a victim of cyber bullying though multiple modalities. First, a Web site was created calling for her to die, the "Kill Kylie Incorporated" Web site. This was accompanied by countless harassing e-mails and phone calls. Furthermore, rumors spread that Kylie was a lesbian, and messages were sent ostensibly from her own instant messaging account asking other girls out on a date. In a news conference on cyber bullying, Kylie described how she was forced to change schools twice and how she had to be home-schooled for one semester because the cyber bullying was so bad. In the news conference, Kylie said "I was scared, hurt, and confused. I didn't know why it was happening to me. I had nowhere to turn except to my Mom" (Gehrke, 2006).

Two Toledo, Ohio, teenagers, aged 16 and 17, were arrested for posting death threats on MySpace against a 15-year-old classmate. They threatened to slit her throat, bash her head in, and discussed going to jail together if they were caught ("Ohio girls sentenced for MySpace threats," 2006).

An 8th grader in Pennsylvania was charged for posting a depiction of "his algebra teacher's severed head dripping with blood, an animation of her face morphing into Adolph Hitler and a solicitation for $20 contributions 'to help pay for the hitman'" (Poulsen, 2006).

In February 2006, five students at Kirkwood High School posted a "hot or not" list of junior girls on Facebook. Once the site was discovered, each of the five boys was given a 10-day suspension from school (Beder, 2006).

16-year-old Jade Prest became a prisoner in her own home and even contemplated suicide in reaction to the relentless cyber bullying she experienced by peers at school. Beginning as a disagreement over a boy at school, the cyber bullying included "midnight prank phone calls, an internet chatroom whispering campaign, abusive text messages, threats, intimidation and the silent treatment" (Crisp, 2006).

In Pennsylvania in 2005, a student created a profile on MySpace ostensibly created by his principal. The profile was highly unflattering and made negative references to the principal's size (Poulsen, 2006).

In New Zealand, a 14-year-old girl's name and cell phone number were posted on Bebo along with offers of sex with no strings attached. The girl was unaware that the message and personal information about her had been posted ("Schools face new cyber bullying menace," 2006).

In the fall of 2005, two students at Oregon City High School were suspended for comments they posted on MySpace about 32 other girls at the school. Included among the comments was the following about one of the students: "Every time you speak all I can think about is where is the closest body of water, so I can tie a brick to your ankle and throw you in. Which would be good exercise because it's hard to pick up fat people" (Pardington, 2005).

Mary Ellen Handy's ordeal started because another student, named Gretchen, liked the same boy as Mary Ellen Handy. Gretchen verbally abused Mary Ellen, and then sent her harassing e-mails. Taking it a step further, she then communicated using IM as if she were Mary Ellen, sending embarrassing and threatening communications to which, not surprisingly, she received insulting responses back. The result for Mary Ellen – she developed an ulcer from the stress. At least two of her friends who were harassed because of their relationship with Mary Ellen switched schools (Levine, 2006).

Ryan Patrick Halligan died by suicide at the age of 13 as a result of being persistently bullied and humiliated by peers at school. The bullying began at school and continued online. Toward the end of 7th grade, it was rumored at school and in IM conversations that he was gay. His father discovered after Ryan's death IMs saved on his computer demonstrating he was cyber bullied in regard to this rumor. His father also discovered that Ryan approached one of the pretty popular girls in his class online during the summer in between 7th and 8th grade, supposedly as a way of combating the gay rumor. Ryan learned on the first day of the school year that the girl only pretended to like him and that she had forwarded their private conversations to others to humiliate him. Two weeks before his death and only four weeks into the school year, Ryan wrote in an IM to a friend: "Tonight's the night, I think I'm going to do it. You'll read about it in the paper tomorrow." The "friend" replied, "It's about f*.* time!" (J. Halligan, personal communication, January 17, 2007)

A female respondent in one of our focus groups described the following: "An ex-boyfriend got kind of crazy once. He started e-mailing me and saying that he was gonna come to my house and kill me and stuff like he was watching [my] sister. I knew he wouldn't do anything but I went ahead and told my mom because he was like a freak. So, it was getting kind of scary. Yeah, he would say stuff to my friends online too so I kind of freaked out."

Overview of the Book

It would be difficult to discuss and understand cyber bullying without a clear understanding of traditional or school-yard bullying. Chapter 2 will provide an overview of traditional bullying – how it is defined, who the victims and perpetrators are, and the effects of traditional bullying on both sources and targets. Chapter 3 will delve into the world of cyber bullying. After defining cyber bullying, we will examine the methods by which people cyber bully, who perpetrates cyber bullying and who is victimized by cyber bullying, and how cyber bullying is similar to and different from traditional bullying. The chapter will end with a discussion of one of the key variables distinguishing electronic and traditional bullying – anonymity and the disinhibition that often results.

Although research on cyber bullying is still in its infancy, Chapter 4 will provide an overview of what extant research says about the topic, including assessments of the prevalence of cyber bullying, methods for studying cyber bullying, and a discussion of gender differences observed with cyber bullying. In particular, we will draw from our own research on cyber bullying with over 3,700 middle school children throughout the country, and from focus groups that we held with middle school students. An examination of the psychological effects of cyber bullying will close out the chapter. Chapters 5 and 6 take an applied look at what parents (Chapter 5) and educators and other adults who work with youth (Chapter 6) can do to deal with cyber bullying. Strategies for dealing with cyber bullying once it has already occurred, as well as prevention methods to deter incidents of electronic violence from beginning at all, are discussed. In Chapter 7 legal and public policy concerns related to cyber bullying will be discussed. In the United States, policy-makers and school personnel have been somewhat slower than those in Canada or the United Kingdom to address cyber bullying in statutes and in school policies (Osmond, 2006). In Chapter 8 we will draw some conclusions and provide some suggestions for future research and policy decisions.

A danger in writing a book on cyber bullying is that we will leave the reader with the impression that technological advances are bad and that children and youth would be better off if they did not have access to the Internet, cellular phones, etc. This is not the message we intend to convey. Indeed, technology can be a good thing. The Internet provides a window to the world for many children and youth. Not only does it open up sources of knowledge to people (adolescents in particular) that might otherwise be too difficult to access, but technology also affords adolescents and adults an easy means of establishing and maintaining social contacts. For some socially anxious individuals, this may be their social saving grace. And, most children and youth when asked about their experiences with the Internet and related technologies rate their experiences positively. One of our former students getting ready to attend graduate school told us how she had already become friends with two or three individuals who would be in her program. Knowing that she could not have met these people in person, we asked her how she had already become friends with them. Her answer: Facebook (A. Scheck, personal communication, August 2, 2006). We couldn't help but think at that moment what a "leg up" these students would all have in moving to a new location and starting a new program simply because they had used a social network site to get acquainted with one another beforehand. Nevertheless, cyber bullying is real, it is occurring with increasing frequency, and the psychological effects may prove to be as devastating, if not more so, than traditional bullying.

Notes

1. Where possible in this book, we have tried to avoid referring to a child as a "bully" or a "victim." We believe that it is critical not to label children as "bullies" or as "victims" or in any way to imply that bullying others or being bullied are indelible traits (which in turn can be quite damaging to children). Instead, we try to refer to "a child who bullies" or "a child who is bullied" and to focus on the bullying behavior of children rather than their status. Where this language becomes unwieldy, we have on occasion used the terms "bully" and "victim." We hope that in these instances, the reader will understand our intent.
2. We do not mean to imply that children have never been bullied while at summer camp. Certainly there are many children who can tell traumatic stories about times when they were mercilessly bullied while away at camp.

2

Children's Experiences with Traditional Forms of Bullying

⌒

"Unless you've been bullied, you really can't understand what it's like and how hard it is to forget. It really leaves a scar that even time can't heal."
(15-year-old focus group participant)

Although the advent of cyber technologies has provided new arenas in which children and youth can bully each other, the phenomenon of bullying is hardly new. In order to better understand cyber bullying, it is important to understand the various dynamics at work in traditional forms of bullying as well as what "best practices" are available for preventing and intervening with traditional bullying.

What is Bullying?

Bullying is aggressive behavior that is intentional and that involves an imbalance of power or strength (Nansel et al., 2001; Olweus, 1993a). Sometimes this imbalance involves differences in physical strength between children, but often it is characterized by differences in social power or status. Because of this imbalance of power or strength, a child who is being bullied has a difficult time defending himself or herself. Typically, bullying does not occur just once or twice, but is repeated over time. Admittedly, sometimes it is quite difficult for adults to know whether behavior has occurred repeatedly, as children are often good at hiding bullying and reluctant to report bullying that they experience or witness. However, it is important to try to determine whether a behavior is a one-time occurrence or whether it is part of a pattern of ongoing behavior. Although adults should intervene *whenever* they observe inappropriate aggressive behavior (even if the behavior appears to be an isolated occurrence), *how* adults respond to bullying versus other aggressive behavior may be different.

What Does Bullying Look Like?

Jack was small and somewhat immature for his age. For the past 2 years (since 2nd grade), Jack had been the target of jokes about his size. Most of the boys in his class called him "midget." He usually tried to laugh off the name-calling, but lately it seemed to be getting even worse. During the past week, several boys had been getting physically rough with him – tripping him on the school bus, and shoving him on the playground when the teachers weren't looking. When he mentioned to his parents that he was being picked on, his father lectured him about ways he could "stick up for himself," so he hadn't brought it up again.

Tara had been attending Grove Street Middle school only 1 month, but she was having trouble fitting in with her fellow 7th graders. Her family was new to town, and Tara didn't know a single student when she walked in the front door on the first day of school. Although kids at school weren't exactly friendly the first couple of days, the bullying didn't start until the second week, during English class. After Tara answered a question from the teacher, a popular girl called Tara a name under her breath, and all the students sitting near them laughed. Before long, several popular boys had started taunting her in the hallways. Each day, when she tried to find a seat in the cafeteria, her fellow classmates made animal noises or blocked open seats with their books. Tara had never experienced bullying at her other middle school, and she was at a loss to know what to do. She had missed a lot of school, complaining of stomach aches and nausea. When her parents insisted on a trip to the doctor, Tara finally broke down and told them what she'd been experiencing. "I hate this school! Please don't make go back – I'd rather die!"

As these stories (composites of real-life children) suggest, traditional forms of bullying include direct behaviors, such as hitting, kicking, taunting, malicious teasing or name-calling, but they also involve indirect (and often less obvious) behavior, such as rumor-spreading, social exclusion or shunning, and manipulation of friendships ("If you're her friend, none of us will talk to you"). The most common forms of bullying (for both boys and girls) involve the use of words, such as name-calling, malicious teasing, or verbal taunts about one's looks or speech (Nansel et al., 2001).

How Common is Bullying?

Although bullying is an age-old phenomenon, it has only been in the past 20 years that researchers have tried systematically to measure bullying. The earliest studies of bullying were conducted by Dan Olweus with children in Norway and Sweden in the 1980s (Olweus, 1993a). In an anonymous survey with over 150,000 children and youth, Olweus found that approximately 15% had been involved in bullying problems with some regularity. Nine percent of children had been bullied by peers, 7% had bullied others, and 2% had been bullied *and* had, in turn, bullied others.

Studies of children and youth in the United States were not conducted until a decade after Olweus' early studies and have typically found significantly higher rates of bullying (Melton et al., 1998; Nansel et al., 2001). The first study of bullying in the U.S. to use a nationally representative sample was conducted with more than 15,000 students in grades 6 through 10 and published in 2001 (Nansel et al., 2001). Using an anonymous self-report questionnaire, Tonya Nansel and her fellow researchers found that, within a single school term, 17% of children and youth said they had been bullied "sometimes" or more often, 19% had bullied others "sometimes" or more frequently, and 6% said they had been bullied *and* had bullied others "sometimes" or more often. Students were asked about the frequency with which they had experienced five specific types of bullying – being "belittled about religion or race," being "belittled about looks or speech," being "hit, slapped, or pushed," being "subjects of rumors," and being "subjects of sexual comments or gestures" – and found that being belittled about one's looks or speech was the most common.

In a more recent U.S. study that involved a wider age range of children, David Finkelhor and his colleagues conducted telephone interviews with children and parents, and found that 22% of children and youth had been physically bullied and 25% had been teased or emotionally bullied during the previous year (Finkelhor, Ormrod, Turner, & Hamby, 2005). The researchers estimated that 13.7 million children and youth were physically bullied and 15.7 million were teased or emotionally bullied each year in the U.S.

How do rates of bullying vary among children in different countries? The most comprehensive cross-national study of bullying and other health behaviors was the Health Behaviour in School-Aged Children (HBSC) Study (Currie et al., 2004; see also Žaborskis, Cirtautienè, & Žemaitienè, 2005) sponsored by the World Health Organization. In 2001–2002 more than 162,000 children and youth (aged 11, 13, and 15) from 35 countries and regions were surveyed about a variety of issues affecting their health and well-being, including bullying. Researchers found that overall 11% of children had bullied others at least twice a month during the previous couple of months, and 11% of students also reported that they had been bullied at least twice a month in this span of time. There was a great deal of variability in rates of bullying others and being bullied across countries. Rates of being bullied ranged from 4% (among girls in Malta and Sweden) to 36% for boys in Lithuania. (Rates of bullying for U.S. children were 10% for girls and 15% for boys.) Similarly, rates of bullying others varied dramatically, from 2% (among girls in Sweden, Ireland, Wales, and the Czech Republic) to 41% for boys in Lithuania. (U.S. rates for bullying others were 8% for girls and 16% for boys.)

Has the Amount of Bullying Increased in Recent Years?

There is no denying that there is much more awareness about bullying today (on the part of media, educators, and policy-makers) than in years past. The massacre at Columbine High School in 1999 seems to have been pivotal in focusing attention on bullying in the United States. Although the specific motivations for this (or other school shootings) may never be fully understood, retrospective accounts in the popular press and in the research literature pointed to bullying as a contributing factor in many of these crimes (Fein et al., 2002; Limber, 2006). To see just how much attention to school bullying has changed in recent years within the United States, we conducted a search of the Lexis/Nexis database, using the search terms "bullying" and "schools" (see Figure 2.1). In 1998, the year prior to the Columbine shootings, school bullying was in the headlines of American newspapers, magazines, and other popular press periodicals 145 times. The following year, the number of articles on school bullying doubled, and, in 2001, shot to more than 750.

Not only has attention to bullying increased remarkably in the popular press since the late 1990s, but there also has been a significant increase in attention to bullying among researchers since that time. To gauge just how much the research focus has changed in recent years, we conducted a search of the Psych Info database (an online social science database of journal articles, books, and other academic publications owned by the American Psychological Association) using "bully" or "bullying" as search terms. As Figure 2.2 illustrates, we found only five publications in 1990. By 2000 (one year post-Columbine) the number increased to 94, and in 2004 there were nearly 250 such publications.

Does the recent attention reflect a dramatic increase in bullying in recent years? According to the supplement to the National Crime

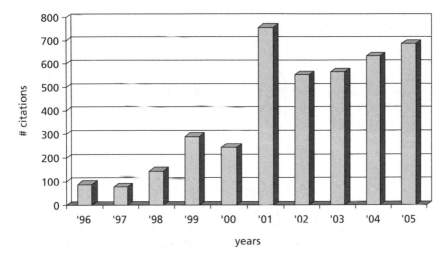

Figure 2.1 The number of Lexis/Nexis citations in which "bullying" appeared in the headlines and "school(s)" appeared in the text of an article

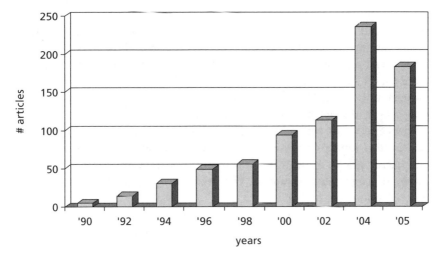

Figure 2.2 The number of PsychInfo citations located that use "bully" or "bullying"

Victimization Survey (DeVoe, Peter, Noonan, Snyder, & Baum, 2005), which asked students if they had been bullied (e.g., picked on or made to do things they didn't want to do) in the previous six months, there was a slight increase in rates of bullying between 1999 and 2001 (by about 3 percentage points) among American school children, but no change between 2001 and 2003. Therefore, much of the recent attention in the United States likely reflects increased interest in (or concern about) the topic of bullying (particularly post-Columbine), rather than a radical change in the likelihood that children are bullied.

Age Differences and Bullying

At what ages are children most likely to be involved in traditional forms of bullying? The answer to this question depends upon whether one is asking about children's experiences of *bullying others* or *being bullied*. Most studies find that children are most likely to be *bullied by others* during elementary grades. They are somewhat less likely to be bullied in middle school, and less likely still to be bullied in high school. For example, in their study of children and youth aged 2–17, Finkelhor and colleagues (2005) found that children aged 6–12 experienced the highest rates of physical bullying. Preschoolers experienced the second-highest rates of physical bullying, and teenagers (13–17-year-olds) experienced the least physical bullying. Children aged 6–12 also experienced the most teasing or emotional bullying of all three groups. Similar results were found by Tonya Nansel and her colleagues in their national study of 6th through 10th graders in the U.S. (Nansel et al., 2001). Although 24% of 6th graders said that they had been bullied sometimes or more often, only 16% of 8th graders and 9% of 10th graders reported that they had been bullied. Rigby (2002) also found decreases in rates of victimization among Australian children in grades 4 through 12, with an important exception. There was a temporary increase in rates of victimization the year that students first entered secondary school.

The picture looks quite different, however, when focusing on children's rates of *bullying others*. Most researchers have found that children are most likely to bully each other (according to anonymous, self-report measures of traditional forms of bullying) during early to mid-adolescence (Eisenberg & Aalsma, 2005; Espelage & Swearer, 2003). For example, in their study of 6th through 10th graders, Nansel and her colleagues found the highest rates of bullying others in 8th grade (24%, compared with 19% in 6th grade and 16% in 10th grade). What accounts for the difference in age trends for bullying others versus being bullied? One likely explanation is that children and youth typically bully peers their same age or they bully *younger* children and youth.

Gender Similarities and Differences in Traditional Forms of Bullying

Although both boys and girls are frequently involved in bullying, there has been debate among researchers about which gender is more likely to engage in and experience bullying. Studies that have used anonymous, self-report measures typically have found that boys are more likely than girls to bully (Currie et al., 2004; Nansel et al., 2001; Olweus, 1993a), but findings are less consistent when looking at gender differences in experiences of being bullied. Some studies have found that boys report higher rates of bully victimization than girls, whereas others have found no gender differences or only slight differences between boys and girls.

Probably more important than comparisons in rates of bullying between boys and girls are comparisons between the *types of bullying* in which boys and girls engage. Boys are more likely to be physically bullied by their peers (Finkelhor et al., 2005; Nansel et al., 2001; Olweus, 1993a; Rigby, 2002), whereas girls are more likely to be bullied through rumor-spreading or through sexual comments or gestures (Nansel et al., 2001). It also is important to note that, although boys are typically bullied by other boys (and rarely girls), girls are bullied by both boys and girls (Finkelhor et al., 2005; Nansel et al., 2001; Olweus, 1993a). Boys who are bullied by boys are more likely to indicate that they were physically and verbally bullied. Girls are bullied by girls more often through social exclusion (e.g., leaving another girl out of a group's social activities, and doing so in a hurtful way and on purpose; Olweus, personal communication, February 23, 2002).

Racial and Ethnic Issues in Traditional Forms of Bullying

Although race and ethnicity clearly play a role in some instances of bullying, there has been relatively little focus on this topic by bullying researchers. Nansel and her colleagues (2001) found that, among 6th through 10th graders who had been bullied, one-quarter said that they had been belittled about their race or religion at least once during the current school semester, and 8% had experienced such bullying once a week or more often.

A number of studies have examined similarities and differences in rates of bullying among children of different races (Graham & Juvonen, 2002; Nansel et al., 2001), but much still has to be learned, such as: (1) Do rates of bullying vary depending on whether children are in the racial majority/minority? And if so, how? (2) Is bullying related to the status hierarchy (e.g., the economic and social mobility) of children of different racial and ethnic groups? (3) How do cultural views of and experiences with aggression influence rates of bullying among peers? (Graham & Juvonen, 2002).

Bullying in Urban, Suburban, and Rural Communities

It is interesting to note that, although bullying has often been seen as a problem primarily for urban schools, there appears to be no support for this view. In fact, bullying has been documented in diverse communities across the U.S. (and around the world). In one of the few studies to examine urban, suburban, and rural differences in rates of bullying, Tonya Nansel and her colleagues (2001) found that students in grades 6 through 10 were just as likely to be bullied in urban, suburban, town, and rural areas. They found only very small differences in students' reports of bullying others, with suburban youth being slightly less likely than others to say that they bullied their peers "sometimes" or more often and rural youth being slightly more likely than others to have ever bullied their peers.

Children Involved in Bullying

Researchers and practitioners have focused much attention recently on understanding the characteristics and experiences of children involved in bullying – including those who are bullied, those who bully, and the majority who are witnesses or bystanders to the bullying.

Children Who Are Bullied

Children who are bullied typically fall into one of two general categories – those who are passive or submissive, and a smaller number who are considered "provocative victims" or "bully/victims." Characteristics and experiences of passive victims will be discussed in this section; those of bully/victims will be discussed later. It is important to note that, although children are frequently referred to in the research and intervention literature as "passive," "submissive," or "provocative," these terms are not intended to be pejorative labels. Nor should they be used in any way to blame children for the bullying that they experience.

Characteristics of bullied children. Although there is no single profile of passive victims of bullying, research suggests that they are likely to have one or more of the following characteristics (Olweus, 1993a):

- They are typically quiet, cautious, sensitive children who may be easily moved to tears.
- They may be insecure, have little confidence, and suffer from low self-esteem.
- They often have few friends and are socially isolated.
- They may be afraid of being hurt.
- They may be anxious or depressed.
- They tend to be physically weaker than their peers (especially in the case of boys).
- They may find it easier to spend time with adults (parents, teachers, coaches) than same-age peers.

As will be discussed later, low self-esteem, anxiety, and depression may be common consequences of bullying, but they also may be precursors to bullying, in some children. Research indicates that children with these characteristics are actually more likely to *become* victims of bullying (Fekkes, Pijpers, Fredriks, Vogels, & Verloove-VanHorick, 2006; Swearer, Grills, Haye, & Cary, 2004). It is likely that anxiety, depression, and poor self-esteem "signal" to peers that children may be easy targets for bullying.

Groups of children at high risk of being bullied. Although any child may be bullied by peers (and while it is not always evident *why* particular children are targeted), recent research has begun to focus attention on groups of children who may be at particularly high risk of being bullied. Relatively little research has been conducted on the relation between learning disabilities and bullying, but early findings suggest that children with learning disabilities are at greater risk of being teased and physically bullied (Martlew & Hodson, 1991; Nabuzoka & Smith, 1993; Thompson, Whitney, & Smith, 1993). Children with Attention Deficit Hyperactivity Disorder (ADHD) also are more likely than other children to be bullied (and to bully their peers; Unnever & Cornell, 2003). Children with special health care needs or chronic diseases may be frequent targets of bullying. For example, researchers have found higher rates of bully victimization among children with conditions that affect their appearance (e.g., cerebral palsy, muscular dystrophy, spina bifida, partial paralysis), and children with diabetes (Dawkins, 1996; Storch et al., 2004a, 2004b; Yude, Goodman, &

McConachie, 1998). Obesity also may place children at higher risk of being bullied. In a study of more than 5,700 Canadian children aged 11–16, researchers found that overweight and obese girls (aged 11–16) and boys (aged 11–12) were more likely than normal-weight peers to be teased or made fun of and to experience relational bullying (e.g., to be socially excluded). Overweight and obese girls (but not boys) were also more likely to be physically bullied (Janssen, Craig, Boyce, & Pickett, 2004). Finally, adolescents who are gay, lesbian, or bisexual, those who may be questioning their sexuality, and those who may be perceived as "too feminine" (boys) or "too masculine" (girls) may be more likely to be bullied (Eisenberg & Aalsma, 2005; Garofalo, Wolf, Kessel, Palfrey, & DuRant, 1998; Harris Interactive & GLSEN, 2005).

Effects of bullying. Research over the past decade confirms that bullying can seriously affect the mental and physical health of children and their academic work. Children who are bullied are more likely than nonbullied children to be anxious (Craig, 1998; Fekkes, Pijpers, & Verloove-Van-Horick, 2004; Juvonen, Graham, & Schuster, 2003; Olweus, 1978), depressed (Craig, 1998; Fekkes et al., 2004; Hodges & Perry, 1996; Juvonen et al., 2003; Kumpulainen, Raasnen, & Puura, 2001; Olweus, 1978; Rigby & Slee, 1993), and to suffer from low self-esteem (Eagan & Perry, 1998; Hawker & Boulton, 2000; Hodges & Perry, 1996; Olweus, 1978; Rigby & Slee, 1993). They also are more likely than other children to think about taking their own lives. For example, in a study of Australian children, Ken Rigby found that those who were frequently bullied (i.e., at least once a week) were twice as likely as other children to wish they were dead or to admit to having recurring thoughts of suicide (Rigby, 1996). Interestingly, the links between bully victimization and depression (and also between bully victimization and suicidal thoughts) are stronger for indirect as opposed to direct forms of bullying (Van der Wal, de Wit, & Hirasing, 2003). In other words, there may be more reason to worry about the psychological states of children who are ostracized by peers ("They pretend they don't see me") than children who are physically bullied ("They hit me"). Because children have such a strong need to belong and to be accepted by their peer group, many find it much more distressing to be excluded by peers than to be battered by them.

Not only may bullied children experience psychological problems as a result of being bullied, but they may experience physical ailments as well. For example, in a study of 2,766 Dutch school children aged 9–12, researchers compared health problems of bullied and nonbullied children and found that bullied children were approximately three times as likely to experience headaches, feel listless, and wet their beds. They were about twice as likely to have trouble sleeping, have stomach pain, feel tense, be tired, and have a poor appetite (Fekkes et al., 2004).

Bullying also may affect the academic work of bullied children. Children who are bullied are more likely than their nonbullied peers to want to avoid going to school (Kochenderfer & Ladd, 1996) and actually have higher absenteeism rates (Rigby, 1996; Smith, Talamelli, Cowie, Naylor, & Chauhan, 2004). They are more likely to say that they dislike school, and their teachers perceive that they are less happy than their nonbullied peers. They also receive lower grades than peers who are not bullied (Arsenault et al., 2006; Eisenberg, Neumark-Sztainer, & Perry, 2003). Most studies linking bullying and poor academic adjustment are correlational; therefore, findings from these studies must be interpreted carefully, because, unlike longitudinal studies, correlational studies do not prove a causal relationship between bullying and academic functioning. In one of the very few longitudinal studies conducted on this issue to date, Buhs and colleagues followed nearly 400 children in the U.S. from kindergarten through 5th grade (Buhs, Ladd, & Herald, 2006). They observed that those children who were rejected by their peers in kindergarten (i.e., their kindergarten classmates said that they did not want to "hang out" with them) were more likely than others to be excluded and picked on by peers throughout elementary school. Children who were excluded by peers were, in turn, less likely to participate in class and ultimately they performed more poorly on a test of student achievement. Students who were picked on were less likely to attend school.

Although more research is needed to better understand the effects of bullying on children's attitudes toward school, their attendance, and their educational outcomes, there is reason for concern that the stress and distractions caused by bullying put children at academic risk. As Nancy Eisenberg and her colleagues speculated, "Young people mistreated by peers may not want to be in school and may thereby miss out on the benefits of school connectedness as well as educational advancement" (Eisenberg, Neumark-Sztainer, & Perry, 2003, p. 315).

For some, the devastating effects of bullying may be felt long after the bullying has ended. For example, in a study of young adults, Dan Olweus found that boys who were bullied in junior high school were likely to suffer from low self-esteem and depression a decade after the bullying had ended (Olweus, 1993b). Other researchers have found that individuals who experienced frequent teasing in childhood were more likely to suffer from depression and anxiety in adulthood (Roth, Coles, & Heimberg, 2002). Roth et al. speculate that "children who are repeatedly teased may develop beliefs that the world is a dangerous place and that they have little control over outcomes in their lives" (p. 161).

Do children tell adults if they have been bullied? Despite the high prevalence of bullying and the harm that it may cause, many children do not report their victimization to adults at school or at home. Research suggests that anywhere from 50% to 75% of students who are bullied *do not* tell a teacher or another adult at school about their experiences (Boulton & Underwood, 1992; Fonzi et al., 1999; Harachi, Catalano, & Hawkins, 1999; Melton et al., 1998; Whitney & Smith, 1993). Older children and boys seem to be particularly reluctant to report being bullied (Melton et al., 1998; Rivers & Smith, 1994; Whitney & Smith, 1993). Children are somewhat more likely to talk with parents or other adults in their home about being bullied (Boulton & Underwood, 1992; Olweus, 1993a; see, however, Ortega & Mora-Merchan, 1999). They may be most comfortable reporting bullying experiences to their friends (Rigby, 2002; Rigby & Slee, 1999). Unfortunately, a worrisome number of children (14–17%) apparently do not tell anyone about their victimization (Harris, Petrie, & Willoughby, 2002; Naylor, Cowie, & del Rey, 2001).

Why are children reluctant to report bullying? For some (particularly older children), negative messages about "tattling" or "snitching" may cause them to think twice about reporting victimization. Boys may feel additional pressures to try to deal with bullying on their own and not to appear "weak" by seeking help from an adult. For other children, their reluctance to report bullying to school staff may reflect a lack of confidence in teachers' and other school authorities' handling of bullying incidents. For example, in a survey of high school students in the U.S., two-thirds of those who had been bullied felt that school personnel responded poorly to bullying incidents at school; only 6% believed that school staff handled these problems very well (Hoover, Oliver, & Hazler, 1992). As a boy remarked during a focus group convened by the developers of the National Bullying Prevention Campaign (Smith, January 3, 2003, personal communication), "Adults either way under-react to bullying or way over-react to it. They hardly ever get it right." With age, children are less and less likely to perceive that adults will help to stop bullying (Fonzi et al., 1999).

In fairness to school staff, it can be extremely difficult for adults to identify bullying, particularly when the bullying is subtle, unreported, or denied by students. Students also may be unaware of efforts of staff to try to address bullying incidents sensitively and confidentially. Nevertheless, adults should take children's concerns to heart if we hope to increase the numbers who will report their victimization experiences.

Warning signs of bullying. Because children often do not report being bullied to adults, it is important for parents, educators, and other adults who work with children to be vigilant for possible signs of bullying. A child may have experienced bullying (or be a victim of ongoing bullying) if he or she:

- comes home with torn, damaged, or missing pieces of clothing, books, or other belongings.
- has unexplained cuts, bruises, and scratches.
- has few, if any, friends.
- seems afraid of going to school, walking to and from school, riding the school bus, or taking part in organized activities with peers (such as clubs).
- takes a long, "illogical" route when walking to or from school.
- has lost interest in school work or suddenly begins to do poorly in school.
- appears sad, moody, teary, or depressed when he or she comes home.
- complains frequently of headaches, stomach aches, or other physical ailments.
- has trouble sleeping or has frequent bad dreams.
- has little appetite.
- appears anxious, has low self-esteem. (Olweus, Limber, & Mihalic, 1999)

If a child shows one or more of these characteristics, it is important to talk with the child (and his or her parents, teachers, and other appropriate adults) to determine whether the child may be bullied by peers and to help address whatever problems he or she may be experiencing (whether or not they are ultimately related to bullying).

Children Who Bully

Just as bullied children do not share all of the same traits or characteristics, there is no single "profile" of children who bully. Nevertheless, research suggests that children and youth who bully often have one or more of the following characteristics (Olweus, 1993a):

- They have dominant personalities and like to assert themselves using force.
- They have a temper, are impulsive and are easily frustrated.
- They have more positive attitudes towards violence than other children.
- They have difficulty following rules.

- They appear to be tough and show little empathy or compassion for those who are bullied.
- They often relate to adults in aggressive ways.
- They are good at talking themselves out of difficult situations.
- They engage in both proactive aggression (i.e., deliberate aggression to achieve a goal) and reactive aggression (i.e., defensive reactions to being provoked; Camodeca & Goossens, 2005).

Children who bully are sometimes stereotyped as "loners" who lack social skills, but this usually is not the case (Cairns, Cairns, Neckerman, Gest, & Gariépy, 1988; Nansel et al., 2001; Olweus, 1978; Juvonen et al., 2003). In fact, research indicates that children who bully are less depressed, socially anxious, and lonely than their peers. Their classmates tend to rate them high in terms of social status, and their teachers confirm that children who bully often are the most popular students in the class (Juvonen et al., 2003). Although not all children who bully are popular, most have at least a small group of friends ("henchboys" or "henchgirls") who support their bullying (Olweus, 1978; 1993a). Children who bully are also good at reading the mental states and emotions of other children and in manipulating them (Sutton, Smith, & Swettenham, 1999a, 1999b).

Why do children bully? There is no simple answer to this question, as children may bully for a variety of personal motivations, because of family dynamics, and even because of school, community, and societal factors. Researchers who have examined personal motivations for bullying have focused primarily on boys. There appear to be at least three primary motivations for boys' bullying (Olweus, 1993a; Olweus et al., 2007) and these may be confirmed for girls as well:

1. They have a need for dominance and power.
2. They find satisfaction in causing suffering or injury to others.
3. They are rewarded for their behavior. These rewards may be material (e.g., money, cigarettes, other possessions taken from their victims) or they may be psychological (e.g., prestige or perceived high social status).

Not only may there be individual motivations for engaging in bullying behavior, but there also may be family factors that increase a child's likelihood of bullying others. These include a lack of warmth and involvement on the part of parents; a lack of appropriate supervision; and inconsistent, physical discipline (Duncan, 2004; Olweus, 1993a; Olweus et al., 1999; Rigby, 1993, 1994). Children who bully are more likely than their peers to be exposed to domestic violence (Baldry, 2003) and be a victim of child maltreatment (Shields & Cicchetti, 2001). They also are more likely than other children to bully their own siblings (Duncan, 1999).

Peer and school influences also can play a factor in a child's propensity to bully. Children who bully tend to associate with other aggressive children who may model or encourage bullying behavior. Bullying also is more likely in certain school settings – namely those in which students and staff have indifferent or accepting attitudes about bullying (Olweus, 1993a), where there is lax adult supervision (Boulton, 1994; Pellegrini & Bartini, 2000; Olweus, 1993a; Smith & Sharp, 1994), and where teachers are ineffective in maintaining control.

Concern for children who bully. There is good reason to be concerned about bullying behavior – not only because of the effect that bullying can have on victims, but also because it can be a sign of other troublesome behavior on the part of children who bully. Children who bully are more likely than their peers to be involved in a host of other antisocial, violent, or worrisome behavior, including fighting, stealing, vandalism, weapon-carrying, school drop-out, and poor school achievement (Byrne, 1994; Haynie et al., 2001; Nansel et al., 2001; Olweus, 1993a). They also are more likely than nonbullying peers to drink alcohol, smoke (Nansel et al., 2001; Olweus, 1993a), and own a gun for risky reasons (i.e., to gain respect or frighten others; Cunningham, Henggeler, Limber, Melton, & Nation, 2000). Bullying also may be an early indicator that boys are at risk of later criminal behavior (Olweus, 1993a; Pellegrini, 2001). In a long-term study conducted by Dan Olweus (1993a) in Norway, boys who were identified as bullies in middle school were four times as likely as their nonbullying peers to have three or more criminal convictions.

Children Who Are Bully/Victims

As mentioned earlier, some children are bullied with regularity but also bully other children. These children, who are frequently referred to as "bully/victims," "provocative victims," or "aggressive victims," tend to be hyperactive (Kumpulainen & Raasnen, 2000), restless, and have difficulty concentrating (Olweus, 1993b, 2001). As a group, they are more clumsy and immature than their peers, and they often have trouble reading the social cues of other children. Bully/victims tend to be quick-tempered and may try to fight back when they feel that they have been insulted or attacked (even when this isn't the case; Olweus, 1993b, 2001). Not only do peers find it difficult to associate with these children, but teachers and other school personnel frequently report that these children are among the most difficult to work with in a school setting.

Research confirms that there is particular reason to be concerned about bully/victims, as they have many of the social and emotional difficulties of "passive" victims of bullying and the behavior problems associated with children who bully. Compared with other children (children who are "passive victims," those who bully, and those who are not involved in bullying), bully/victims fare more poorly in a variety of areas, including problem behaviors, self-control, social competence, deviant peer influences, school adjustment and bonding, and depression (Haynie et al., 2001). In a study of nearly 2,000 6th grade students, Juvonen and colleagues (2003) examined self-reports, peer reports, and teacher ratings of bully/victims compared with other students. The bully/victims were the group of children singled out by their peers as the most avoided students at school. Teachers rated them as being very unpopular, having many conduct problems and being disengaged from school. Disturbingly, bully/victims also are more likely than other children and youth to report suicidal or self-injurious behavior and suicidal thoughts (Kim, Koh, & Leventhal, 2005). Finally, the authors of two retrospective studies of violent acts at school (including, but not limited to, school shootings) have noted that many of the violent youth in their studies had also been bullied (Anderson et al., 2001; Fein et al., 2002). Anderson and his colleagues speculated that these children "may represent the 'provocative' or 'aggressive' victims . . . who often retaliate in an aggressive manner in response to being bullied" (p. 2702).

Children Who Witness Bullying

Adults often view bullying as a problem between two children – a child who bullies and his or her victim. But bullying is more accurately understood as a group phenomenon in which children may play a variety of roles. Olweus (1993a; Olweus et al., 1999) described eight such roles as part of a continuum that he referred to as the Bullying Circle:

1. The child who initiates the bullying.
2. Followers or henchmen, who actively take part in the bullying but do not initiate it.
3. Supporters, who openly support the bullying (e.g., they laugh or otherwise call attention to the bullying) but do not take an active role.
4. Passive supporters, who enjoy the bullying but do not openly support it.

5. Disengaged onlookers, who neither get involved nor feel responsible for stepping in to stop the bullying.
6. Possible defenders, who dislike the bullying and think they should do something to help, but do not.
7. Defenders, who dislike the bullying and try to help those who are bullied.
8. The student who is bullied.

It is important to note that these roles (particularly roles 3–7) are not static but rather may change from one situation to the next. In one situation, a child may be a passive supporter of bullying that involves a new student whom she doesn't know; in another she may defend a friend who is being bullied. During physical education class, a child may be a victim of bullying. Later that day, the same child may pick on younger students on his school bus. Children's roles depend on the particular social setting, and the interaction of students within that setting.

Children's attitudes toward bullying. Because bullying thrives in settings in which children and adults have indifferent or accepting attitudes towards bullying, it is important to understand how children view bullying. Most children have fairly negative reactions to bullying and positive or sympathetic feelings towards children who are bullied (Baldry, 2004; Rigby & Slee, 1993; Unnever & Cornell, 2003). Unfortunately, sympathy often does not translate into action. For example, in a study of middle school students, Unnever and Cornell (2003) found that the vast majority of students reported feeling sorry for victims of bullying. However, two-thirds also admitted that students at their school rarely tried to prevent bullying. If most children are disturbed by bullying, why don't they try to put a stop to it? Many may be uncertain about how best to respond to the bullying or are afraid that they may make the situation worse for the victim. Others may feel that their actions would be fruitless unless other students supported them, and they doubt that they would find many supporters. Many likely are afraid that they will become targets themselves if they take action to stop bullying.

The reasons for children's inaction illuminate some of the negative effects that bullying can have on bystanders. As witnesses to bullying, they may feel afraid, powerless to change the situation, and guilty for their inaction. Over time, if they do not see adults or other children intervening to stop bullying, they may feel less empathy for children who are bullied. ("If they have been bullied all this time, maybe they deserve it!") If unchecked in school (or in other environments where children gather), bullying can seriously affect the silent majority of students who are bystanders to bullying. In so doing, it can erode the social climate of the school.

Conditions Surrounding Bullying

In order to prevent bullying, it is important to better understand typical conditions that surround bullying incidents, including common locations for bullying, and the number and identify of perpetrators.

Where Does Bullying Take Place?

Bullying tends to thrive anywhere in a school or a community where adults are not present or are not vigilant. Although "hot spots" for traditional forms of bullying may vary somewhat from school to school and from community to community, some consistent areas of concern emerge. From self-report surveys, children tell us that traditional forms of bullying are more common at school (in the school building or on school grounds) than on the way to and from school, such as on the school bus, at the bus stop, or elsewhere in the community (Harris et al., 2002; Nansel et al., 2001; Olweus, 1993a; Rivers & Smith, 1994; Unnever, 2001). Common locations for bullying at school include the playground and/or athletic fields (especially among elementary school children), the classroom, the lunchroom, hallways, and bathrooms.

Number and Identity of Perpetrators of Bullying

Children who are bullied typically indicate that they are bullied by one other child or by a very small group of peers (Melton et al., 1998; Olweus, 1993a; Unnever, 2001). It is much less common for children to be bullied by large groups, although children who are bully/victims may be the exception to this rule. Bully/victims may, in some cases, be bullied by many peers – occasionally an entire class. Most often, children are bullied by same-age peers or older children. As noted earlier, boys are typically bullied by other boys, whereas girls are bullied by both boys and girls.

Effective Bullying Prevention

In response to concerns about bullying, school personnel have adopted a variety of strategies to address traditional forms of bullying, including: (a) efforts to raise awareness about bullying (e.g., during school assemblies, staff in-services, PTA meetings); (b) efforts to report and track bullying incidents at school; (c) therapeutic interventions for children who bully and children who are bullied; (d) peer mediation and conflict resolution to address bullying; (e) curricula focused on bullying; and (f) comprehensive bullying prevention programs.

What are Common Misdirections in Bullying Prevention and Intervention?

Unfortunately, a number of misguided intervention and prevention strategies have been developed in recent years by well-intentioned adults (Health Resources and Services Administration, 2006; Limber, 2003, 2004).

Zero tolerance policies. Some schools and school districts have adopted zero tolerance or "three strikes and you're out" policies towards bullying, under which children who bully others are suspended or expelled. At first glance, and in light of recent tragic school shootings, these approaches may appear to make sense. However, these policies raise a number of concerns. First, they potentially affect a very large number of students. Approximately one in every five students tells us that they have bullied other students with some regularity. Clearly, it would be bad policy to expel every fifth child from our schools. Second, a goal of bullying prevention initiatives should be to encourage students to report known or suspected bullying among their peers. Threatening to severely punish students for bullying may have an unintended consequence of discouraging children and adults from reporting bullying. Finally, as noted earlier, children who bully their peers are at risk of engaging in other antisocial behaviors (such as truancy, fighting, theft and vandalism). Children who bully need positive, prosocial role models, including peers and adults at their school. Suspension and expulsion of students may be necessary in a small number of cases to keep children and adults safe at school, but these practices are not recommended as a bullying prevention or intervention strategy.

Group treatment for children who bully. Other, less drastic measures call for children who bully to be grouped together for therapeutic treatment, which might include anger management, empathy-building, or skill-building. Unfortunately, these groups are often ineffective, even with well-intentioned and skilled adult facilitators, and they may actually make bullying worse, as group members may reinforce each others' bullying behaviors. Rather, children who bully need to be exposed to prosocial peers who can model positive behavior and help send a message that bullying is not acceptable behavior.

Conflict resolution/peer mediation. Because of the popularity of conflict resolution and peer mediation programs to address conflict among students, many schools use these techniques to address bullying problems as well. This practice is not recommended. Why? First, as we discussed earlier, bullying is a form of victimization, not conflict. Second, mediation may further victimize a child who has been bullied. It can be extremely painful for a child who has been bullied to have to face his or her tormentor in mediation. Finally, mediating a bullying incident may send inappropriate messages to the students who are involved. The message should not be, "You are both partly right and partly wrong, and we need to work out this conflict between you." Rather, the appropriate message for the child who is bullied should be, "No one deserves to be bullied, and we are going to see that it ends." The message for children who bully should be, "Your behavior is wrong, it against our school's rules, and it must stop immediately."

Simple, short-term solutions. With increasing pressures to address bullying at school, many educators are (understandably) searching for simple, short-term solutions. Bullying may be the topic of a school-wide assembly, addressed in a once-a-month curriculum, or the focus of a staff in-service. Although each of these efforts may represent important pieces of a comprehensive, long-term bullying prevention strategy, they probably will not significantly reduce bullying if implemented in a piecemeal way.

What Works in Bullying Prevention?

In its landmark National Bullying Prevention Campaign, the Health Resources and Services Administration (HRSA), identified 10 strategies that represent "best practices" in bullying prevention and intervention (2006).

1. Focus on the school environment. What is needed to reduce bullying in schools is nothing less than a change in the climate of the school and in the social norms. As the HRSA campaign notes, "It must become 'uncool' to bully, 'cool' to help out kids who are bullied and normative for staff and students to notice when a child is bullied or left out" (2006). Doing so requires the efforts of everyone in the school environment – teaching staff, administrators, nonteaching staff, parents, and, students.

2. Assess bullying at your school. Because adults often are not very good at estimating the nature and amount of bullying at their school, it is helpful to assess perceptions of bullying among the student body, staff, and parents.

One effective way of doing this is by administering an anonymous survey. Findings from the assessment can help motivate adults to take action against bullying that they otherwise may have overlooked or downplayed. These data also can help staff to tailor a bullying prevention strategy to the particular needs of the school. Finally, these data are important in helping administrators measure progress in reducing bullying over time.

3. *Garner staff and parent support for bullying prevention.* Bullying prevention should not be the sole responsibility of any single administrator, counselor, teacher, or individual at a school. In order to be effective, bullying prevention efforts usually require support from the majority of the staff and from parents.

4. *Form a group to coordinate the school's bullying prevention activities.* Bullying prevention efforts appear to work best if they are coordinated by a representative group from the school. This coordinating group (which might include an administrator, a teacher from each grade, a member of the nonteaching staff, a school counselor or other school-based mental health professional, a school nurse, a school resource officer, and a parent) should meet regularly to review data from the school's survey; plan bullying prevention policies, rules, and activities; motivate staff; get feedback from staff, students, and parents about what is working and what is not working; and ensure that the efforts continue over time. A student advisory group also can be formed whose purpose is to focus on bullying prevention and provide suggestions and feedback to educators.

5. *Train school staff in bullying prevention.* All administrators, faculty, and staff at a school should be trained in best practices in bullying prevention and intervention. Appropriate training can help staff to better understand the nature of bullying, its harmful effects, how to respond to bullying, and how to work with others at the school to help prevent bullying. Administrators should make an effort to train all adults in the school who interact with students, including teachers, counselors, nurses, media specialists, lunch room and recess aides, bus drivers, custodians, and cafeteria workers.

6. *Establish and enforce school rules and policies related to bullying.* Most school behavior codes implicitly forbid bullying, but many do not use the term "bullying" or make it clear how students are expected to behave with regard to bullying (as witnesses as well as participants). Developing simple, clear rules about bullying can help to ensure that students are aware of adults' expectations that they refrain from bullying and help students who

are bullied. School rules and policies should be familiar to staff, and posted and discussed with students and parents. Appropriate positive and negative consequences should be developed for following/not following the school's rules against bullying.

7. Increase adult supervision in places where bullying occurs. Because bullying thrives in places where adults are not present (or aren't vigilant), school personnel should look for creative ways to increase adults' presence in "hot spots" that students identify for bullying.

8. Focus some class time on bullying prevention. Bullying prevention programs should include a classroom component. Classroom meetings, which focus on bullying and peer relations at school, can help teachers to keep abreast of students' concerns, allow time for honest discussions about bullying and the harms that it can cause, and provide tools for students to address bullying and other social problems. Antibullying themes and messages also can be effectively incorporated throughout the school curriculum.

9. Intervene consistently and appropriately in bullying situations. All staff should be able to intervene on the spot to stop bullying. Designated staff (e.g., school counselors or administrators) should also hold sensitive follow-up meetings with children who are bullied and (separately) with children who bully. Parents of affected students should be involved whenever possible and appropriate.

10. Continue these efforts over time. There should be no "end date" for bullying prevention efforts. Bullying prevention should be woven into the everyday fabric of the school and continue over time.

Comprehensive Approaches to Bullying Prevention

In recent years, a number of school-wide, comprehensive bullying prevention programs have been developed that include classroom-level interventions but also include interventions targeted at the broader school environment.[1] Among these programs, the oldest, and probably the most widely researched, is the Olweus Bullying Prevention Program (see Table 2.1). The Olweus program includes school-wide components, interventions within the classroom, individual interventions, and community-level components (Olweus et al., 2007):

Developed and initially researched in Norway, this elementary and middle/junior high school program has been implemented and evaluated

Table 2.1

Components of the Olweus Bullying Prevention Program

School-level components:
- Establishment of a bullying prevention coordinating team to meet regularly and coordinate the program.
- Administration of a student bullying questionnaire for students in grades three and higher.
- Committee and staff training on bullying prevention.
- Ongoing staff discussion groups on bullying prevention.
- Development of school rules and discipline procedures surrounding bullying.
- A supervisory system that includes a special focus on bullying.
- Kick-off events to launch the program with students and parents.
- Parent involvement.

Components at the classroom level:
- Posting and enforcement of school-wide rules against bullying.
- Holding regular classroom meetings on topics of bullying and peer relations.
- Holding regular meetings with parents, if possible.

Individual components:
- Supervision of students' activities.
- Effective on-the-spot interventions to address bullying.
- Follow-up meetings with students who are bullied and (separately) with students who bully.
- Meetings with parents of involved students.
- Individualized intervention plans for involved students.

Community components:
- Involvement of community members on the Bullying Prevention Coordinating Committee.
- Development of partnerships with community members to support the school's program.
- Spreading of anti-bullying messages and principals of best practice in the community.

in the United States, Canada, Great Britain, and Germany, and has been found to result in significant reductions in students' reports of bullying and victimization (Black, 2003; Black & Jackson, in press; Charach, Pepler, & Zieler, 1995; Olweus, 1993a, 1994, 2004a, 2004b; Limber, 2006; Limber, Nation, Tracy, Melton, & Flerx, 2004; Melton et al., 1998; Whitney, Rivers, Smith, & Sharp, 1994). It also has resulted in improvements in students' perceptions of the social climate of the classroom, and in reductions in students' reports of antisocial behavior (such as vandalism, fighting, truancy, and theft). Comprehensive bullying prevention programs that embrace principles of best practice hold the most promise for significantly reducing bullying behavior among school children.

Summary

Although the experiences of children like Jack and Tara are not new, it has only been in the past decade that the research community (with several notable exceptions) and members of the popular press have focused attention on their plight. Numerous studies conducted since the early 1990s have confirmed that bullying affects millions of school children each year – either directly or indirectly. Victims of bullying can suffer serious physical health, mental health, and academic consequences. Children who bully are at higher risk of being involved in a wide variety of antisocial, violent, or otherwise troubling behaviors. The effects of bullying also can "bleed" into the school environment as a whole, affecting bystanders and adults as well. As Limber (2006) noted, "Although being bullied, harassed, and excluded are common experiences for many school children, we need not and should not accept that they are *inevitable* experiences" (p. 326). In fact, comprehensive school-based approaches have been shown to reduce bullying among students at school when they are implemented with fidelity. While more research is needed to better understand and address the many different risk and protective factors for bullying, including the broader societal or cultural influences on bullying, researchers have made important strides over the past decade in understanding this phenomenon.

We know far less about the very new phenomenon of cyber bullying, however. Research into this new modality for bullying is clearly in its infancy. In Chapters 3 and 4, we will outline what currently is known about the nature and prevalence of cyber bullying, as well as ways in which it is similar to and different from more traditional forms of bullying.

Note

1. For a listing and description of comprehensive (as well as curricular) approaches to bullying prevention, visit: http://www.bullyingresources.org/stopbullyingnow/indexAdult.asp?Area=ProgramResources.

3

What is Cyber Bullying?

Source: © Milt Priggee, 2007

> Technology . . . has all but erased the reflection time that once existed between planning a silly prank (or a serious act) and actually committing the deed.
>
> (Franek, 2005/2006)

Ten years ago, this book wouldn't have been written because no one would have needed it. A decade ago, technology had not advanced to the point where cyber bullying was even an issue. Times have changed, however, and, unfortunately, kids are keeping pace with the changes much more readily than adults. As a testament to this, ask any child or adolescent about the abbreviations in Table 3.1. Most will immediately know what these abbreviations mean. Ask adults, and you will be met with blank stares.

Table 3.1

Popular Internet acronyms

121	one to one
411	information
AAR	at any rate
A/S/L	age, sex, location
BAK	back at the keyboard
BF	boyfriend
BRB	be right back
CUL	see you later
DKDC	don't know don't care
DQMOT	don't quote me on this
EMFBI	excuse me for butting in
IHAIM	I have another instant message
JK	just kidding
JT	just teasing
LMIRL	let's meet in real life
LSHMBB	laughing so hard my belly is bouncing
NIFOC	nude in front of computer
NP	nosy parents
NTK	nice to know
PA	parent alert
P911	my parents are coming!
PAW	parents are watching
PIR	parent in room
POS	parent over shoulder
RBAY	right back at ya
RBTL	read between the lines
TAW	teachers are watching
TTYL	talk to you later
YGBK	you gotta be kiddin

Source: www.missingkids.com/adcouncil/lingo.
html

Although school-yard bullying such as that described in the previous chapter still regularly occurs, kids today are experiencing a new type of bullying that has been made possible through technological advances, such as cellular phones and the Internet. In addition, with the accessibility of free e-mail services, such as Hotmail and Yahoo ("Internet bullies," 2006), a single child who cyber bullies can communicate with a victim using multiple identities and multiple e-mail addresses. As mentioned in Chapter 1, this new type of bullying is known as cyber bullying, online social cruelty, and electronic bullying. One Web site devoted to educating parents about cyber bullying appropriately defined it as "social terror by technology" ("Cyber bullying," 2006). On an ABC *Primetime* news segment (Ross, 2006), Diane Sawyer referred to cyber bullying as "emotional wilding" and "going for the emotional jugular." Whatever the specific phrase used to capture its essence, cyber bullying, broadly defined, refers to bullying that involves the use of e-mail, instant messaging, text digital imaging messages and digital images sent via cellular phones, Web pages, Web logs (blogs), chat rooms or discussion groups, and other information communication technologies (Health Resources and Services Administration, 2006; Patchin & Hinduja, 2006; Shariff & Gouin, 2005; Willard, 2006).

Much of the attention in the popular press and professional literature has focused on sexual predators that seek out their victims through online venues such as Facebook and MySpace. This focus on sexual predators is not all that surprising given the seriousness of the issue, and the legal resources available to handle such cases when they do arise. In addition, most parents and teens understand the significance of and discuss the dangers of sexual predators. The same cannot be said of cyber bullying. Significantly less attention – popular, academic, and/or legal – has been devoted to the topic of cyber or electronic bullying. The reality, however, is that the majority of children are more likely to be targeted by a person who cyber bullies than by a stranger they have met on the Internet who is trying to arrange an offline meeting.

Defining Cyber Bullying

Whenever researchers begin working in a new area, there are, not surprisingly, conceptual issues that need to be worked out. Cyber bullying has certainly been no exception. Defining the parameters of cyber bullying (e.g., which communication technologies are involved, how they are misused, what is said to whom and with what effect) has proven somewhat difficult, in part because the methods used to cyber bully are varied. Complicating matters further, cyber bullying can sometimes be ambiguous in much the same way that interpersonal teasing is ambiguous. Is a heated exchange between two people IMing each other cyber bullying or simply an argument in print? As with interpersonal teasing, whether something is considered cyber bullying likely depends on who you ask. Targets of vicious e-mails or "verbal lynchings" as Diane Sawyer referred to them (Ross, 2006) are far more likely than perpetrators to identify the behavior as cyber bullying (see also Kowalski, 2000).

There is also confusion surrounding the ages at which cyber bullying may take place. According to Parry Aftab, a lawyer who specializes in Internet safety and who is the executive director of wiredsafety.net, one of the leading Internet sites devoted to cyber bullying, cyber bullying must occur between minors. When an adult becomes involved, the behavior is labeled *cyber harassment* or *cyber stalking*. According to Aftab (2006), "adult cyber-harassment or cyberstalking is NEVER called cyber bullying." We would like to suggest that this behavior, while certainly deserving of the labels of cyber harassment and cyberstalking (and the legal remedies that follow), is also a type of cyber bullying. Indeed, the British National

Association of Schoolmasters/Union of Women Teachers (NAS/UWT) highlighted the fact that teachers are often cyber bullied by their students. In one particular instance, the NAS/UWT was lobbying for the rights of a teacher to be able to refuse to teach a student who had photographed her cleavage and distributed the image to classmates. Similar cases in which head shots of teachers have been superimposed on nude bodies had also been reported ("Pupils not the only victims of cyber bullies," 2006). More recently, a survey conducted by the Teacher Support Network and the Association of Teachers and Lecturers showed that 17% of teachers had been cyber bullied (Smith, 2007). One of us recently had a conversation with a newspaper reporter who talked about the dozens of e-mails she frequently gets haranguing her over a story she has written. Having been a reporter for many years, she said the viciousness of people's e-mails far surpasses anything they would write in snail mail letters or say to reporters over the telephone. As she related several examples of these e-mails, they were clearly examples of cyber bullying.

Conceptual confusion about cyber bullying also stems from the fact that cyber bullying, like more traditional forms of bullying, can be both direct and indirect. Aftab (2006) draws an interesting distinction between *direct cyber bullying* and *cyber bullying by proxy*, or indirect cyber bullying. She defines direct attacks as sending messages direct to other children or youth. Cyber bullying by proxy involves "using others to help cyber bully the victim, either with or without the accomplice's knowledge;" in other words, getting someone else to do the dirty work (Aftab, 2006). Aftab argues that the latter is more dangerous because adults can get involved in the harassment. Most of the time, they are unwitting accomplices and don't know they are being used by the cyber bully. What Aftab refers to as "Warning" or "Notify Wars" are an example. Kids click on the warning buttons on their instant message (IM) screen or e-mail or chat screens and alert the Internet Service Provider (ISP) that there is objectionable content in something the target has written. Targets who receive enough warnings eventually lose their accounts with a particular site. Cyber bullies often set up their victims by making them angry so that they respond with an irate or hateful remark. Once the target responds this way, the perpetrator "warns" or "notifies" them. An unsuspecting adult then terminates the account, becoming an accomplice in the cyber bullying incident.

Cyber bullying by proxy also may occur when someone hacks into the victim's account and sends out harassing, inappropriate, and hateful messages to friends and family on the buddy list. (A buddy list, most often associated with American Online [AOL] and related Internet Service Providers [ISPs] is a window that comes up that includes the screen names of friends, family, coworkers, and acquaintances whom you have chosen to

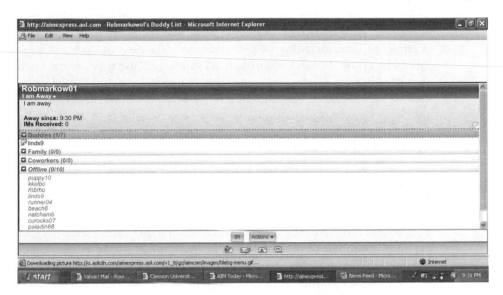

Figure 3.1 Sample buddy list

include in the list and wish to be able to communicate with instantly once they sign onto the ISP; webopedia.com; see Figure 3.1). Alternatively, the cyber bully may be a friend with whom the target has shared his or her username and password, so access to the account is even easier. Recipients of the harassing messages assume that they are coming from the original user of the account (i.e., the target), who subsequently may lose friends, feel humiliated, and have his or her trust destroyed (Aftab, 2006).

In other instances of cyber bullying by proxy, cyber bullies may reset passwords on the target's account so that even the target is blocked from accessing his or her own account. Importantly, and highlighting the diffi- culty in always clearly identifying when cyber bullying has occurred, some individuals may reset a friend's password just in fun. What distinguishes "playful teasing" from cyber bullying is the aggressive intent behind cyber bullying. But, again, intent is in the eye of the beholder. Just as someone who realizes that his or her teasing has gone too far can say "I was only teasing," so, too, a person who cyber bullies can deny that there was any malicious intent behind the behavior; in other words, the target was being too sensitive.

In even more threatening situations, children who cyber bully will sometimes post information about their victim online that places their victim at considerable risk of harm. For example, they may post "informa- tion in child molester chat rooms and discussion boards, advertising their victim for sex. They then sit back and wait for the members of that hate group or child molester group to attack or contact the victim online and, sometimes, offline" (Aftab, 2006). Recently, just such a situation occurred. A family of four, including 14-year-old twin girls, their mother and step-father, had moved from California to Montana because they felt the town they lived in wasn't "white enough." The twin girls, Lynx and Lamb Gaede, created a band called Prussian Blue so they could use music to disseminate their views on the supremacy of the white race. Neighbors in the Montana town, concerned with the views of the new residents, posted fliers through-out the town that said "No Hate Here." However, according to news reports, Web sites, including hate groups, linked to the Prussian Blue site then posted names, addresses, and phone numbers of individuals who had handed out the fliers (Redeker, 2006).

It should be clear now, why coming up with a single sentence or two that defines cyber bullying is difficult. Cyber bullying casts a wide net that captures a number of different types of behaviors. Still, at its core cyber bullying involves bullying through the use of technology such as the Inter-net and cellular phones. As with traditional bullying, cyber bullying also exists on a continuum of severity. On the less extreme end of this contin-uum, cyber bullying may, at times, be difficult to identify. At the other extreme, cyber bullying has led to murder and suicide (see, for example, www.ryanpatrickhalligan.org). As will be seen in the sections that follow, the methods that people use to perpetrate cyber bullying are as varied as the different types of behaviors that constitute it.

Types and Methods of Cyber Bullying

A distinction needs to be made between the methods by which cyber bul-lying is carried out (e.g., e-mail, chat rooms, etc.), and the kind of behavior or exchange being transmitted via that method that leads to a label of cyber bullying. First, we will discuss behaviors that are likely to be classified as cyber bullying regardless of the specific means by which they are executed. Then, we will turn our attention to some of the most common mechanisms used to cyber bully others.

In one of the first books to address the topic of cyber bullying, *Cyberbul-lying and Cyberthreats*, Nancy Willard (2006), an attorney who is the Direc-tor of the Center for Safe and Responsible Internet Use, outlined a number of behaviors that she argues constitute cyber bullying. Included among these are flaming, harassment, denigration, impersonation, outing and trickery, exclusion, and cyberstalking. To this list, we will add happy slap-ping. Each of these will be discussed.

Flaming

Flaming refers to a brief, heated exchange between two or more individuals that occurs via any communication technology. Typically, though, flaming occurs in "public" settings, such as chat rooms or discussion groups, rather than private e-mail exchanges. If a series of insulting exchanges ensues, then a flame war has started (Willard, 2006).

At first blush, flaming would seem to occur between two individuals who are on an equal playing field with one another. However, an unsuspected aggressive act by one individual may create an imbalance in the playing field that is made all the greater by the fact that the target, at least in the short term, is unsure who else the perpetrator might bring into the flame war. So, what may appear to observers to be a level playing field may not be perceived that way by the individuals directly involved in the insulting exchange.

Harassment

Some writers and researchers have used the terms harassment and cyber bullying interchangeably. We mentioned earlier in this chapter Aftab's (2006) use of the term cyber harassment to refer to electronic bullying among adults. *Black's Law Dictionary* (2004, p. 733) defines harassment as "words, conduct, or action (usually repeated or persistent) that, being directed at a specific person, annoys, alarms, or causes substantial emotional distress in that person" and further notes that some but not all types of harassment are actionable (i.e., persons may file suit). In the cyber bullying literature, cyber harassment generally is viewed as a unique form of cyber bullying that involves repetitive offensive messages sent to a target. Most often harassment occurs via personal communication channels, such as e-mail, but harassing messages may also be communicated in public forums, such as chat rooms and discussion groups. One form of harassment, referred to as text wars, involves one or more perpetrators and a single target. The perpetrator(s) sends hundreds or thousands of text messages to the target's cellular phone, leaving the target not only with a slew of harassing messages but with a sizable phone bill as well.

Although conceptually similar, harassment typically differs from flaming in two ways. First, harassment is longer term than flaming. Second, harassment is more one-sided, with at least one offender and a single target. With flaming, on the other hand, there is a mutual exchange of insults between the individuals involved.

Harassment also occurs among a special group of online bullies known as griefers. Griefers are individuals who deliberately harass other players in multiplayer online games. A griefer is less concerned about winning a particular game than he or she is about ruining the playing experience for other players (Pham, 2002; Swartz, 2005). Several participants in our focus groups indicated that either they had been cyber bullied in this way or that they had friends who had been cyber bullied by griefers.

Denigration

Denigration is information about another that is derogatory and untrue. The information may be posted on a Web page or it may be disseminated to others via e-mail or instant messaging. Included within this category of cyber bullying is posting or sending digitally altered photos of someone, particularly in a way that portrays them in a sexualized or harmful manner. In a cyber bullying case that was relayed to us, classmates recorded a song making fun of another classmate. They then placed the song on a Web site so that other classmates could listen to it. One of our focus group participants related a story about a classmate who was cyber bullied by other classmates who posted a picture of her online that was designed to make her look pregnant.

Online "slam books," which are created to make fun of students, represent a form of denigration. Students create a Web site where classmates' names are listed and students write mean and nasty comments about targeted students. Similar to this are negative lists that are posted online. For example, one individual created an online list of students that she identified as "ho's" of the school. Other lists may post information related to who is believed to be sleeping with whom.

Impersonation

With impersonation, the perpetrator poses as the victim, most often by using the victim's password to gain access to his or her accounts, then communicating negative, cruel, or inappropriate information with others as if the target himself or herself were voicing those thoughts. In one case, a password was stolen to a student's instant message account and sexually explicit messages were sent to his classmates by someone posing as this student. The student was humiliated and lost many friendships over the incident.

Additionally, the perpetrator may steal the target's password in order to be able to change the target's personal profile on buddy lists or on a social network site so that inappropriate or offensive information is included. Or they may steal the password so that they can send harassing e-mails to others as if they were coming from the target himself or herself. As noted earlier, at the extreme a cyber bully impersonator may post an offensive remark or comment on a hate group or some other type of group's message board pretending to be the victim, including the name, address, and phone number of the victim should members of the hate group decide to track him or her down. At this level, impersonation truly puts the victim's life in danger.

Outing and Trickery

Outing refers to sharing personal, often embarrassing information with others with whom the information was never intended to be shared. This may take the form of receiving an e-mail or instant message from a target that contains private, potentially embarrassing information and/or photos and then forwarding that e-mail on to others. Trickery refers to tricking someone into revealing personal information about themselves and then sharing that information with others

Exclusion/Ostracism

Whether in the online or offline world, children often perceive that they are either "in" or "out". If they are not in the in-group, then they are in the out-group. Social psychologists have determined that people have a basic human need to be included by other people. Much of our social behavior is guided by our attempts to be included by others and to avoid being excluded, referred to by some as "social death" (Sudnow, 1967; Williams, Cheung, & Choi, 2000). Not surprisingly exclusion in the online world, or cyber-ostracism, can have a serious emotional impact. Dr Larry Koenig (September 28, 2006, personal communication), a former family therapist and a leader in the development of programs for parents and children, summed it up well when he said "with cyber bullying you can absolutely destroy a child emotionally."

Online exclusion can occur in any type of password-protected environment or by a target being knocked off of buddy lists. In some instances, the ostracism may be perceived rather than real, as when someone doesn't respond as quickly to an IM or e-mail as you would like them to. According to Bill Belsey, the creator of www.bullying.org, a leading online source for information about bullying, and www.cyberbullying.ca, the first Web site devoted specifically to cyber bullying, not responding promptly in the online world is viewed as a "real social faux-pas."

Kip Williams and his colleagues (2000) conducted two studies looking at the effects of cyber-ostracism. In the first study, participants played a disk toss game in cyber space ostensibly with two other players. In fact, the players were created by the computer. The researchers manipulated the degree to which the participant was included or excluded in the disk toss game. The more people were ostracized from the game, the worse they felt and the more their self-esteem dropped.

In a second study, the researchers used a simulated ball toss paradigm to determine the relationship between exclusion and the desire to reestablish social connections through conformity. As in the first study, researchers manipulated the degree to which participants were included or excluded in the ball toss game. The more excluded participants were, the more likely they were to conform to members of a completely different group than the group that had ostracized them.

Interestingly, this suggests that people who are cyber bullied, particularly through the method of cyber-ostracism, may join other groups online more readily than individuals who are not ostracized. These groups could be discussion groups or chat rooms, or they could be groups designed to seek revenge on the original source. Joining other groups and feeling connected again may help to alleviate some of the negative feelings associated with having been cyber bullied and ostracized. In addition, there is safety in numbers. Feeling connected to a group of other people may lead the victim to feel empowered to retaliate either individually or by enlisting the help of members of the new group.

Cyberstalking

Cyberstalking refers to the use of electronic communications to stalk another person through repetitive harassing and threatening communications. *Black's Law Dictionary* (2004, p. 1440) defines "stalking" as: "(1) The act or an instance of following another by stealth. (2) The offense of following or loitering near another, often surreptitiously, with the purpose of annoying or harassing that person or committing a further crime such as assault or battery." Although clearly related to harassment, cyberstalking involves more threats than pure harassment. A counselor in the district where we conducted focus groups shared a story of a female band member who was stalked by a fan after posting her e-mail address on the band's Web site. A focus group participant, also a victim of cyberstalking, related the following story: "My ex-boyfriend got kind of crazy once. He started e-mailing me and saying that he was going to come to my house and kill me and stuff like he was watching my sister."

Happy Slapping

Happy slapping is a relatively new method of cyber bullying that began on subway trains and that has taken hold in England. People, usually teenagers, walk up and slap someone, while another individual, also usually a teenager, captures the violence using a camera phone. The behavior often involves more than a "slap," however, and often constitutes assault with associated legal ramifications. A variant of happy slapping, known as hopping, that typically involves direct assaults, is showing up with increasing frequency in the United States and elsewhere (Kohler, 2007). With both happy slapping and hopping, the video that is taken of the incident is then downloaded onto the Web for thousands to see. The victim could be someone known or unknown to the perpetrator. In one incident, an 11-year-old boy was mercilessly attacked in the hallways of his school while observers recorded the incident on their cell phones. Pictures of the boy were then e-mailed to friends of the perpetrator and observers (Blair & Norfolk, 2004). In another incident, Triston Christmas died as a result of happy slapping. Triston was 18 years old when he was hit so hard that he was knocked backwards and hit his head on a concrete floor. The cell phone images show him bleeding as he tried to speak (Watt, 2006). He didn't die until a week later. While he lay on the ground after being attacked, his killer and the killer's friends went to a party and posted the image of Triston online.

In still other incidents, children have committed suicide as a result of being happy slapped. In one instance in April, 2005, a 14-year-old named Shaun Noonan hanged himself after being physically bullied and happy slapped ("Bullycide memorial page," 2006). In a Web-based discussion forum on happy slapping, one respondent stated: "I live in London and can confirm this – I've seen this happen a couple times. It's sad but true. They generally 'attack' in groups and think it's really funny. But I've seen some people really messed up and scared by it" (Dybwad, 2005). Some schools in England have "banned camera phones because of worries that the fad was leading to an increase in playground bullying" (Honigsbaum, 2005). As is true for other types of bullying behavior, depending upon the nature of the situation happy slapping incidents also may constitute crimes.

Communication Modalities for Cyber Bullying

Although it is clear from the descriptions of these behaviors that they can be carried out through any of a number of different communication modalities, some behaviors lend themselves more readily to some venues than others. For example, flaming is more likely to be carried out over public communication venues whereas harassment is more likely to be limited to personal communication modalities such as e-mail. Because of the diversity of communication technologies that can be used to cyber bully others, we will briefly describe the most commonly used methods.

Instant Messaging

As will be discussed in Chapter 4, instant messaging represents one of the most common ways in which teenagers cyber bully one another. Instant messaging, or "IMing", refers to real-time communication via the Internet with individuals on one's buddy or contact list. Cyber bullying through instant messaging can take a number of different forms (Aftab, 2006). Most obviously, perpetrators may send angry or threatening messages to someone else. Alternatively, they may create a screen name that closely resembles the target's screen name or they may use the target's actual screen name. They then send inappropriate communications to others as if they were the target. They may also send compromising photos or videos of another person via IM.

Electronic Mail

Electronic mail, or e-mail, is one of the most frequently used means of digital communication. E-mails are a frequent method of cyber bullying others for two primary reasons. First, a single e-mail can be sent to hundreds and even thousands of people with a single keystroke. Someone wishing to harass or humiliate another individual can send an e-mail containing pictures or objectionable information about someone to hundreds or thousands of people at one time. Second, although e-mails are generally easily traceable, there is no certainty that the person from whose e-mail account the e-mail originated was actually the individual who sent the e-mail. In some instances, individuals who cyber bully may sign up their targets on various pornographic sites and marketing lists so that they are barraged with offensive and harassing e-mails.

Text Messaging

Text messaging is also known as Short Message Service (SMS). The speed with which kids today can send text messages to one another via cellular phones is astounding. Although not a method of real-time communication, text messaging is still an important mode of communication, particularly among teenagers. While certainly an invaluable tool for keeping in contact with others, cellular phones and text messaging also have a downside. Many a naïve college professor has realized only too late that pictures have been taken of a test via cellular phone and transmitted to others, or that students outside of class have text-messaged answers to test questions to their friends in the class.

Outside the academic setting, text messaging can also be used to cyber bully others. Countless stories abound of adolescent girls and boys receiving hundreds if not thousands of text messages because they upset someone. In addition to the harm caused by the messages themselves, there is a financial cost associated with receiving the text messages.

Social Networking Sites

As of April, 2006, there were approximately 200 social networking sites, millions of registered users, and hundreds of thousands of new people registering each day ("Social networking sites," 2006). The number of people communicating with one another via this modality is truly staggering. Social network sites go by many different names. Among the most popular are Facebook, MySpace, LiveJournal, Friendster, Nexopia, Xuga, Xanga, Imbee, and Bebo. As defined by the Federal Bureau of Investigation ("Social networking sites," 2006), social networking sites are "websites that encourage people to post profiles of themselves – complete with pictures, interests, and even journals – so they can meet like-minded friends. Most also offer chat rooms. Most sites are free; some restrict membership by age."

As noted by Swinford (2006), social network sites provide a "window on youth culture." Social network sites allow us to see who is doing what, where, and with whom. The recent news feed changes made to Facebook allow almost real-time insight into what is happening in the lives of Facebook users (see Figure 3.2). Through these news feeds, we know who is friends with whom, who has ended a relationship with whom, who has posted new pictures, and who is having a bad day, to give just a few examples.

Any changes made to an individual's profile are made readily available to "friends" who have access to that person's profile. Even the users of Facebook themselves say it's too much of a window on what Facebook users are doing in their day-to-day lives.

And, it's often a cruel window on what children and youth are doing. Swinford (2006) cites Chris Cloke, head of child protection at the National Society for the Prevention of Cruelty to Children (NSPCC), as noting that: "[i]t's a completely unregulated world out there. I'd compare it to a modern-day Lord of the Flies. Children say things that are much more extreme and vindictive than they would in their everyday lives."

Adding additional fuel to an already combustible situation, the owners of Facebook, Inc., in conjunction with executives at Verizon Wireless, Cingular, and Sprint Nextel, are making it possible for people to post messages on Facebook or search for phone numbers and e-mail addresses from

```
News Feed
  ⚏
Collin Leary joined the group Coastal Carolina Chanticleers 2010. 8:15pm
  ⚏
Ginger Lijewski and Kristina Wright are now friends. 6:39pm
  ⚏
Richard Reams and Kristy Kelso are now friends. 3:30pm
  ⚏
Natalie Irby joined the group Clemson is Going To Win The ACC Championship in 2006. 1:56pm
  ⚏
Melinda Keith joined the group Virginia Tech in Our Prayers. 10:52am
  ⚏
Caroline King wrote on Whitney Chamber's wall, 8:15pm
  ⚏
Sarah Bagwell King joined the group CU Bound. 9:21am
  ⚏
Kelly Finnegan and Melissa Redfearn are now friends. 2:15am
  ⚏
Kelly King is heading back to Clemson for an alumni weekend visit! 1:55am
  ⚏
Amy Scheck and Cathy Litty are now friends. 1:02am
  ⚏
Karissa Chorbajian posted on Sarah Eisner's wall. 12:42am
  ⚏
Noah Britt and Jordan Britt joined the group Twins are Awesome, 7:01pm
  ⚏
Erin Hunter and Lindsey Sporrer are now friends. 9:28pm
  ⚏
Frances Bagwell and Randolph Kowalski are now friends. 8:14pm
  ⚏
Jim Merck tagged Suzanne Tripp in the note It was a blast... And I thank you all. 7:54pm
```

Figure 3.2   Sample news feed

their cellular phone. MySpace has made a similar agreement with wireless company Hello Inc. (Yuan, 2006).

A variant of social network sites are social Web sites where people can upload, share, and comment on videos. Referred to as YouTube, Google Video, and the like, these sites are becoming increasingly popular with teens. YouTube was founded in February 2005 by three PayPal employees. In about a year-and-a-half, it has grown to over 50 employees, and is currently listed by the Web information company Alexa as the 15th most popular Web site. Approximately 65,000 new videos are uploaded daily, around 20 million people visit the site monthly, and over 100 million video clips are viewed each day (YouTube, 2006). Although some of the videos are intended to be funny, others are in very poor taste. Not surprisingly, a cursory search of YouTube will quickly reveal instances of cyber bullying. A site very similar to YouTube known as Kazaa, although traditionally used to share music, was the Web site on which the video of the Star Wars Kid described in Chapter 1 was originally posted (Dyrli, 2005).

Variants of social network sites have also been created in memory of deceased individuals who had profiles on social network sites. For example,

MyDeathSpace.com contains tributes to former members of MySpace who are no longer living. Clicking on the individual's photo takes you to their MySpace page where people continue to post messages to the person. Although perhaps these sites provide cathartic value for some survivors, the sites also provide an opportunity for people to post comments and replies, many of them negative and inflammatory. It only takes a few minutes to find multiple instances of cyber bullying on the Web site, not all that surprising given that there is a section for hate mail. Posted within this part of the site's discussion forum are hate emails that have been sent to the Web site. In one instance, a mother, whose daughter had died and whose picture and MySpace page were posted on MyDeathSpace.com, had posted a comment about how offensive she found the site to be and how she would do everything in her power to have the site removed. A torrent of responses from proponents of MyDeathSpace.com followed, many of which fit the definition of cyber bullying.

Chat Rooms

Chat rooms are places where people can go in virtual reality to talk with one another about any of a number of issues. Typically, a chat room will, at least on the surface, be designed to focus on a particular topic or topics. Participants type in comments that then appear on the screens of other individuals signed into the chat room. Other chat rooms, however, are designed purely to provide people with a place where they can meet other individuals and communicate with them in real time. In some of these chat rooms, people pick an avatar or a symbol (e.g., an animal or a character) that they feel represents them. It is via this avatar that they communicate with others in the chat room (www.netlingo.com). As with any other virtual communication in real time, however, chat rooms provide a forum in which cyber bullying can occur. Members of the chat room can begin to denigrate a particular individual, they may ostracize a member of the chat group, or particular members may get into a flame war with one another.

Complicating matters further, people often assume identities in chat rooms that are very different from their real-world identity. They may fabricate their age, gender, occupation, or any other personally identifiable feature. Although this can be cathartic for the person trying to pretend to be someone other than whom they really are, in some instances cyber stalkers and sexual predators seek out their unsuspecting victims by fabricating their identities. Furthermore, in spite of the cathartic value to the communicator of taking on an assumed identity, fellow chatters often become angry if and when they later find out they have been duped and communicating with someone other than whom they thought they were communicating with. For example, people in chat rooms and discussion groups often report communicating differently with another individual as a function of whether they believe that person to be male or female, presumably engaging in more self-disclosure with females than males. One can imagine the chagrin and anger of an individual who has been communicating with a "woman" only to later find out it was a man. Such circumstances might set up a cyber bullying situation fueled by the anger of the individual who felt "duped."

Blogs

Blogs, or Web logs, refer to online journals. Blogs are extremely popular. In fact, it is estimated that a new Web log is created every second (www. netlingo.com). One Web site devoted solely to tracking blogs, Technorati. com, searches Web sites according to blog topic. The purpose is to allow users to see what is being said about any of a number of topics and then weigh in with their own comments. Current estimates are that Technorati. com has on average 1.2 million new blog posts daily (www.netlingo.com). Although blogs can be used for any of a number of positive functions, they can also be used to cyber bully others. Kids may use these blogs to damage other kids' reputations or invade their privacy. For example, in some cases, jilted boyfriends or girlfriends may post a series of blogs containing degrading and embarrassing information about the ex-partner, even getting their friends to post negative information on the site as well.

Web Sites

Web sites are places or locations on the World Wide Web that contain a home page, in addition to links to other possible pages. Many people have their own personal home pages used to promote their businesses, post personal information for the benefit of family and friends, or sell products. Web sites can also be set up, however, for the purposes of cyber bullying. In many instances, Web pages are created for the sole purpose of posting offensive information and/or pictures about another individual. For example, pictures may be taken of a classmate and then doctored in a way that portrays that individual in a sexually provocative manner. Personal contact information for that individual, including name, address, and phone number then may be provided on the Web site.

In other instances, Web pages are established to set up Internet polls. Internet polling may be used for the purpose of humiliating a target. Students, for example, might be encouraged to go to the Web site and vote for the ugliest girl in the class, or the fattest kid at school. Although sites that exist for the purpose of setting up such Web pages have abuse policies and reporting systems, they are often not closely regulated (Belsey, 2006).

Bash Boards

Although often equated with chat rooms because they afford people the opportunity to have a virtual chat with one another, bash boards more closely resemble Internet polling sites. In fact, they are online bulletin boards where people can post any information that they want to about any person or any topic.

Internet Gaming

Many kids today play online interactive games on gaming devices such as X-Box Live and Sony Play Station 2 Network. (Many also play games on their home computers, in some instances paying a monthly subscription fee to participate.) Some of the games are single-player, text-based games, whereas others are complex, interactive, multiplayer games in a virtual world. Just as people expressed their frustration 20 years ago when playing Nintendo games, online players also vent their dissatisfaction with the playing of others. However, consistent with most other types of cyber bullying, the expression of dissatisfaction and frustration in the cyber world where people communicate anonymously using pseudonames tends to be more abusive, threatening, and demeaning. In addition, players can block other players from the game and they can gain unauthorized access to their game accounts (Aftab, 2006). One of the most popular massive multiplayer online games is World of Warcraft. Players join guilds in order to complete various tasks. Players can be promoted by the guild leader, but they can also be kicked out of the guild or demoted. This may cause quite a bit of emotional distress for some players.

Who Cyber Bullies?

Unfortunately, although there is much speculation about "cyber bullies" in the popular press, we actually know very little about the characteristics of these individuals or their various motivations. Below we will discuss what little is known from the research literature about children who cyber bully, and we also will share speculations (our own and those of others), which will need to be further explored by research.

Characteristics of Children Who Cyber Bully

In Chapter 2 we explored common characteristics of children who bully, which included (Olweus, 1993a):

- They have dominant personalities and like to assert themselves using force.
- They have a temper, are impulsive and are easily frustrated.
- They have more positive attitudes toward violence than other children.
- They have difficulty following rules.
- They appear to be tough and show little empathy or compassion for those who are bullied.
- They often relate to adults in aggressive ways.
- They are good at talking themselves out of difficult situations.
- They engage in both proactive aggression (i.e., deliberate aggression to achieve a goal) and reactive aggression (i.e., defensive reactions to being provoked) (Camodeca & Goossens, 2005).

Although it is reasonable to assume that children who cyber bully share some (or even many) of these characteristics, it is also likely that there are some important differences that will need to be explored through future research.

In Chapter 2, we also explored gender differences in traditional forms of bullying and noted that boys are more likely than girls to engage in bullying at school. When looking at similarities and differences in the types of bullying that boys and girls experience, research suggests that boys are more likely to be physically bullied by their peers (Finkelhor et al., 2005; Nansel et al., 2001; Olweus, 1993a; Rigby, 2002), whereas girls are more likely to be bullied through some indirect forms of bullying, such as rumor-spreading, as well as through sexual comments or gestures (Nansel et al., 2001). Interestingly, girls are more likely to report being both victims and perpetrators of cyber bullying. However, among those individuals who engage in cyber bullying, boys do so with greater frequency than girls. We will return to the issue of gender and cyber bullying again in Chapter 4.

Because of the suggestion that socially anxious individuals might be more likely to (a) use technology as a means of communicating with others and (b) engage in cyber bullying as revenge for bullying at school, we examined the relationship between a person's dispositional tendency to experience social anxiety and their experiences with cyber bullying (Kowalski & Limber, 2006). As will be discussed in more detail in Chapter 4, our data showed that, among perpetrators, the highest levels of social anxiety were reported by 8th graders who cyber bullied others at least twice a month. The more frequent the cyber bullying, the higher the level of social anxiety, supporting our hypothesis that cyber bullying and social anxiety are linked. Importantly, however, in a comparison between individuals who cyber bully and those who are cyber bullied, social anxiety scores are higher among victims than perpetrators.

Although there are a number of other personality traits that might be shared by many children who cyber bully, there probably is no single profile of such a child. Some engage in electronic violence somewhat inadvertently without realizing that what they are doing is actually cyber bullying, particularly when they are simply responding in kind to negative comments that have been sent to them in e-mails or instant messages. Other individuals, however, cyber bully with the express purpose of hurting and humiliating their victims. Still other children and youth cyber bully because they are bored and simply think that sending threatening or demeaning messages to another person would be fun. Their focus is on alleviating their own boredom, rather than thinking about the effects that their behavior could have on their victims.

What Motivates Children to Cyber Bully?

Asking the question of "who cyber bullies?" also raises the question of "what motivates someone to engage in such a behavior?" Just as there is a variety of possible motives for engaging in traditional forms of bullying (see Chapter 2), there also is a long list of reasons why adolescents might engage in cyber bullying. Some may cyber bully as a way of asserting power or channeling their aggressive energy. Others may gain satisfaction, prestige, or other rewards from cyber bullying. Still others may bully as a way to act out aggressive fantasies online. Parry Aftab (2006) recounted a meeting with a young boy who was what some might call the "perfect child" in real life – well behaved, polite, and a good student. However, online this boy became someone completely different – violent and aggressive. When asked why, his response was, "Because I can." Nevertheless, in our focus group interviews with middle and high school students, a discrete number of motivations continued to emerge. These motives included: boredom, power, meanness, as retaliation for being bullied, for attention, looking cool and tough, and jealousy. Other key reasons included that cyber bullying was safer than traditional bullying because it was anonymous and they were less likely to get caught and it was easier because it didn't involve face-to-face confrontations. Another motive is the pleasure of inflicting pain. As noted by Alex Pham (2002), a writer for the *Chicago Tribune*, in his analysis of griefers: "For a griefer, it's not the killing that is fun, because combat is inherent in many of these games. It's the misery it causes other players. 'Griefers feed on the negative reactions of the people they kill,' said Frerichs, who savors his evil online persona and saves every nasty e-mail he gets from the people he has antagonized. 'There's nothing sweeter than when you kill someone, and they spout insults at you for hours. That's when you know you got him. It sounds really cruel, but it's fun.'"

Parry Aftab (2006) has delineated four types of children who cyber bully: (a) the vengeful angel, (b) the power-hungry, (c) mean girls, and (d) the inadvertent cyber bully or "because I can." Although these four categories may provide a useful heuristic for considering different motives of children who cyber bully, empirical evidence is needed to bear them out.

According to Aftab (2006), the "vengeful angel" views himself or herself as seeking justice to right wrongs that have been inflicted on them or others. Many of these cyber bullies are children and youth who have been victims of bullying at school and who are now retaliating. They may be the outcasts who have been victims of traditional bullying at school (Willard, 2006). Support for the fact that children often retaliate in one form or another after being bullied can be found in a study by the U.S. Department of Education and the U.S. Secret Service that showed that 75% of school shooters had been victims of traditional bullying (Fein et al. 2002; see also Leary, Kowalski, Smith, & Phillips, 2003). The Internet postings of Eric Harris and Dylan Klebold, who gunned down students and staff at Columbine High School, dramatically recounted their anger at being bullied. Similarly, Kimveer Gill, who killed one student at Dawson College in Montreal, Canada, in September, 2006, had numerous postings on vampire-freaks.com in which he wrote of his anger at being bullied: "Stop bullying. It's not only the bully's fault you know!! It's the teachers and principals fault for turning a blind eye, just cuz it's not their job . . . Stop making fun of each other because of the clothes you wear or the way people talk or act, or any other reasons you make fun of each other. It's all the jock's fault" (Lackner, 2006).

The "power-hungry cyber bully," according to Aftab (2006), most closely resembles the prototypical school-yard bully in his or her desire to exert control, power, and authority over others. Whereas the traditional bully often uses, in addition to indirect strategies, direct verbal attacks or physical aggression to induce fear in others, the cyber bully uses threats or humiliating postings to create fear. Unlike the vengeful angel, who most often acts alone, the power-hungry cyber bully thrives with an audience to watch or reinforce his or her actions. Aftab hypothesizes that there is a subset of power-hungry cyber bullies that seeks power over others but as a way of compensating for their own perceived inadequacies. These individuals may be victims of traditional bullying and may be smaller and weaker than many of their peers. Cyber bullying may be a means to retaliate and appear bigger than they really are, using technology at which they may be particularly skilled.

Included within the category of power-hungry cyber bullies are children and youth who have not been subjected to bullying at school but who bully online just to vent anger or hostility (Levine, 2006). These children may feel that their life is out of control for reasons that have nothing to do with peers at school or with school-yard bullying (e.g., divorce, separation, illness of a parent). Cyber bullying may provide a way for these children and youth to release the anger they have in response to their current life situation and to feel in control of something (or someone).

Aftab's (2006) category "mean girls" is used to refer to children who cyber bully out of boredom. As noted earlier, cyber bullying that is motivated by boredom occurs more for the pleasure and entertainment of the cyber bully than for any particular desire to hurt the victim, although clearly part of the entertainment value of cyber bullying would lie in knowing that their bullying had embarrassed or humiliated another person.

This description, however, highlights the fact that the name "mean girls" is something of a misnomer. First of all, although cyber bullying is more common among girls than boys (see Chapter 4), boys engage in cyber bullying out of boredom as well. Second, the title implies that there is an inherent meanness in children and youth who are motivated to cyber bully because they are bored. Long before technology became what it is today, children and youth got into all kinds of trouble because they were bored. Boredom, however, does not equate with meanness. While it is certainly true that many people who cyber bully engage in the behavior to harm others, it would be inappropriate (and not very useful) to label children who cyber bully as "mean."

The "inadvertent" cyber bully consists of those individuals who become cyber bullies as they respond in kind to negative communications that they receive, or who are inadvertently brought into cyber bullying through cyber bullying by proxy.

How Cyber Bullying Differs from Other Types of Bullying

Aware that knowledge about cyber bullying is still in its infancy, Parry Aftab (2006) stated that: "the motives and the nature of cyber communications, as well as the demographics and profile of a cyber bully, differ from their offline counterpart." Yet, cyber bullying, by its very name, remains a form of bullying. Therefore, it shares in common with traditional bullying the three primary characteristics of bullying that were discussed in Chapter 2, albeit in slightly different ways: (a) the behavior is aggressive; (b) there is a power imbalance between the victim and the perpetrator; and (c) the behavior is repeated. Importantly, a power imbalance may be somewhat different in cyber space than it is in a face-to-face interaction. Because of the nature of cyber space (and particularly the anonymity it may present, something we will return to below), a child who might wield little power over a victim face-to-face may wield a great deal of power (and fear) in cyber space. More specifically, there is power in being anonymous, in assuming a false identity, in having the ability to spread rumors and lies to a wide audience, and in being able to harass a victim anywhere and any time.

Furthermore, although typically bullying is defined as not occurring once or twice, but as being a repeated behavior, the picture becomes a bit murky in cyber space. A single act (e.g., a nasty e-mail or an inflammatory text message) may be forwarded to hundreds or thousands of children over a period of time. From a victim's perspective, he or she may feel repeatedly bullied, to say nothing of the fact that the victim may reread the e-mail or text message himself or herself multiple times, again leading to the feeling of being bullied repeatedly. Even though there may have been only one initial act, it may have been perpetrated through many people and over time.

Although certainly, as their names and this brief discussion imply, traditional bullying and cyber bullying share features in common, they also clearly differ from one another in important ways. We will discuss four of these differences.

The Enemy You Know . . .

As bad as the thug in the school yard may be, at least he or she is a known entity. He or she usually can be readily identified, and potentially avoided. The cyber bully, on the other hand, is often anonymous. Thus, the victim is left wondering if the cyber bully is a single person or a group of people. Is it a girl or a boy? Is it a friend or an enemy? A stranger or an acquaintance? Someone older or younger? Someone from school or elsewhere? Later in this chapter, we will return to this issue of anonymity and the implications it may have for both the victim and the perpetrator.

Accessibility

Most children who use traditional ways of bullying, terrorize their victims at school, on the school bus, or walking to and from school. Although bullying also may happen elsewhere in the community, there usually is a circumscribed period of time during which traditional bullies have access to their victims. (And at the very least, most children who are bullied by peers can find respite at home, unless they also are bullied by siblings.) Children who cyber bully, on the other hand, can wreak havoc 24/7. A child in a study conducted by Glenn Stutzky, an instructor at Michigan State University, summed it up well when he said: "It's like being tethered to your tormentor" (Meadows et al., 2005, p. 152). In fact, most cyber bullying happens not at school but off school grounds. Although certainly children and youth who are cyber bullied can turn their computers and their cellular phones off, as soon as they turn them back on the messages reappear, the comments continue to be posted on Web sites, and e-mails have accumulated.

The fact that cyber bullying happens most often away from school as opposed to at school also limits the role that schools can play in intervening in cyber bullying situations. If the cyber bullying occurs using school computers, then school administrators can enact punitive measures. If the electronic violence occurs off of school grounds, even though it may affect school performance and relationships, school personnel may feel less obligation to intervene. We will talk more about this in Chapters 6 and 7.

Punitive Fears

One way in which traditional bullies wield their power is by threatening their victims if they tell anyone or if they fail to bring money or perform certain tasks. Thus, victims of traditional bullying may be most fearful of the bullying escalating if they tell someone about their victimization. Although fears of retribution also accompany cyber bullying, the fear of having computer and phone privileges revoked is even greater for many victims of cyber bullying. For many parents who hear that their child is a victim of electronic violence, this is, at first blush, the most logical initial step. However, given that the computer and cellular phone are key elements of the child's social life, to revoke technology privileges is to punish the victim (again!)

Bystanders

Most traditional bullying episodes occur in the presence of other people who assume the role of bystanders or witnesses. Although some of these bystanders may egg on the bully or defend the victim, most stand by and simply witness the event. Their presence, however silent, still speaks volumes to both the victim and the perpetrator. To the perpetrator, the silence of a passive bystander comes across as support; to the victim, the mere presence of the bystander may amplify an already painful and humiliating situation.

With cyber bullying, bystanders play a slightly different role and may be willing or unwilling bystanders. The role that a bystander plays also depends on the medium by which the cyber bullying occurs. In chat rooms, for example, a bystander could simply witness an exchange between a victim and a perpetrator or he or she could join in on the electronic bullying. In other instances, a cyber bully may use the screen name of an unassuming "bystander" to bully someone else, creating a cyber bullying by proxy scenario described earlier in the chapter. Although empirical data are needed to support or refute this statement, we would venture to guess that bystanders to cyber bullying are more likely to eventually take part in the cyber bullying themselves than are bystanders of traditional bullying. Why? First of all, cyber bullying requires neither the physical capabilities nor the social prowess that may be needed with traditional bullying. For example, size doesn't matter in cyber bullying; the smallest child could easily join in cyber bullying others. Second, as mentioned at other points throughout the book, the anonymity associated with the Internet, and the tendency to forget the human side of the target of cyber bullying, make it easier to join in on cyber bullying than traditional bullying.

The Phenomenon of Disinhibition

The anonymity afforded by the Internet can lead people to pursue behaviors further than they might otherwise be willing to do. When they cannot be identified, people will often say and do things that they would not do if their identities were known, a phenomenon known as disinhibition. In a classic study within social psychology, Williams, Harkins, and Latané (1981) found that participants reduced the amount of effort they put into a group activity as long as they thought no one could single them out as withholding effort or engaging in social loafing. Once their identity became known, however, the participants exerted maximum effort. Ironically, it is their very anonymity that allows some individuals to bully at all. Children and youth who are smaller and physically weaker than many of their peers tend to bully others at school less frequently for the simple reason that they are outsized. Yet with electronic communications, they can hide behind an assumed identity and wreak havoc.

Because of the ability of people to hide behind pseudonames on the Internet as they bully others, some have referred to cyber bullying as the "cowardly form of bullying" (Belsey, 2006). Others have suggested that the anonymity associated with cyber technologies provides perpetrators with a "cloak of invisibility" (Carrington, 2006). Without the threat of punishment or social disapproval, people may carry their actions much further than they normally would. Interestingly, however, this anonymity is more illusion than reality. As noted by Nancy Willard (2006, p. 47), "people are not totally invisible or anonymous when they use information and communication technologies. In most cases, they leave 'cyberfootprints' wherever they go." Still, even if they are identified, perpetrators can always claim that someone else was using their screen name, so that they can distance themselves from any personal responsibility.

The anonymity afforded by electronic communications is a much bigger factor than one might think at first blush, and may be responsible for cyber bullying having such a strong intimidation factor associated with it. In a survey that we conducted examining the incidence of cyber bullying among over 3,700 middle school children, close to 50% of the individuals did not know the identity of the perpetrator.

A respondent in one of our focus groups said: "I personally think cyber bullying is not something you think about and say oh I feel like cyber bullying someone. It might even be accidental but you might say something to someone that really hurts them and you might just keep at it. You might think you are having fun but you can't hear their tone of voice over AIM or e-mail so you don't even know if you are doing it." As conveyed in this statement, because cyber bullying occurs via technology as opposed to via face-to-face interactions, perpetrators cannot see the emotional reactions of their victims. In many face-to-face interactions, people will modulate their behavior when they see the effect that their behavior is having on others (e.g., nervousness, increased anxiety, etc.). In other words, our behaviors in real life are often modulated by the emotional reactions of others. When we good-naturedly tease someone else, but realize based on their facial reactions that our tease has been misinterpreted or taken too far, we usually apologize and stop engaging in that behavior. When we cannot see that person's emotional reactions as is the case with cyber technologies, there is no emotional meter that serves to temper our behaviors. As stated by a high school student being interviewed about cyber bullying: "It's hard to remember that the other person is really seeing it." It is almost as if some perpetrators fail to remember that they are actually communicating with another human being, albeit unseen.

The inability to read the emotional reaction of the other also extends from victim to perpetrator. There are no contextual cues for the victim to use to interpret the messages that they are receiving. In face-to-face interactions, victims can scan the faces of potential bullies or individuals they perceive to be hurting their feelings for signs that a tease is really just a tease. Teases that are accompanied by winks, smiles, or the like may convey information to the target regarding the prosocial nature of a tease. When communicating electronically, however, targets cannot see the faces of the perpetrator. Thus, they have no means of "reading" the intentions of the perpetrator through nonverbal behaviors. With the exception of emoticons (e.g., smiley faces), e-mail, for example, is devoid of nonverbal communication. As noted by Kruger and his colleagues (2005, p. 926), "this limitation is likely to be fertile ground for miscommunication and, in particular, a lack of awareness of that miscommunication."

In two studies investigating the discrepancy between how well people thought they communicated over e-mail and how well they actually communicated, Kruger et al. (2005) found that people believe they communicate better over e-mail than they actually do. In one of these studies, 12 participants were asked to write two statements about each of 10 topics (e.g., dating, Greek life). One statement was to be a serious statement and the other was to be a sarcastic statement. The sentences were then e-mailed to another participant who was asked to identify which statements were serious and which were sarcastic. Although participants estimated that 97% of their statements would be correctly identified by the receiver, in fact only 84% were correctly labeled as serious or sarcastic. The researchers concluded that e-mail senders overestimated their ability to communicate clearly because of egocentrism; in other words, because a message was clear to them, they assumed that it would also be clear to the receiver. When we communicate sarcasm, for example, over e-mail, we can "hear" the sarcasm in the sentences as we type them. However, the same sarcastic tone is not being played for the receiver. Thus, what may begin as "innocent" teasing over e-mail or instant messaging may be taken for something other than what was intended. The result could be a flaming war or some other type of cyber bullying.

Summary

One of the difficulties in discussing cyber bullying and in attempting to design intervention and prevention programs related to it, is that there is no simple definition of cyber bullying nor is there a single profile of the cyber bully. Rather, cyber bullying is a behavior that can occur through multiple modalities (e.g. instant messaging, e-mail, chat rooms), appear in a number of guises (e.g., harassment, flaming, impersonation), and be perpetrated anonymously by individuals you would least suspect of bullying someone else. With time, however, and continued research, we should be able to better identify the circumstances under which cyber bullying is most likely to occur. Additional research related to cyber bullying will be discussed in the next chapter.

4

Current Research on Cyber Bullying

〜

Relative to research on traditional bullying, only a handful of studies have focused specifically on cyber bullying among children and youth. Those that have been conducted have used a variety of methods to obtain information about the frequency of cyber bullying, how children and youth are cyber bullying one another, and the effects of cyber bullying on both the victim and the perpetrator. The end result is that there are some slight inconsistencies in the actual numbers (e.g., frequencies) that are reported across studies. Although we will discuss many of these studies and report their findings, the variability in the precise frequency with which cyber bullying occurs, for example, is far less important than the consistent conclusions from the studies that cyber bullying is a problem, that it is increasing among children and youth, and that more research needs to be conducted and policies developed to deal with the problem.

Important considerations to keep in mind when comparing studies are cultural similarities and differences in both the prevalence of research on the topic of cyber bullying and the prevalence of cyber bullying itself within a particular culture. Although clearly the frequency of cyber bullying is directly correlated with the availability of technology in a particular culture, among developed cultures cyber bullying is nonculture specific. In other words, cyber bullying is increasingly becoming an issue in most, if not all, developed countries. Reports on the increasing prevalence of cyber bullying have emerged from all corners of the world, including the United Kingdom, Australia, Japan, Canada, Korea, and the United States, to name a few. Kraft (2006) recently summarized worldwide trends in cyber bullying and examined cross-cultural variations in the effects of cyber bullying. She found that victimization reports varied between 10% and 42%, and that, whereas the most popular medium for cyber bullying in Australia and the United Kingdom was the cellular phone, in the United States and Canada it was the Internet.

Methods of Studying Cyber Bullying

Most existing research on cyber bullying, whether in the United States or abroad, has relied on surveys. Some of these have been anonymous paper and pencil surveys (e.g., Kowalski & Limber, 2006), others have been completed online (e.g., Kowalski & Witte, 2006), and still others have been conducted via the telephone (e.g., Ybarra, Mitchell, Wolak, & Finkelhor, 2006). One of the primary reasons for the extensive reliance on surveys is that they are easy to administer and can be completed by a large number of people in a relatively short period of time. However, surveys are not without their problems, as discussed in Box 4.1.

Another reason for the popularity of surveys is the difficulty associated with trying to recreate cyber bullying within a laboratory setting. In spite of this difficulty, however, such a situation was actually created by the producers of the ABC News show *Primetime*, with very interesting results (Ross, 2006). In consultation with three researchers at Brigham Young University and Teri Schroeder, the head of i-SAFE, an organization devoted to Internet safety education, the producers created a role-play situation that lasted over the course of a weekend. The purpose was to see whether or not cyber bullying would emerge among strangers over a relatively short period of time. Eleven previously unacquainted teenage girls were provided with cellular phones, computers with Internet access, and Web cams. A second, mixed-sex group of slightly older individuals represented a "popular" group. As summarized by ABC reporter Keturah Gray (September 14, 2006), "over the course of the weekend, the girls put their arsenal to full use, working diligently to reach the top of the social hierarchy." The girls "competed" for the attention of those in the popular group and resorted to cyber bullying tactics when necessary to achieve a desired social status. In a debriefing following the role-play, one of the girls commented that she had no idea she could be so mean.

One additional method that has been used to study cyber bullying has been focus groups. In our own research using focus groups, a series of questions were created to allow investigators to probe not only the frequency of cyber bullying but more specific information about actual incidents of cyber bullying that the adolescents had experienced or witnessed. A female and a male interviewer conducted 12 focus groups with small numbers of female and male students, respectively, from four suburban

Box 4.1	Popularity and problems of surveys

In spite of the popularity of survey use in investigations of cyber bullying, and most other research topics for that matter, there is no research that is devoid of problems, including methodological issues, sampling issues, and analytical issues. Research on cyber bullying is no exception to this. Two of the primary online surveys that have been done are good exemplars of this: Parry Aftab's online survey found at www.wiredsafety.org, and our survey (Kowalski & Witte, 2006) found at www.camss.clemson.edu/KowalskiSurvey/servlet/Page1. Both of these surveys have provided very useful data related to cyber bullying that will be discussed in the pages that follow. The online nature of these surveys meant that anyone could go to the Web site and complete the survey. At first blush, this would seem to be an ideal situation that would increase the representativeness of the sample and the number of people who could respond. However, the wiredsafety.org survey was housed on the Web site itself. Thus, people who were going to access the site to fill out the survey represented those individuals who were probably already concerned about the issue of cyber bullying or who were interested in learning more about it. With our own survey (Kowalski & Witte, 2006), a link to the survey was posted on two social network sites: LiveJournal and Nexopia. Although a useful way to gain access to individuals willing to complete the survey, the fact that they were on a social network site when they saw the link to the survey suggests that they might have been more regular Internet users than someone who did not regularly access a social network site.

We mention these difficulties so that readers may engage in critical thinking as they evaluate any research study, whether related to cyber bullying or not, whether written in a book, the popular press, or an academic journal article.

Georgia middle and high schools representing different socioeconomic backgrounds. Additional individual interviews were conducted with targets and perpetrators of cyber bullying as well as with the mothers of individuals who had been cyber bullied. As will be seen throughout the chapter, a key advantage of focus groups is that they provide much more information about specific incidents and feelings related to cyber bullying than can be conveyed on a survey.

Prevalence of Cyber Bullying

As the methods used to study cyber bullying have been somewhat variable, not surprisingly exact statistics related to the prevalence of cyber bullying are difficult to obtain. Reported frequencies of cyber bullying depend on the country in which the data are collected, how cyber bullying is defined, whether participants are asked if they have *ever* been cyber bullied or been cyber bullied *within the past couple of months*, and the ages of the respondents. With those caveats in mind, however, there is still remarkable consistency across studies in the prevalence rates of cyber bullying reported by victims and by perpetrators and in the most frequent methods by which people experience cyber bullying as victims and as perpetrators. In the pages that follow, we will provide a brief synopsis of the primary findings from each of the major studies that was designed to focus exclusively on cyber bullying, plus one of our own studies that examined cyber bullying in addition to Internet use more broadly (Kowalski & Witte, 2006). Table 4.1 provides a summary of the prevalence data from these studies.

National Children's Home (NCH) Study

In the first study to systematically investigate cyber bullying, researchers with the National Children's Home in Great Britain (NCH, 2002) surveyed children and youth between the ages of 11 and 19 and found that 16% had *ever* been bullied via mobile phone text messaging, 7% via Internet chat rooms, and 4% through e-mail. Of those who had been cyber bullied, 69% had told someone of the bullying. The most likely confidantes were friends (42%) and parents (32%), followed by siblings (14%), teachers (12%), and police (7%). Girls were almost twice as likely as boys to say they had been bullied via text messaging (21% vs. 12%). Conversely, boys were almost twice as likely as girls to report being bullied via Internet chat rooms (9% vs. 5%). Females (3%) and males (5%) varied little in the rates at which they were victimized via e-mail.

Between March and April of 2005, NCH teamed up with Tesco Mobile to conduct a mobile bullying survey ("Putting U in the picture – Mobile bullying survey 2005," 2005). In response to a paper and pencil survey, 20% of the children and youth aged 11–19 said that they had *ever* been cyber bullied. Fourteen percent had been bullied via text messaging, 5% in chat rooms, and 4% through e-mail. Twenty-six percent did not know the identity of the perpetrator, and 28% had never told anyone about being cyber bullied. Eleven percent of the respondents admitted to ever cyber bullying someone else.

Table 4.1

Key investigations of cyber bullying

Study	Year	No. of participants	Ages	% cyber bullied*	% who bullied*
National Children's Home (NCH)	2002	856	11–19	16% via txt msg; 7% via chat rooms; 4% via e-mail	–
Mobile Bullying Survey	2005	770	11–19	20%	11%
Anti-Bullying Alliance	2006	92	11–16	22%	–
Online Victimization Survey	2000	1,501	10–17	6%	–
YISS-1	2004	1,501	10–17	4%	12%
YISS-2	2006	1,500	10–17	9%	–
Patchin & Hinduja	2006	384	<18	29%	11%
Colorado Multi-site Eval. Study	2006	>3,000	Grades 5, 8, 11	21%	18%
Fight Crime Preteen	2006	503	6–11	17%	–
Fight Crime Teen	2006	512	12–17	36%	–
Kowalski & Limber	2006	3,767	Grades 6–8	18%	11%
Agatston & Carpenter	2006	257	Grades 6–8	18%	5%
Youth Internet Survey	2006	>700	>11	11%	3%
WiredSafety	2006	>900	>7; 44% >16	53%	23%

*Refer to the text for definitions and time periods of responses

Anti-Bullying Alliance Study

In another British study (Smith, Mahdavi, Carvalho, & Tippett, 2006), 22% of the participating students, ranging in age from 11 to 16, reported that they had been cyber bullied at least once *in the two months preceding the survey*. The most common methods by which the cyber bullying had occurred were phone calls, text messaging, and e-mail. Rates of victimization were significantly higher among girls than boys. About a third of the victims had not told anyone about the cyber bullying, and many did not know the identity of the perpetrator.

Online Victimization Survey

A study sponsored by the National Center for Missing & Exploited Children found that 1 out of 17 American respondents (6%) between the ages of 10 and 17 reported having been threatened or harassed via the Internet, with boys and girls being victimized at approximately equal rates (Finkelhor, Mitchell, & Wolak, 2000). The researchers defined harassment as "threats to assault or harm the youth, their friends, family, or property as well as efforts to embarrass or humiliate them." Almost three-quarters (70%) of the harassment episodes had occurred to children who were at least 14 years of age. Perpetrators were primarily male (54%), juveniles (63%), and unknown to the target (72%). The most common means by which the harassment had occurred were instant messaging (33%) and chat rooms (32%), followed by e-mails (19%; Finkelhor et al., 2000).

Youth Internet Safety Survey

During the fall of 1999 and the spring of 2000, data were collected from 1,501 regular Internet users in the United States between the ages of 10 and 17, along with one parent or guardian of each participant, to compare characteristics of aggressors, targets, and aggressor/targets (individuals who were both victims and perpetrators of Internet harassment or online bullying; Ybarra & Mitchell, 2004). Nineteen percent of the respondents had *ever* been involved in online aggression (i.e., threats or harassing comments made via the Internet), 4% as online victims only, 12% as online aggressors only, and 3% as aggressor/targets only. Few of the victims knew the harasser in person (31%), yet 84% of the perpetrators reported knowing their target. Most victims (55%) had been harassed more than once by the same person; 16% had been cyber bullied four or more times by the same individual. A third of those who were bullied online reported feeling emotionally distressed as a result of the bullying, with bully/victims report-ing the highest levels of distress.

In a follow-up study, the second Youth Internet Safety Survey (YISS-2; Ybarra et al., 2006), 9% of the respondents, aged 10–17, indicated that they had been threatened or harassed over the Internet during the previous year. Ybarra et al. noted that this was a 50% increase over the frequency of Internet harassment found in the YISS-1 study. Close to half (45%) were acquainted with the perpetrator prior to the incident, and two-thirds had reported the incident to someone else. Almost a third (32%) of the victims reported that they had been harassed at least three times in the previous year. Although the trend was that more girls reported being victimized than boys, the difference was not significant. Thirty-eight percent of the targets indicated that they had felt distressed following the online harassment.

Patchin and Hinduja Study

Building on the research of Ybarra and Mitchell (2004), Patchin and Hinduja (2006) conducted an Internet-based survey of cyber bullying. A link to the survey was provided on the Web site of a popular female vocal-ist. Although anyone with access to the Web could respond to the survey, the majority of the respondents were from English-speaking countries, most notably the United States (59.1%), Canada (12%), and the United Kingdom (9.1%). Among respondents younger than 18, 11% confessed to perpetrating cyber bullying, and 29% reported having been the target of cyber bullying. Almost half (47%) of the under-18 population indicated that they had observed cyber bullying while online. Among victims, the most common venues for cyber bullying were chat rooms (21.9%), fol-lowed by instant messaging (13.5%), and e-mail (12.8%). Perpetrators were most likely to cyber bully via chat rooms (7.6%) and instant messag-ing (5.2%).

The Colorado Multi-site Evaluation Study

The Colorado Multi-site Evaluation Study is a 3-year bullying prevention initiative sponsored by schools and community-based organizations in 32 counties throughout Colorado. Williams and Guerra (2006) surveyed over 3,000 students in grades 5, 8, and 11 regarding their experiences with physi-cal, verbal, and Internet bullying. The researchers also examined the vari-ables that might predict involvement in each of the three types of bullying as either a victim or a perpetrator. The data from the first year of the study revealed that 21% of the students had *ever* been cyber bullied and another

18% had cyber bullied others. The incidence of cyber bullying peaked in middle school and dropped off among the 11th graders.

Fight Crime Preteen and Teen Studies

Telephone surveys conducted with preteens between the ages of 6 and 11 living in the United States showed that 17% had been cyber bullied *within the previous year* (www.fightcrime.org/cyberbullying/cyberbullyingpreteen. pdf). Of these cyber bully victims, 23% reported that the cyber bullying had occurred via e-mail, 12% via instant messaging, 19% through comments posted on a Web site, 18% in a chat room, 11% via embarrassing photos distributed without the victim's consent, and 7% through text messaging. Almost half (45%) of the targets did not know who had cyber bullied them. Sixteen percent of the victims had not discussed the cyber bullying with anyone. Among those who had told someone about being bullied online, 51% told their parents, 44% a friend, 31% a sibling, 27% a teacher, and 11% another adult.

A similar study conducted with *teens* between the ages of 12 and 17 (www.fightcrime.org/cyberbullying/cyberbullyingteen.pdf) indicated that 36% of the teenagers had been cyber bullied *within the previous year*. The means by which the cyber bullying had occurred included: 44% via instant messaging, 34% through e-mail, 30% through comments posted on a Web site, 19% via text messaging, 14% in chat rooms, and 13% through the distribution of embarrassing photographs of the victim without his or her consent. Twenty-six percent did not know the identity of the cyber bully. Sixteen percent had not disclosed their victimization to anyone. Among those who did tell someone, 72% told a friend, 35% their parents, 34% a sibling, 9% a teacher, and 11% another adult.

Cyber Bullying Among Middle School Children

In our own research (Kowalski & Limber, 2006), 3,767 students in grades 6 through 8 completed an anonymous pencil and paper questionnaire asking them about their experiences with traditional bullying and with cyber bullying. The students completed a revised version of the Olweus Bully/Victim Questionnaire (Olweus, 1996/2004) consisting of 39 questions examining their general bullying experiences. Another 23 questions were created that focused specifically on cyber bullying (e.g., "How often have you been electronically bullied in the past couple of months?"). We defined electronic bullying as bullying through e-mail, instant messaging, in a chat room, on a Web site, or though a text message sent to a cell phone. Participants in the study also completed the Interaction

Anxiousness Scale (Leary, 1983) and the Rosenberg Self-Esteem Scale (Rosenberg, 1965).

Eighteen percent of the students reported having been electronically bullied at least once *within the previous two months* and 6% had been electronically bullied at least 2–3 times a month. Eleven percent of the students reported having electronically bullied someone else at least once in the previous two months and 2% had electronically bullied at least 2–3 times a month. Of those students who reported having been electronically bullied at least once, students indicated that they had been cyber bullied most frequently by a student at school (52%) followed by a friend (36%). Just over 13% reported that they had been electronically bullied by a sibling. Importantly, almost half (48%) indicated that they did not know who had electronically bullied them. Similarly, of those perpetrators who had electronically bullied others at least once, 41% reported cyber bullying another student at school, 32% had bullied a friend, and 12% had bullied a brother or a sister. Although beyond the scope of this chapter, these data have interesting implications for research on sibling bullying, given the relatively high prevalence rate of cyber bullying among siblings.

A comparison of the statistics from our own research with those of other studies show that our frequencies are, typically, lower in terms of the overall incidence rates of cyber bullying, which is not surprising since we used a different metric of time than did a number of other researchers. Our questions asked participants whether they had been involved with cyber bullying during the previous two months. Most other studies (see, however, Smith et al., 2006) have not put a time limit on participants' responses, but rather asked them whether they have *ever* experienced cyber bullying. Parry Aftab (2006) estimates that around 85% of 12- and 13-year-old kids have ever had experience with cyber bullying.

In the Kowalski and Limber (2006) study, instant messaging was the most common venue by which the middle school children reported being victims and perpetrators of cyber bullying. Among the middle school targets, 67% had been bullied through instant messaging, 25% had been bullied in chat rooms, and 24% had been bullied through e-mail messages. Perpetrators, similarly, reported using instant messaging (56%) most frequently to cyber bully others, followed by chat rooms (23%), and e-mail messages (20%).

A related study (Agatston & Carpenter, 2006) involving an anonymous survey administered to 257 middle school students showed that 18% of the students (27% of the females and 9% of the males) reported having been cyber bullied *at least once in the previous two months*. The most common means by which the cyber bullying had occurred were instant messaging (52%) and via Web sites (52%). The increased prevalence of Web sites as a vehicle for cyber bullying among targets in the sample compared to the Kowalski and Limber (2006) study, whose data had been collected in 2005, likely reflects the increasing prevalence of social network sites as tools of interpersonal communication among adolescents.

Youth Internet Survey

Additional data were collected by one of the authors of this book through an online survey examining over 700 respondents' (predominantly college students) use of personal pages and their experiences with cyber bullying (Kowalski & Witte, 2006). Unlike in the Kowalski and Limber (2006) study, a time limit was not placed on when the cyber bullying had to have occurred. The data revealed that 11% of the participants reported *ever* having been cyber bullied, with only 3% reporting that they had ever cyber bullied someone else. As with our survey of middle school children, instant messaging was the most common venue for victimization, with 42% of the respondents saying they had been cyber bullied through instant messaging, followed by chat rooms (23%), and e-mail (13%). Perpetrators of cyber bullying equally favored instant messaging (33%) and chat rooms (33%). Table 4.2 contains a sample of the content of some of the cyber bullying that occurred.

We also asked participants whether their friends had ever cyber bullied or been cyber bullied and, if so, how. Participants with friends who had been victims of cyber bullying reported that those friends had been cyber bullied primarily through instant messaging (37%), followed by social network sites (33%), and e-mail (10%). Fifty percent of the friends who had perpetrated cyber bullying had done so through instant messaging.

Wired Safety Survey

Parry Aftab hosts an extensive Web site devoted to providing tips and resources related to online safety. As part of this, she created an online survey examining people's experiences with online bullying (https://www.wiredsafety.org/forms/interactive/poll_archive/poll.html). Participants included over 900 individuals with a minimum age of 8; almost half of the respondents (44%) were over 16. The rates of cyber bullying reported by Aftab are markedly higher than those found in most other studies, with 53% of the respondents saying they had been bullied online. Twenty-three percent said they had bullied someone else online. Fifty-five percent had never told anyone about the cyber bullying, and the majority of those who had told another person informed their friends (54%). Fifty-seven percent did not know the identity of the cyber bully.

Table 4.2
Content of cyber bullying

Victims
- "A death threat."
- "Angry and malicious things said that wouldn't have been said in person."
- "I was mocked. Anything I said would be insulted. Anything about me was insulted, i.e., physical features, personality, the way I speak, etc."
- "Just threatening to beat me up and shoot me."
- "This guy was mad at me and threatened to make me out to be a whore and get his new girlfriend to beat me up and stuff like that."
- "Me trying to cheer someone up, and them saying I was full of crap for saying they weren't worthless . . . that I knew nothing . . . then came personal attacks against me."
- "Sexual stuff."
- "Someone knows my friend's screen name and is using it against her. This person is ruining her reputation and says things that my friend would never say."

Perpetrators
- "I made fun of them."
- "I used to find random people's screen names through chat rooms, and if they had the name of their girlfriend/boyfriend in their profile, I would IM them pretending to be that person and then I would pretend to dump them."
- "Calling them a noob."
- "My friend got on Facebook and changed some detailed information on the person's profile."
- "It was actually a website, like www.hatedevin.com (that wasn't it, but it was similar). Mostly how much a kid in their class annoyed them."

Gender Issues and Cyber Bullying

Over the past two to three decades, research on aggression has shown that males engage in more direct forms of aggression, such as hitting one another, and females engage in more indirect forms of aggression, such as gossiping or spreading rumors about one another (Bjorkqvist, Lagerspetz, & Osterman, 1992; Lagerspetz, Bjorkqvist, & Peltonen, 1988). Interestingly, the definition advanced by Bjorkqvist and his colleagues for indirect aggression sounds remarkably similar to that proposed by Parry Aftab for cyber bullying by proxy (see Chapter 3). Bjorkqvist et al. defined indirect aggression as "a kind of social manipulation; the aggressor manipulates others to attack the victim, or, by other means, makes use of the social structure in order to harm the target person, without being personally involved in attack" (p. 52).

A qualitative analysis of why girls are more likely than boys to engage in indirect aggression revealed some interesting insights. Owens, Shute, and Slee (2000) conducted focus groups with 54 teenage girls in Australia. The researchers concluded that girls engage in indirect aggression to eliminate boredom and because of friendship processes, including attention seeking, assuring that they are a member of the in-group as opposed to the out-group, belonging to the right group, self-protection, jealousy, and revenge.

In keeping with this, it is not all that surprising, then, that cyber bullying overall seems to occur more frequently among girls than among boys (E. Mishkin, personal communication, January 20, 2006). Among the middle school students who completed our survey about cyber bullying (Kowalski & Limber, 2006), 25% of the girls and 11% of the boys said that they had experienced cyber bullying *at least once* in the previous two months; 5% of girls and 2% of boys indicated that they had experienced cyber bullying "2 or 3 times a month", and 3% of girls and 2% of boys said they had been cyber bullied about "once a week" in the previous two months. However, at the highest frequency level – those electronically bullied "several times a week" – boys (1.4%) slightly outnumbered girls (1.2%).

Thirteen percent of the girls and 9% of the boys said that they had perpetrated cyber bullying *at least once* within the previous two months. An equal percentage of girls and boys (1%) said they had electronically bullied others "2–3 times a month." Fewer girls (.7%) than boys (1.2%) said they had engaged in electronic bullying "once a week" in the previous two months. Twice as many boys (.8%) as girls (.4%) reported that they had electronically bullied others "several times a week."

For comparison purposes, we assessed the frequency of traditional bullying among girls and boys in our study (Kowalski & Limber, 2006). We found that 40% of the girls and 38% of the boys reported having been bullied at school *at least once* during the previous two months. A breakdown of prevalence rates at higher frequency levels showed that an equal percentage of girls and boys (6%) reported having been bullied "2 or 3 times a month;" 3% of girls and 4% of boys said they had been bullied "about once a week;" 3% of girls and 5% of boys indicated that the bullying occurred "several times a week."

Among perpetrators, 27% percent of the girls and 35% of the boys indicated that they had bullied someone else *at least once* within the previous two months. Observations at the higher frequency levels showed differences between girls and boys; however, these differences were not statistically significant. Three percent of girls and 5% of boys had bullied other students "2 or 3 times a month;" 1% of girls and 1% of boys had bullied others "about once a week;" twice as many boys (2%) as girls (1%) had bullied others "several times a week."

Although some studies have found no significant differences in cyber bullying between males and females, others have obtained results that parallel those in our own research. For example, Smith et al. (2006) found that girls were significantly more likely than boys to be cyber bullied. In terms of specific methods, they found that incidence rates for girls surpassed those for boys for all methods except for Web pages and picture editing.

Data from the Fight Crime surveys with preteens and teens (www. fightcrime.org) show mixed findings regarding gender differences. In the preteen survey, no significant differences in the frequency of experiencing cyber bullying were observed between boys and girls. Fifteen percent of the boys and 19% of the girls reported having been cyber bullied within the previous year. Among teens, however, a significant difference was obtained. Almost twice as many females (44%) as males (28%) reported having been cyber bullied within the previous year.

Participants in our focus groups acknowledged the link between gender and cyber bullying. When asked what can be done to prevent cyber bullying, respondents in one of our focus groups said the following: "It depends on if it's a guy or a girl or how mean they are. Some people are just going to do it anyway. Girls are harder to stand up to. Cause like guys can be like 'stop bothering me.' I'm not afraid that a guy is going to hit me, but girls are like catty. They get back at you in a more subtle way."

In keeping with this, a male focus group respondent, when asked what he would do if he were cyber bullied at home by a student, said he would "print out the pages and say – 'what's up, man?'" Another male student responded similarly: "Just go up to them and be like 'how come you didn't say it to my face?'" None of the female focus group respondents indicated a similar response.

As some of these data show, in examining gender differences in cyber bullying, it is important to bear in mind the method by which the cyber bullying is executed. Even though females may outnumber males in terms of the overall frequency with which cyber bullying occurs, as noted in the Smith et al. (2006) study, variations also occur with the method used (see also Keith & Martin, 2005).

Developmental Trends and Cyber Bullying

Research has evidenced age-related variations in the prevalence rates of traditional bullying. As discussed in more detail in Chapter 2, rates of victimization from traditional bullying are higher in elementary school, with decreases in frequency in middle and high school (Finkelhor et al., 2005). However, the frequency of perpetrating traditional bullying peaks in late middle and early junior high school. Support for this was found in the Kowalski and Limber (2006) study. Among individuals who had bullied others at school at least once (through "traditional" means), 8th graders bullied significantly more frequently than either 6th or 7th graders.

As with traditional bullying, there appear to be age-related variations with cyber bullying. Middle school seems to be the peak time during which problems with cyber bullying emerge. The Fight Crimes survey (www.fightcrime.org) with preteens supports this conclusion. Among preteens, children in the 6–8-year-old range were significantly less likely than children in the 9–11- year-old age range to have been cyber bullied within the previous year (13% and 21%, respectively).

Even among middle schoolers variations in rates of cyber bullying are observed. In our own research (Kowalski & Limber, 2006), we found significant differences by grade in the frequency with which youth had cyber bullied others, with 8th graders cyber bullying more frequently than 6th or 7th graders (see also Williams & Guerra, 2006). We did not find any differences among 6th, 7th, and 8th graders in the frequency with which they were the targets of cyber bullying. However, grade differences were observed among victims as a function of the method by which the cyber bullying occurred. Eighth graders reported being victimized through instant messaging at a significantly higher rate than 6th or 7th graders. Similarly, 8th graders also reported a higher rate of victimization via text messaging than 6th graders. Sixth graders used instant messaging to perpetrate cyber bullying less frequently than 7th or 8th graders. Sixth graders also used text messaging less often than 8th graders did.

Characteristics and Experiences of Children Involved in Cyber Bullying

A cursory look at the references accompanying this book or the dates of the studies on cyber bullying that have been conducted highlights the infancy of this line of investigation. Although we are getting a good picture of the frequency with which cyber bullying occurs, we know less about the characteristics of targets and perpetrators of cyber bullying, a topic to which we now turn our attention. One feature that has received increasing attention is the overlap between children's experiences with both cyber bullying and traditional bullying.

Overlap with Traditional Bullying

Ybarra and Mitchell (2004) found that many of their respondents who were cyber bullies or victims were also targets of conventional bullying. Fifty-six percent of aggressors/targets of online aggression also reported being the target of offline bullying (compared with 49% of the aggressor-only and 44% of the victim-only respondents). As the authors note, "for some youth who are bullied, the Internet may simply be an extension of the schoolyard, with victimization continuing after the bell and on into the night" (p. 1313). For others who have been victims of conventional bullying, the Internet may provide them with a means to bully others "as compensation for being bullied in person" (p. 1313). Importantly, consistent with research on traditional bully/victims, Ybarra and Mitchell (2004) found that cyber bully/victims experienced a higher frequency of problem behaviors (e.g., drinking, smoking) and poor psychosocial functioning (e.g., depression).

In our own research (Kowalski & Limber, 2006), to assess more directly the links between traditional bullying and cyber bullying, we examined participants' responses to the two questions asking them whether they had been bullied at school or had bullied someone else at least once. Based on these responses, participants were divided into four categories: victims (21%), bullies (13%), bully/victims (18%), and neither (48%). Because we were interested in the relationship between traditional bullying and cyber bullying, we examined the percentage of individuals within each of these four categories who had been electronically bullied at least once and the percentage of individuals within each of the categories who had electronically bullied others at least once. Among victims of traditional bullying, 9% had cyber bullied and 23% had been cyber bullied. Among traditional bullies, 20% had cyber bullied and 19% had been cyber bullied. Bully/victims reported the highest percentages associated with being a victim of cyber bullying (36%) and with perpetrating cyber bullying (23%). Among individuals who had not experienced traditional bullying, only 5% had cyber bullied and 9% had been cyber bullied. (See Table 4.3.)

Similarly, based on whether they had been the victim of, or perpetrated, cyber bullying at least once, we divided our participants into four cyber bullying groups: cyber victim, cyber bully, cyber bully/victim, or neither. We then examined the percentage of individuals within each of these four

Table 4.3

Relationship between traditional bully status and cyber bullying experience

Traditional bullying status	Cyber bully victim	Cyber bully perpetrator
Victim only	23%	9%
Bully only	19%	20%
Bully/victim	36%	23%
Not involved	9%	5%

Table 4.4

Relationship between cyber bully status and traditional bullying experience

Cyber bullying status	Traditional bully victim	Traditional bully perpetrator
Victim only	61%	39%
Bully only	39%	55%
Bully/victim	64%	66%
Not involved	33%	25%

groups who had been the victim of, or perpetrated, bullying at school at least once. Among the victims of cyber bullying, 61% had been a victim of school-yard bullying and 39% had perpetrated bullying at school. (See Table 4.4.) Among cyber bullies, 39% had been victims of traditional bullying, whereas 55% had perpetrated traditional bullying. Bully/victims again stood out as the most problematic group. Sixty-four percent of individuals who were both victims and perpetrators of cyber bullying were also victims of traditional bullying. Sixty-six percent perpetrated traditional bullying. A third of respondents (33%) who had not been involved with cyber bullying had been a victim of traditional bullying, and a quarter (25%) had perpetrated traditional bullying.

The disinhibition effect described in Chapter 3 may account, at least in part, for the strong relationship between cyber bully status and experiences with traditional bullying. Once individuals have anonymously perpetrated cyber bullying and experienced the feeling of power associated with doing so, as well as the reinforcement from peers, perpetrating traditional bullying at school becomes easier (and vice versa). In addition, the ease with which people can victimize one another via the Internet and cellular phones easily sets the stage for conflicted relationships at school that might otherwise have remained neutral to friendly.

Importantly, we also examined the relationship between being a cyber bully and being cyber bullied, as well as between being a traditional bully and being bullied at school. The correlation between cyber bullying and being cyber bullied ($r = .43$) was quite high. In other words, cyber bullying and being a target of cyber bullying tended to go along together. Conversely, the correlation between being a traditional bully and being traditionally bullied was much lower at only .22.

Characteristics of Victims and Perpetrators

In addition to gender, research on cyber bullying and Internet harassment suggests that there are other characteristics that may be linked to being a victim or a perpetrator of cyber bullying. Significantly more research attention has examined characteristics associated with targets as opposed to perpetrators of cyber bullying. Li (2006) found that half of the victims of cyber bullying had above average grades, whereas fewer than a third of cyber bullies had above average grades. Ybarra et al. (2006) noted that victims of Internet harassment were more likely than individuals who were not victims to harass others online, to have social problems, and to be victimized in other situations. They were also more likely to use instant messaging, blogs, and chat rooms, a finding not all that surprising given what we now know about the preferred venues for cyber bullying. Parallel findings were obtained in Kowalski and Witte's (2006) online study. Relative to nonvictims, targets were more likely to spend time using e-mail, instant messaging, online shopping, blogging, Web surfing, personal pages, and gaming. No differences were found between the two groups in the amount of time they spent doing research online or talking in chat rooms.

Our own research (Kowalski & Limber, 2006) has found a relationship between social anxiety, self-esteem, and cyber bullying. As noted earlier, in addition to completing measures of traditional bullying and cyber bullying, nearly 4,000 middle school students completed Leary's (1983) Interaction Anxiousness Scale and Rosenberg's (1965) Self-Esteem Scale. The Interaction Anxiousness Scale is a 15-item measure of an individual's dispositional level of social anxiety: how nervous they typically feel in social situations. A representative item includes "I often feel nervous in casual get togethers." Scores are summed and can range from 15 to 75, with higher numbers indicating higher levels of social anxiety. Rosenberg's Self-Esteem Scale is a 10-item measure of how an individual feels about himself or herself. A representative item from this scale is "I feel that I have a number of good qualities." Participants' scores on the self-esteem scale can range from 10 to 50, with higher scores indicating higher self-esteem.

We compared the levels of social anxiety and of self-esteem among individuals who were cyber bullies, cyber victims, cyber bully/victims, and those not involved in cyber bullying. We conducted these analyses twice for social anxiety and twice for self-esteem to allow us to examine levels of these individual difference measures among individuals who reported experience with cyber bullying at least once within the previous two months and those who had experienced cyber bullying at least 2–3 times a month within the previous two months. The data from these analyses are shown in Table 4.5. Using the criterion of occurring at least once in the previous two months, victims of cyber bullying had higher social anxiety scores than children not involved with cyber bullying. Children who were not involved with cyber bullying had higher self-esteem than children in all of the other

Table 4.5
Cyber bullying status, social anxiety, and self-esteem

Status (involved at least once)	Social anxiety score
Cyber bully only	35.4
Cyber victim only	38.2
Cyber bully/victim	37.4
Not involved	36.3

Status (involved at least 2–3x/month)	Social anxiety score
Cyber bully only	36.7
Cyber victim only	40.5
Cyber bully/victim	41.6
Not involved	36.3

Status (involved at least once)	Self-esteem score
Cyber bully only	20.4
Cyber victim only	19.2
Cyber bully/victim	19.2
Not involved	22.7

Status (involved at least 2–3x/month)	Self-esteem score
Cyber bully only	20.8
Cyber victim only	18.1
Cyber bully/victim	15.1
Not involved	22.1

three groups. Using the more stringent criterion of cyber bullying occurring 2–3 times a month or more, cyber victims and cyber bully/victims had higher social anxiety scores than cyber bullies and those children not involved with cyber bullying. Cyber victims and cyber bully/victims had lower self-esteem compared with children not involved with cyber bullying and also with children who bullied.

Children and youth who experience social anxiety may choose to avoid friends and withdraw from social situations as a means of avoiding the socially anxious feelings associated with those situations. Unfortunately, as reported throughout this book, the fact that cyber bullies can attack 24/7 and that much "social" interaction for adolescents now takes place online makes it difficult for youth to completely avoid "social" settings that produce adverse feelings. Because parents and educators seldom want to encourage children and youth to avoid social situations when they are anxious or to turn to the Internet for "social contact," knowing that they might be further isolated and victimized, the results of this study suggest that social skills training and practice in safe settings may be in order for children who are cyber bullied. Because of the correlational nature of these findings, it is not possible to know whether anxiety and low self-esteem may lead to cyber victimization or whether they might result from being cyber bullied (a focus of the next section).

Possible Effects of Cyber Bullying on the Victim and Perpetrator

As little research exists on cyber bullying itself, even less examines the effects of cyber bullying on the victim and perpetrator. Complicating matters even further, the effects of cyber bullying on the victim are highly variable and range from victims committing suicide, as in the case of Ryan Patrick Halligan, or murder, as in the case of a 6th grader in Japan who retaliated against a friend and classmate who had made derogatory comments about her on a Web site ("Archive of CRN home page topics," 2004), to the cyber bullying having little to no effect.

More commonly, however, the effects of cyber bullying tend to parallel those of traditional bullying. Victims of traditional school-yard bullying often report feelings of depression, low self-esteem, helplessness, social anxiety, reduced concentration, alienation, and suicidal ideation (see Chapter 2). Although very little research exists to date, victims of cyber bullying seem to report similar effects of their victimization (Ybarra & Mitchell, 2004). A respondent in one of our focus groups, in talking about the effects of cyber bullying on one of her friends, said: "It made them be mean for a while. They just didn't want to do anything with anyone, they didn't want to deal with it. It affected their mood, their relationships. It affected them academically. They stopped coming to school for a few days." The long-term effects of being a victim of cyber bullying stem in part from the intentional nature of the behavior. "It's not just the fact of getting hurt . . . people get hurt in accidents. It's the fact that someone made a choice to intentionally hurt you" (Akwagyiram, 2005).

Data from Kowalski and Witte's (2006) online study highlight the emotional toll that being a victim of cyber bullying can take. When asked, "How did you feel when you were cyber bullied?," participants reported feeling angry, sad, depressed, hurt, stressed, and confused. One participant wrote that she felt "meek and small . . . very alone and helpless." Alternatively, another respondent, although clearly in the minority, stated that he felt "engaged, like in a fight or combative sports activity." This individual went on to say: "I look at what most consider 'bullying' as a challenge or invitation to 'play'." Another respondent recounting the effects of cyber bullying on his friend said: "She actually has been thrown into a sort of a depression and contemplates suicide very often." Similar findings have been reported by Patchin and Hinduja (2006).

An interesting comparison is the responses of perpetrators to the question "How did you feel when you cyber bullied someone?" Among the responses in Kowalski and Witte's online study (2006) were the following: aggressive, vindictive, happy, pleased. Another individual said: "Right, as they deserved it, like I was giving them a taste of their own medicine."

Although longitudinal data do not yet exist providing empirical support for this, many researchers and writers on cyber bullying (e.g., Ybarra & Mitchell, 2004; Willard, 2006) believe that the long-term effects of cyber bullying are just as bad if not worse than those that accompany traditional bullying. One reason is that adolescents cannot escape cyber bullying. A child who is bullied at school is at least free from the actual bullying when he is away from school or not riding the school bus. A child who is electronically bullied is never really free unless he or she ceases to communicate electronically, a behavioral choice that has other implications, such as cutting off the child's social communication network. Therefore, even as the teen sleeps, he or she could be inundated with text messages or e-mails containing harassing or denigrating communications.

Also, in comparison to traditional bullying, the public nature of cyber bullying increases the potential negative impact of the cruelty relative to traditional bullying. As horrible and embarrassing as it is to be humiliated and belittled in front of one's peer group at school, such humiliation may be multiplied by hundreds of thousands in cases like the Star Wars Kid described in Chapter 1. Indeed, in cases such as the Star Wars Kid, scenes from the original video continue to appear in unexpected places, such as, most recently, in a segment of "Weird Al" Yancovic's music video "White and Nerdy" (http://video.google.com/videoplay?docid=138427770645115 7121&q=white+and+nerdy, 2006). Instead of knowing who the bully and the observers were, cyber bully victims walk around often unsure of who the bully is and most definitely unsure of how many countless people are aware of, or have contributed to, their humiliation.

Depending on the modality that cyber bullying takes, in some instances the danger associated with cyber bullying can be very real indeed. Perpetrators who impersonate another individual and post hate messages (and personally identifying messages) in chat rooms may be placing that individual's life at risk. Discussants in the chat room offended by the hate messages may decide to use the identifying information to track down the person ostensibly posting the message.

There has been some discussion, although as yet no empirical data, regarding the extent to which social networking sites may facilitate a "suicide contagion effect" (Zayas, 2006). Previous research on copycat suicides that was published long before the existence of social network sites showed an increase in suicides following the publicizing of a suicide on the front page of a newspaper. Referred to as the Werther effect (Becker & Schmidt, 2005), researchers found that individuals who had been contemplating suicide were more likely to actually make the attempt if they saw a newspaper story about an individual who resembled them in some way. The Internet suicide contagion effect would work in much the same way. One MySpace user changed his screen name to Goodbye immediately before committing suicide. Another left a message on his My Space page for his friends and family not to be sad when he was gone (Zayas, 2006). Of course, the idea is that psychologically vulnerable people with characteristics similar to these individuals might view these sites and decide that they, too, could be successful at a suicide attempt or be somehow "better off."

An additional consequence of cyber bullying for at least some perpetrators is guilt and regret. Although, certainly, some people who bully, either electronically or in the traditional sense, feel no remorse for their actions, others do, particularly those who are more tuned in to the negative effects that bullying has on the victim. One of our focus group interviews that was conducted with a person who had cyber bullied a student at another school highlights this regret. When asked how he or she felt about the content of what they wrote, the perpetrator stated: "Well, now I realize. . . . how bad it really did sound. I mean, I know this sounds totally lame, but I really did not realize how threatening it really was." In response to the question "Do you regret what you did?," the person who cyber bullied responded: "Yeah, one because it probably, I mean, not scarred her for life, but because it probably did something to her mentally or something, like made her more scared or something, and two because I lost some of my parents' trust and I have to regain that again and who knows how long it's going to take."

Conclusions

As research on the topic of cyber bullying continues to develop, presumably programs and policies will be put in place with the intent of decreasing the incidence of cyber bullying. As with traditional bullying, however, it is unlikely that cyber bullying will disappear completely. Thus, additional research using a variety of methodologies is needed to investigate the characteristics of targets and perpetrators of cyber bullying, as well as bystanders. We need to know more about who does what to whom with what effect, so that prevention and intervention efforts, such as those that will be discussed in the next two chapters, can take a more focused approach to increase their effectiveness.

5

What Parents Can Do

Brandy[1] is a 9th grader at a large suburban high school outside of Atlanta, Georgia. She is pretty, popular, and a cheerleader. She also has a Web site on a social networking site called Xanga that includes pictures of herself and diary type entries of her personal interests and activities. One day over the summer break, she receives a post to her site that says, "Go to my Xanga, bitch!" When she clicks on the link, she is connected to another blog site that is dedicated to her. This blog, also on Xanga, contains profanity and demeaning language describing her as an ugly, fat whore. The tone of this blog is very dark, and sinister music begins playing as the screen comes up. The headline of the Xanga site reads, "Tomorrow You Will Die." The screen name of the person who owns this blog is listed as F*** you, F*** me. The unidentified blogger has listed his or her personal interests as "stalking and murder."

Though Brandy is upset about the content, she decides to keep it to herself and not respond to the postings on the blog because she thinks the person just wants to get a reaction out of her. She avoids telling her parents about the incident as well.

Six weeks later, another posting is added to the Xanga site dedicated to Brandy that reads, "Hey you f****** bitch. I know where you were the other night. You will f****** well die if I can help it . . . How does it feel to be so hated . . . You tell me when I see you tomorrow . . . I'll see you tomorrow because I'll be beating the s*** out of you!!! Enjoy living, whore, enjoy living while you can. You won't be living for long. I'll make sure you die s-l-o-w-l-y. F****** die ass***e!!!"

Brandy McClain did what many young people do when they receive cyber bullying messages on a Web site, or in an instant message, text message or e-mail. She told a friend, but avoided telling her parents. Fortunately for Brandy, her friend thought it was serious enough to tell her own mother, who in turn told Brandy's mother about the site.

Imagine for a moment that you are Brandy's mother, Mrs McClain. After the call from another parent, you access the social networking site called Xanga and are confronted with a dark screen that threatens to kill your daughter the next day. Imagine the fear and pain such a site would cause you. As Mrs McClain said later, "I didn't know whether to let her go to school the next day. She was supposed to be in a pep rally. Would someone try to kill her?" Mrs McClain also described the flood of emotions and panicky thoughts going through her mind. "You start to become paranoid. You begin wondering about all of your child's friends and look at them differently. Everyone is a suspect when you don't know who wrote such a thing. I started wondering if I should home school my child!"

What did Mrs McClain do? She started where many parents start when they are concerned about a threatening message targeting their child. She called the school counselor at Brandy's high school. Unfortunately, many school counselors are not sure what to do when confronted with this new form of bullying. Many believe that, if cyber bullying happens outside of school, there is little that the school can do to assist the families. Although the school may have limited options in terms of what it can do regarding disciplining the offender (see also Chapter 7), there are always steps the school can take to assist the family of the victim. Chapter 6 will discuss the steps that school administrators and counselors can take to help students affected by cyber bullying. This chapter will focus on steps that families can take to prevent and address cyber bullying problems.

Admittedly, Brandy's school counselor faced a difficult challenge. She didn't know who posted the threatening site targeting Brandy and whether or not the offender was a fellow student. Fortunately, the school counselor referred Mrs McClain to the school district's student assistance program, knowing that it led many of the bullying prevention efforts for the school district and was beginning to focus attention on cyber bullying as well. The counselor also did a very wise thing: she suggested that Mrs McClain contact the police because the posting involved a physical threat.

Parental Involvement in the Prevention/ Intervention of Cyber Bullying

The students in our focus groups indicated that most cyber bullying occurs outside of school hours, when children are at home under their parents' supervision. This is consistent with the Fight Crime: Invest In Kids (2006) survey data that report that *teens* received 70% of harmful messages at home, and 30% of harmful messages at school. However, their data on preteens suggest a more equal distribution, with preteens reporting they were as likely to receive harmful messages at school (45%) as at home (44%). While the current generation of parents has been termed "helicopter parents" for their tendency to "hover" unnecessarily over their children's school and extracurricular activities, this does not apply to parents supervising their children's online activities.

Parents Often Aren't Present in the Online Environment of Children

A survey by i-SAFE America (2005–2006) found that, while 93% of parents felt they had a good idea of what their child was doing on the Internet, 41% of students in grades 5–12 said they did not share with their parents what they do or where they go online. Another i-SAFE survey (2004–2005) also indicated that over half (52%) of children prefer to surf the Internet alone. In addition, social networking sites such as MySpace and Xanga have grown immensely popular among teens and young adults. Older adults are less familiar and less likely to have a profile on a social networking site, thus leading to a situation where young people are virtually unsupervised as they develop their online profiles.

Parents who routinely discuss bike helmet safety and "home alone safety tips" with their children are often silent when introducing a new piece of technology such as a cellular phone or computer into the home environment.

Why Don't Children Report?

In our case example, Brandy avoided telling her parents about the cyber threats she was receiving. It is very likely that children will avoid telling their parents about a cyber bullying incident unless families have discussed cyber bullying ahead of time. The Fight Crime: Invest In Kids survey found that, although 51% of *preteens* who had been cyber bullied told their parents, only 35% of cyber bullied *teens* had done so (2006). Communication with a daughter or son is the key. Parents need to listen closely to what children say about their online experiences, and familiarize themselves with the sites and modalities children are using for online interaction.

The students in our focus groups gave interesting responses as to why they and their friends don't always tell their parents about such incidents. Here are some of the student responses when asked why their friends didn't tell:

"She was afraid if she told her parents she would get restricted, so [she] didn't want to let them know." "Yeah – or [their parents] would make them quit using [a social networking site]." – *middle school female*

"They might be scared to tell their parents, because they might say, 'I told you so, I told you not to have that blog.'" – *high school female*

"If you tell your parents a lot of times they'll want to get involved." – *middle school boy*

"They overreact." – *middle school boy*

The students' fears were supported by one middle school focus group participant who shared that she was not allowed to instant message anymore because she had received intimidating instant messages from a former classmate.

It is tempting to view these new technologies in black or white terms, as good or evil, and to react accordingly. But children rarely benefit or learn when parents are reactive and respond immediately by restricting or punishing them. They benefit most when parents are proactive and educate. While parents may be inclined to blame technology and the Internet for putting their children at risk of harm, being antitechnology is unproductive. The reality is that the Internet is here to stay and is a valuable tool. While a child who abuses others over the Internet may need some consequences, such as restriction from certain sites or functions, the victim who did nothing wrong should not be punished by losing such privileges. Otherwise, the child may not tell a parent about the next incident.

Knee-jerk responses by parents that blame the victim are, of course, not limited to instances of cyber bullying. Consider, for example, the reactions of some parents to a child's disclosure of sexual abuse or assault. If a child tells her parent that someone touched her inappropriately, a parent may instinctively become upset and respond with a statement such as, "What do you mean? Why didn't you tell them to stop?" This or similar responses may further victimize a child by blaming him or her for someone else's actions. It also sets up the likelihood that the child will avoid such a parental reaction in the future by not sharing any information that could prompt such a response, such as having been at a party where drinking or drug use occurred.

Parents may benefit from beginning every response to disclosures, no matter how upsetting, with, "Thank you for telling me that. You did the right thing by letting me know." As challenging as it may be, parents who remain calm during disclosures will ensure that the lines of communication remain open with their child, and the parents will be in a position to provide guidance in the future when their child is faced with various challenges. Children tend to share more when they have learned that their parents can be trusted to respond in a stable and reassuring manner.

Warning Signs that a Child May Be a Victim of Cyber Bullying

Because many young people are reluctant to tell an adult about cyber bullying, there are some warning signs that may indicate a child is being victimized, although these may also be signs of other problems.

- Child appears upset after being online.
- Child appears upset after viewing a text message.
- Child withdraws from social interaction with peers.
- Possible drop in academic performance.

The most obvious sign of a cyber bullying incident is when a child becomes visibly upset or withdrawn after being on the computer. They may also show signs of emotional distress after viewing a text message. A drop in grades or performance at school also could be a warning sign of cyber bullying (see, e.g., Willard, 2005a, 2005b). However, as it also may be a sign of so many other troubles, it may not be a very useful indicator. Some students in our focus groups seemed to minimize the impact that cyber bullying had on the academic performance of friends who had been cyber bullied, claiming their friends could separate cyber bullying from their schoolwork, as seen in the following comments.

> *Interviewer:* Do you think the cyber bullying impacted their school work?
> "No – I don't think so." – *high school female*
> "No change." – *high school male*
> "Maybe, it depends on what was said." – *middle school girl*

However, one student discussed how her friend *had* been affected academically:

> "It affected [her] academically. [She] stopped coming to school for a few days."

These students readily admitted, however, that the cyber bullying affected their friends' social relationships and that they felt distrustful and fearful

of others in their social circle (especially if the cyber bullying was anonymous). Here are some of the comments from a high school girls' focus
group about their friends' social and emotional responses to being cyber
bullied.

> "She thought the girls who did it were her friends, so she lost those
> friendships."
> "[She was] upset. She just wasn't friends with those people anymore."
> "She was scared, looking around all of the time."
> "He said, 'I don't even know who this person is.' I think he was kind of
> scared."

A middle school boy said the following:

> "[It] makes them think less about themselves. Because whenever
> someone is mad they say things they shouldn't and then they [the
> targets] think less of themselves."

This comment came from a high school boy:

> "The kid I'm talking about takes everything too seriously. He got
> all . . . he started crying and stuff. It upset him."

It seems difficult to imagine being able to give the strongest academic performance when a student is fearful, anxious, and distrustful of peers at
school.

Thus, paying attention to a child's social relationships and any changes
in these relationships can help alert parents to cyber bullying instances.
Some parents choose to read all of their child's e-mail and instant messages,
but this can be construed as a huge invasion of privacy by young people,
and rightly so. It is more helpful for parents to spend time talking with
their children about the appropriate way to interact online, and about their
family guidelines for computer use. It is important for parents and children
to reach consensus about the circumstances under which the children
should notify the parents if they receive negative messages or view harmful
material online. It also makes sense that if a son or daughter posts information to a social networking site, such as MySpace or Xanga, for the general
public to see, the parent will view it occasionally. It is helpful if parents let
their children know ahead of time that they will occasionally monitor their
social networking site, but that they do not plan to read all of their children's communications on a daily basis. However, if the parents are alerted

to instances of cyber bullying, they will need to monitor their children's communications more closely.

Suggestions for Addressing Cyber Bullying that Children Have Experienced

What can parents do if their child is a victim of cyber bullying? Because cyber bullying instances can vary dramatically from one another in method, intensity, and duration, there is no set course of action that parents can follow. However, we will provide some basic steps, as well as response options, that parents should consider when responding to cyber bullying directed toward a child.

Saving the Evidence

Parents must teach their children to save any evidence of cyber bullying. While ignoring or blocking a sender's messages may be the best response for minor incidents of cyber bullying, it could still be useful to have copies of instant message conversations should things escalate. Unless parents have added a specific program that routinely saves instant messages, most computers will not automatically save instant messages that are sent to a child.

Children should be taught to print out any threatening or harassing e-mails or instant messages that they receive. They should avoid deleting the e-mails. All instant message programs also have a "save" feature, but children may need help in knowing how to do so. Parents should ask that children show messages to them that include threatening or harassing statements. If the parent and child do not know who sent the messages, the parent should save the messages to the computer's hard drive and then forward these communications to the Internet service provider in order to try to trace the perpetrator.

Children also need to know that if they ever receive offensive pictures or are directed to a Web site that is offensive or frightening, they should turn off the monitor (not the computer) and notify a parent. Often children will respond by shutting down the computer, which may erase the evidence. By turning off the monitor but leaving the computer on, they can stop viewing the upsetting material, but it will still be present for a parent to review (and if necessary save evidence). Older children can be instructed to save the Web pages and print out copies of offensive Web sites or social networking sites. It is important that they are told not to respond to the offensive comments unless they have conferred with an adult.

When to Ignore, Block, or React

An instant message from a friend that reads, "You idiot!" may seem upsetting to a child but may just lack a few critical words (e.g., "just kidding" or "jk") that would have conveyed quite a different sentiment. In such a situation, an appropriate response might be to ask for clarification or ignore the message. An individual who regularly communicates through the use of profanity or obscenities should be warned, and, if necessary, blocked from sending instant messages to a child. Instant message screen names and cellular phone numbers (used to send text messages to cellular phones) can be blocked. Of course, some users will set up new screen names to harass others. At that point, the cyber bullying has become harassing in nature and will need to be addressed more directly by contacting the parent of the cyber bully, possibly the school counselor if the bully attends the same school, and maybe the police. Contacting the parent of the cyber bully will be discussed later in this chapter.

Usually, the best response to a mean or nasty comment is no response. Students in our focus groups shared that responding often just aggravates the situation. Here are some of their responses to the question, "What would you do if you were cyber bullied by someone you knew?"

> "Delete it." – *high school female*
> "Ignore it." – *middle school male*
> "I wouldn't pay attention unless it happened frequently." – *high school female*
> "Ignore them. Block them." – *high school male*
> "Block them so they couldn't e-mail me." – *middle school female*

A person who sends one mean e-mail, text message, or instant message can be ignored. Often this will end the cyber bullying, whether the identity of the individual is known or not. If the messages continue, the sender's messages can be blocked by using the blocking feature on an instant message account. WiredSafety.org explains how one can avoid receiving text messages temporarily by turning off the incoming messages function for a couple of days. This may stop the person from sending the text messages as he may think the phone number has been changed. E-mails accounts can also be set up to block incoming messages from certain senders.

Of course, ignoring or blocking offensive messages may not always stop them from coming. Occasionally, cyber bullying continues through the creation of new accounts and new screen names. Because the identity of the sender cannot be confirmed, the parents of the cyber bully cannot be contacted. If, despite ignoring mean comments and blocking the sender's messages, the cyber bullying continues, parents may find it helpful to send one message indicating that the authorities will be contacted if the messages persist. Responding assertively has been helpful in some instances of cyber bullying. We give an example later in this chapter of a situation where this was used effectively by a parent.

Tracing E-mails and Text Messages

It is possible to identify the senders of e-mails and text messages in many situations. Students in our focus groups were asked, "What would you do if the cyber bully was someone you *didn't* know?" Some of their responses:

"Block them." – *high school male*
"Trace them." – *high school female*
"I worry about stalking. I might tell my parents just so they would know it was happening." – *high school female*
"I would wonder how they got my number if it were a text message." – *middle school female*

It is encouraging that some students are aware of such options as tracing and blocking inappropriate messages. Parents and children should also attempt to identify the individual doing the cyber bullying.

If threatening messages are coming through a cellular phone via text messaging, the phone number can be traced and reported to the mobile phone provider. Again, while one or two mean text messages would best be ignored, if continued harassment is occurring the abuse should be reported and if necessary the phone number can be changed. The Center for Safe and Responsible Internet Use recommends that abuse that occurs through e-mail be reported to the Internet service provider of the perpetrator (Willard, 2005a). A copy of the abusive e-mail can be forwarded to their provider. The forwarded e-mail can be sent to support@internetserviceprovider. An example would be: support@aol.com. There may also be a specific e-mail address listed on the support page of the Internet service provider that provides instructions for reporting abuse. Keep in mind the importance of reporting inappropriate messages as soon as possible. Internet service providers may only be able to trace information for a certain period of time.

Tracing and Responding to Postings to Social Networking Sites and Web Sites

Mrs McClain was asked by the student assistance counselor (and coauthor of this book) if she had contacted the police and she replied positively that she had spoken with a detective at the high-tech crimes unit. He was pursuing a subpoena as required by Xanga.com in order to release the name of the Internet service provider that was used to post the material on the Xanga Web site. It was suggested by the author that she also let the school resource officer at the high school know about the threats, so that he could monitor the situation at the school in case the threats were from a classmate. Mrs McClain assumed that the offender was another student at her daughter's school. She was surprised to learn a few days later from the high tech crimes detective that the cyber bully was, in fact, a 9th grade female student attending a different high school. The two students had been in middle school together previously. "They knew each other," Mrs McClain stated in a puzzled voice, "but they weren't really even friends."

Mrs McClain was fortunate to be able to identify the perpetrator of the cyber threats toward her daughter by contacting a high-tech crimes unit at her local police department. Many cities are adding cybercrime units and training detectives in cybercriminal behavior (Franek, 2005/2006). However, not every threatening statement posted on the Internet will be specific enough or deemed severe enough for the courts to allow law enforcement to pursue the identity of the perpetrator. The Center for Safe and Responsible Internet Use recommends that, if a site entry about an individual includes threats of violence, stalking, extortion, harassment, or is obscene or pornographic, the police should be notified (Willard, 2005a).

Another parent who was interviewed for this book discovered an entry on a social networking site dedicated to her daughter, titled "Lisa Smith must die." The entry included comments about hating Lisa; however, there were no specific threats posted. Mrs Smith was still referred to the high tech crimes police unit, but the district attorney's office would not issue a subpoena in this case. While Mrs Smith was disappointed in this outcome, she was successful in having the site shut down by posting the following assertive message on the Web site: "This is Lisa Smith's mother. This will be handed over to the police tomorrow. I will also be turning this in to the school. Your parents would not be proud. If you were smart, you would find better things to do with your time."

The next day, the site had been shut down by the person who had created it. In addition, it was suggested by one of the authors that Mrs Smith meet with the 7th grade counselor at Lisa's school to show her a printed copy of the Web site, and ask for her help. Mrs Smith was pretty sure some classmates were behind the Web site, and the counselor was more than willing to talk with teachers to ask them to be on the lookout for any incidents of bullying and listen for classmates' statements that might target Lisa. Regardless of whether one can determine the identity of the perpetrator, there are always steps to take to address the behavior.

As with instant messaging, text messaging, and e-mails, it is generally not recommended that the victim or the victim's parent respond to any of the mean comments or offensive material posted on the Web site. However, when the identity cannot be confirmed and the comments are continuing, it can be helpful for a parent to post one assertive comment as Mrs Smith did. Unfortunately, if the targeted child responds to the mean comments, the response often adds fuel to the fire, where the perpetrator(s) will respond in more aggressive ways once the victim tries to defend himself or herself.

Request that the Web Site or Social Networking Site Remove the Offensive Material

As mentioned previously, minor incidents of cyber bullying such as one or two mean instant messages, posts, or a nasty text message are often best ignored. Information posted on a Web site, however, can continue to victimize a student when it is left up for everyone to see. Although parents may want to find the perpetrators and make sure they are punished, the child often simply wants the bullying to stop. Lisa, for example, just wanted the Web site to come down. Fortunately, her mother's post was successful in having the perpetrators remove the offensive material. She could also have requested that the domain host remove the offensive material.

Most social networking sites (as well as instant messaging programs) now have profile settings that allow a user to block other users from contacting them or posting comments on the user's Web site. If a user has set up a threatening Web site targeting a child, the parent or child can request that the social networking site remove the offensive Web site. The parent should also contact law enforcement in such instances. Most Web sites have an abuse policy that allows individuals to complain about material posted on the site. Parents can usually find the abuse policy as a link, or sometimes under the "FAQ" (frequently asked questions) section on a site. Anyone can complain about an offensive site and request that it be shut down. Most sites have a link to their customer service department that allows individuals to report an offensive Web site in order to have it removed from the site.

Two of the popular social networking sites mentioned in our focus groups were MySpace and Xanga. MySpace has recently partnered with WiredSafety.org to provide safety tips for its users, as well as links to report cyber bullying. Xanga.com lists the following reasons for which they will shut down a site:

- It exists solely to abuse or stalk another person or ethnic group.
- It is blatantly pornographic.
- It contains an explicit death threat (or physical threat) to another person.

Though not a social networking site per se, YouTube.com has become a popular site among young people for uploading and sharing videos that users have made. We observed some video clips that targeted classmates and that involved bullying. YouTube.com has a feature in place that allows users to report such offensive videos that do not meet the site guidelines for appropriate videos.

Should Children Be Banned from Social Networking Sites?

Although many parents respond to cyber bullying by banning the use of social networking sites altogether, by doing so they are asking their children to avoid a hugely popular pastime among students that allows for identity development and self-exploration. Younger children probably do not have the judgment to safely use such sites, but older teens enjoy expressing themselves and exploring their identity online. Parents may allow access, but they need to set some guidelines and occasionally visit the site. According to their Web site, www.MySpace.com, the current age limit for MySpace is 14; however, it is easy for children to lie about their age and set up a profile. A parent should give approval for the social networking site only if their child agrees to the Web site guidelines, and gives the parent their profile name and password. The child and parent should also agree that the parent will view the profile on occasion, at least until the child is in his or her later teens. There are also sites being developed now for young teens only that market a safer online experience, such as YFLY.com. WiredSafety. org partnered with YFLY.com to provide safety tips for its teen users, and its use is currently restricted to 13–19-year-olds. BlogSafety.com also has helpful tips for teens on safe and appropriate blogging. Parents may find it helpful to use these sites as a training ground for a child to learn about safe posting.

Social networking sites continue to be hugely popular during the college years (when a son or daughter is no longer under their parents' roof or control), so providing teens with age-appropriate rules for using social networking sites may be the best response among parents. The key for parents is to help their children understand that they are building a reputation in cyberspace that will follow them into the future. This will be discussed further in the section on monitoring a child's online reputation.

Contacting the Parents of the Cyber Bully

Authors of bullying prevention programs generally argue that it is risky or ineffective for the parent of a victim to contact the parent of a perpetrator of traditional bullying (e.g., Olweus, 1993a). Often the parents of the child who bullied are unresponsive or are defensive about the bullying and label their child's behavior as "kids being kids." It is not uncommon for parents to make statements such as, "I prefer to let the kids work it out," which assumes a level playing field for the parties involved. Unfortunately, with bullying we know that there is no level playing ground; it is an abuse of power similar in some respects to child abuse and domestic abuse (Olweus, 1993a).

Cyber bullying may be unique in that students who would not typically bully feel empowered to engage in bullying behaviors over the Internet. While rates of traditional bullying are higher among males (Nansel et al., 2001; see Chapter 2), cyber bullying appears to be more common among females (Kowalski & Limber, 2006; see Chapter 4). Reactive cyber bullying occurs when children who feel victimized or discouraged in their day-to-day life lash out, often anonymously, over the Internet.

Because the dynamics of cyber bullying are somewhat different from traditional bullying, it is appropriate to encourage parents of the victim to share evidence of the cyber bullying with the parents of the bully *in some situations*. The language of cyber bullying is often very threatening, offensive, and filled with profanity. It is hard for the average parent to defend their child when faced with a copy of such offensive language.

After discovering the identity of the perpetrator, Mrs McClain was confused about what her next step should be. The detective stated that while she could press charges against the 9th grade female per-petrator, the student was basically a "good kid" from a "good family" who attended an honors program at a local high school. "I don't want to press charges," Mrs McClain confided to the author, "but I want to do something. I don't want her to think this is acceptable. Do you think it would be alright if I contacted her parents? The detective gave me their name and phone number. He said the mother was very responsive." "I think it would be alright," the author told Mrs McClain. "I would also be willing to meet with all of you if you think it would be helpful – a sort of mediation or accountability circle, if everyone is willing. Brandy can choose whether or not to be present. We don't want her to feel revictimized in any way."

In Mrs McClain's situation, the mother of the perpetrator, Mrs Jones, was very concerned about her daughter's behavior and very responsive to meeting in order to address the situation. After Mrs Jones agreed to meet Mrs McClain, the assistance program counselor contacted both parties and arranged to meet with both sets of parents as well as the student who made the threatening profile at an agreed location. Brandy did not want to be present during the session, but her parents did.

Mrs Jones was concerned about the cyber bullying incident when noti-fied of its occurrence, yet when she went to view the actual Web site, it had been removed. After she was shown a printed copy of the blog entries that Mrs McClain had saved, Mrs Jones was shocked and outraged by her daughter's behavior. It was one thing to hear that her child had threatened another student; it was another to see a profanity-laced entry filled with shocking brutality. Few parents could justify such entries as just "kids being kids." As a result of viewing the evidence, Mrs. Jones was very motivated to take steps to address the cyber bullying and monitor her child's online behavior.

In traditional bullying situations where the offenses happen at school, the school counselor or administrator usually contacts the parents of both the victim and the perpetrator. Parents of a child who has been bullied at school need to know that their concerns are being addressed, that the administration is meeting with the parents of the perpetrator, and that, if applicable, there will be consequences for the bullying behavior. These parents also can work with the administration to develop a "safety plan" that includes increased adult supervision and possible schedule changes of either party to help minimize their child's exposure to bullying behavior. Parents of the child who bullied need to be made aware of the situation and be aware of any consequences for current or future bullying behavior instigated by their child.

Cyber bullying, because it frequently happens outside of school, may require a different response. It often takes place between classmates but can also occur between students attending different schools, as our case example demonstrates. Thus, it may be appropriate in some cases for the parents of the victim to contact the parents of the perpetrator. There is no guarantee that the parents of the perpetrator will respond in a helpful manner, but often the parents of the perpetrator will take the situation seriously when provided with visual evidence of the bullying. In some cases, it may be effective to send a letter to the parents with a copy of the cyber bullying and a written request that the offensive messages stop. Parents of the victim should outline their next steps if the cyber bullying continues, such as contacting law enforcement or an attorney (where appropriate), but this needs to be done in a sensitive and calm manner. Parents are advised to *describe* the bullying behavior, rather than labeling another child a bully.

Requesting Intervention Assistance from the School

Students in our focus groups shared that they would be more likely to tell a parent than any other adult about a cyber bullying situation. Parents may be able to investigate and handle the cyber bullying situation on their own or with community assistance, but in some situations parents may need the school's assistance to determine if cyber bullying or traditional bullying is occurring on campus. The school may also be able to provide resources and intervention assistance.

Share Evidence with the School

Schools *need* to be aware of bullying situations that involve students at their school in order to effectively monitor the safety of students. It is helpful if parents print out a copy of the evidence of cyber bullying and share it with a school counselor or administrator, whether they know the identity of the perpetrator or not. The designated counselor or administrator can investigate whether bullying is occurring at school as well as over the Internet. Although schools may not be able to administer consequences for cyber bullying occurring outside of the school day (see Chapter 7), it is possible that incidents (either cyber bullying or traditional bullying) are occurring on campus as well. In such situations, the school may have policies in place to address bullying and cyber bullying that occur on campus.

School Personnel Can Help Monitor the Situation

Sharing the evidence with the school will enable the administration to monitor potential bullying situations more closely and, where necessary, set up a school safety plan for the student. If offenses are determined to be occurring using school technology, the school district has a responsibility to address the situation. These incidents should be documented by the parent to provide the counselor or administrator with as much information as possible about when and where the incidents are occurring. If one student is using a cellular phone to cyber bully another student while at school, the administration may be able to intervene as well.

Requesting Assistance from the School in Contacting Parents

If parents of a bullied child have reason to doubt that the parents of the cyber bully will respond appropriately to their requests that the cyber bullying cease, or if the cyber bullying is accompanied by traditional bullying at school, parents may need to request that the school counselor or administrator at a child's school contact the parents of the perpetrator to notify them of the incident. Be aware, however, that while public schools may be able to assist by alerting the parents of those involved through a phone call or letter sent home, they may not be legally able to discipline students for online comments or postings that occur at home, for fear of violating students' rights to freedom of speech and expression under the First Amendment (see Chapter 7). Private schools have more options in this area, and may be in a position to levy consequences for cyber bullying that occurs off campus. If the offenses are criminal in nature, the school resource officer may be able to assist or refer parents to the appropriate law enforcement official. Schools may also be able to provide educational materials or resources for parents on cyber bullying and Internet safety.

A school district may have counselors who are willing to assist the parties involved by arranging an informal resolution meeting. Chapter 6 of this book includes tips for counselors who wish to mediate an informal resolution or "accountability circle" strategy that is helpful in some situations, and which was used successfully with the McClain case.

Legal Options

Mrs McClain did not want to press criminal charges against the 9th grader who targeted her daughter, but she could have. Sometimes threatening to call the police or contact an attorney is enough to ensure that the cyber bullying stops. Police should be contacted if cyber bullying includes such things as:

- threats of physical harm to an individual
- stalking or harassment
- pornographic images
- extortion (Willard, 2005a).

In rare cases, parents may choose to file a lawsuit against the cyber bully or the cyber bully's parents. Courts have ruled in some jurisdictions that the parents of minors can be held financially responsible if the minor engages in wrongdoing that is a result of parental lack of supervision (Willard, 2005a). Parents may wish to consult with a personal injury attorney if their child has been harassed or threatened in such a manner as to cause severe emotional distress, or if the child's reputation has been severely damaged by posting false information online. The parent of a child engaged in cyber bullying who has not been responsive to complaints will likely be more responsive to the situation when confronted with a letter from a parent or an attorney outlining possible legal actions.

Parents will find it well worth their time to monitor and guide their children's activities on the Internet, when faced with the prospect of being sued in response to statements written by their child online or having criminal charges filed against their son or daughter. This is another reason for parents to be proactive in educating themselves about the Internet and communicating their guidelines and expectations for how their children conduct themselves online. It would be a shame for a child's actions to lead to a criminal record for the child or other legal actions for the parent, but, unless parents take reasonable responsibility for their child's actions and recognize that parenting must continue in the virtual world, this is a possibility. Box 5.1 provides a summary of legal and other tips for responding to cyber bullying. (See Chapter 7 for more in-depth information on legal issues and cyber bullying.)

Box 5.1	Intervention tips for responding to cyber bullying

- Save the evidence. Print copies of messages and Web sites. Use the save feature on instant messages.
- First Offense (if minor in nature) – ignore, delete, or block the sender. Instant message programs, e-mail, and cell phones usually have blocking features.
- If a fake or offensive profile targeting your child is set up on a social networking site, report it to the site. The link for reporting cyber bullying and fake profiles can be found under the help sections of many Web sites. MySpace has a help center on its site that provides a link for reporting offensive profiles. Make sure to copy the link (the Web site address) to the site for reporting purposes.
- Investigate your child's online presence. Set up an alert on Google, or search your child's name occasionally through a variety of search engines.
- If the perpetrator is another student, share evidence with the school counselor. Check to see if any bullying may be occurring at school.
- If the perpetrator is known and cyber bullying is continuing or severe, contact the child's parents and share your evidence (if you are comfortable doing so). Ask that they ensure that the cyber bullying stop and any posted material be removed.
- If the parent of perpetrator is unresponsive and the behavior continues, the parent of the target may wish to contact an attorney or send a certified letter outlining possible civil/legal options if the behavior does not stop or material is not removed.
- Report the cyber bullying to the police or high tech crimes unit in your area if the cyber bullying contains threats, intimidation, or sexual exploitation.
- If your child expresses emotional distress or thoughts of self-harm seek help from a school counselor or other mental health professional immediately.

Suggestions for Addressing Cyber Bullying that Children Engage in or Witness

Research on bullying has demonstrated that most young people do not find themselves in the role of bully or victim (Olweus, 1993a). The majority of young people are witnesses to bullying. They may play a variety of roles as witnesses or bystanders, including disengaged onlookers or possible defenders (a child who sees the bullying behavior and dislikes it, but is not sure what to do about it). Adults need to help young people understand that they have important roles to play as bystanders. Parents can talk with their children about the various options available to them when they see bullying behavior in the real world and cyber bullying in the virtual world. Too often young people witness bullying, feel badly, and do nothing.

Here are some of the students' comments about their feelings when witnessing cyber bullying behavior:

"I was surprised and stuff because I was friends with them and I knew they didn't like her but I thought it was lame to do that, I thought it was mean, so I was surprised they would do it." – *high school female*
"I felt bad for her because they were saying things about how she looked and stuff, and she couldn't help it." – *high school female*
"I just felt really bad because everyone was being so mean." – *middle school female*
"I felt bad for [her], because it was multiple girls doing it to one girl . . . on MySpace." – *middle school boy*
"I was mad." – *middle school boy*

Despite being upset or disappointed in their friends' actions, the bystanders did not tell an adult about the cyber bullying in the vast majority of the cyber bullying situations discussed in our focus groups. Thus, it is critical for parents to talk to their children about what to do when they witness cyber bullying.

If Your Child Witnesses Cyber Bullying

Parents can help their children to become "empowered" bystanders by discussing the following strategies with their children.

1. Speak out against the cyber bullying. Children can let cyber bullies know that they think their actions are wrong and that they need to stop bullying others. This may or may not be a safe option for some bystanders. While it will certainly not help if the cyber bully turns on them, some young people will feel comfortable speaking out against others who bully. These young people are assertive enough and have enough social support to do so. There is strength in numbers. One student may not wish to discourage the cyber bully on his or her own, but having a group of friends approach the cyber bully face-to-face or online can bring positive results.

2. Support the student being bullied. Talking to victims face-to-face (or in cyberspace) and letting them know that their peers think that the cyber bullying is wrong can provide much needed emotional support for the victims. In the face of silence, many children who are bullied feel that everyone else believes, likes, or takes the side of the cyber bully. It is easy for a victim to feel friendless in such a situation. In the case of Lisa Smith (whose "Lisa Must Die" Web site was discussed earlier), her friends posted positive comments to the site to counteract the negative messages. In a follow-up interview about the incident, Lisa's mother commented that it helped her daughter weather the storm when she saw her friends' positive comments and messages of support posted online.

3. Tell an adult. Unfortunately, many bystanders as well as victims avoid telling an adult about cyber bullying incidents. As mentioned earlier, some are afraid to tell because they think they will lose their online privileges. Parents may find it helpful to clarify with their children that they will not be punished for another person's bullying behavior or their own reluctance to help stop the cyber bullying. A parent's goal should be to help improve the situation, not to find fault. Parents can also discuss with their children which adults they feel they can trust or talk to when they need help or advice. While parents often prefer that their children come to them with a problem, it is helpful for young people to have a wider circle of adults to whom they can turn for support. If a classmate is being cyber bullied, the most appropriate adult to seek out may be the school counselor or a helpful teacher. Parents should explain to their children that these adults need to know about the situation so they can help stop the bullying.

The toughest social dilemmas that many children face are in the roles of a witness or a bystander. It is one thing to avoid engaging in mean, dishonest, or unethical behavior. It requires even greater moral fiber to take action when young people observe others engaging in such behavior. Parents may find it helpful to admit to their children that sometimes adults also fail to speak up or act when they witness inappropriate behavior. Think about how reluctant Parent A is to call Parent B even though she knows Parent B's child is engaged in harmful behavior that could be damaging to the child or to others. Parents may need to look in the mirror to make sure that they are leading by example.

If Your Child Engages in Cyber Bullying

Imagine that the school counselor calls you to let you know that your daughter participated with her classmates in designing a Web site to make fun of a fellow classmate. On the Web site, students posted negative comments about the girl's physical appearance and called her sexually derogative terms. Because the pages were printed out and shared at school, administrators are taking the position that the students should be disciplined for engaging in bullying behavior, and they request that you come to school for a meeting. How will you respond?

- You deny that your daughter could ever be involved in such behavior and threaten to get to the bottom of this. You ask for any proof they have that your child was involved and threaten a lawsuit if they are wrong.
- You accuse the school of overreacting and explain how this is just "kids being kids." You point out that slam books have existed forever and, even if it's mean, it's not that big a deal. "Do we really have to meet about this?"
- You listen carefully to their findings and express concern about your daughter and her classmates' behavior. You agree to come to the meeting and assure the school that you support its position to take cyber bullying seriously. You plan to have a serious discussion with your daughter as well, in order to better understand her role in the incident.

Few parents want to admit that their children are capable of cruel or bullying behavior. It has been our experience that many educators are very hesitant to use the term bullying in describing children's behavior to parents, because parents react so strongly to the term. "My child is not a bully!" and "Are you calling my child a bully?" are common responses from parents. Rather than becoming defensive, parents of students who engage in bullying behavior should recognize that most individuals are capable of either supporting or directly engaging in bullying behavior at some point in their lives. A child who engages in bullying behavior is not necessarily a "bully" every day of his or her life. The advent of the Internet and electronic communication, combined with the opportunity to post information anonymously, has influenced some young people to make negative statements online that they would be much less likely to make if their name were attached to the comment.

That being said, some young people who cyber bully also engage in other forms of bullying. If an investigation into the cyber bullying suggests that a child has bullied another student at school as well as online, the parents face a serious situation that may best be corrected through a combination of consequences, counseling, and possibly community service. The consequences and counseling should focus on correcting mistaken beliefs of entitlement, and the community service (if used appropriately) may help teach empathy. It also is important in this situation to monitor a child's Internet use much more closely. Installing tracking software is one way to verify that a child is only corresponding in a positive manner online and only accessing agreed upon Web sites.

If the child appears truly remorseful for his or her actions, it would be appropriate for him or her to write and apologize to the child who was bullied and the other family members that have been hurt. Forcing an apology is never a good idea, however, and will do more harm than good. The child who has been cyber bullied will recognize that the effort is insincere and may feel further victimized by the incident. The parents of the child engaged in the cyber bullying may want to have a school counselor review the apology note to make sure it appears sincere and appropriate before giving it to the family of the targeted child.

Parents should remember that every challenge that children face is also an opportunity for learning. Consider the lessons that children may learn from such an event. When parents catch a child experimenting with alcohol or other drugs or engaging in some other high risk behavior, it is common to be reactive and look at only the negative aspects of the incident. It is much more useful, however, to recognize that an opportunity is available to correct a situation that needs attention. This is an opportunity to teach again, guide again, and communicate values again to children who need to hear these messages. Parents may reflect that it is time to focus closely on issues that are important to them as a family. The alternative is for parents to take the position that their child should not be held accountable for his or her actions and that school administrators or other parents are overreacting. In this case, a child may conclude that his or her misbehavior was okay, but that being caught was unacceptable. Such lessons will do little to curb bullying and other antisocial behavior.

By teaching empathy and modeling compassion for others, parents will be less likely to see their children engage in bullying behavior. There is no guarantee, however, that, when faced with the dynamics of a peer group, children will always choose not to engage in bullying and other negative actions. Thus, parents need to actively discuss bullying behavior and bystander strategies to prepare their children for the situations they may encounter.

If Your Child is Bullied But Also Engages in Retaliatory Cyber Bullying

"One time I cyber bullied this person because [he] spread rumors about me . . . I put up a whole Xanga about [him]. I started a rumor that he cheated on his girlfriend, and his girlfriend actually broke up with him."
– *high school male*

There are some incidents of cyber bullying that occur when a student who has been the victim of bullying at school decides to retaliate online. A

student who lacks the social support or assertiveness skills to confront bullying behavior at school may occasionally use the anonymity that the
Internet provides to respond to or attack a perceived bully. If a parent finds
that his or her child has engaged in cyber bullying behavior, it is important
to make sure that the child wasn't the recipient of other bullying behavior
at school. A child who engages in retaliatory cyber bullying may fit the
category of the "bully/victim" or "provocative victim" discussed in Chapter
2. These children may have poor social skills that put them at greater risk
for being bullied at school and may benefit from a school-based support
group that emphasizes the development of social skills (such as "friendship
skills"). These children may also benefit from individual counseling, particularly if group supports are not available.

While retaliating online is not to be condoned, addressing the bullying at
school will reduce the likelihood of retaliation online. Parents need to
emphasize that such retaliation is inappropriate, yet empathize with the
frustration their son or daughter may be feeling. It will be critical to request
the school's help in addressing the bullying situation on campus; however,
the parent of the child engaged in cyber bullying needs to take whatever steps
are necessary to ensure that the cyber bullying ends. Parents will also need
to support the school's policies around cyber bullying if it has occurred on
campus or through the use of school technology. Yet they should also make
sure that the school is aware of the bullying that influenced the retaliation.

Parents can request a meeting with the school to identify an appropriate
adult for their son or daughter to approach should they experience additional bullying behavior at school. As mentioned previously, the school
counselor or administrator can assist the parents and child in developing
a school safety plan that includes increased adult monitoring of situations
where bullying behavior typically occurs. This may include schedule adjust-
ments (for either party, but preferably for the student engaged in bullying
behavior), if necessary.

In addition, parents can set up a written agreement at home with a child
that defines appropriate computer use and clarifies that using the Internet
to harass or demean others is not acceptable. The agreement needs to
provide clear consequences, such as a loss of online privileges, should such
behavior occur again. Parents can have their child sign a copy of the agreement and keep it for reference in case any other computer infractions occur.

Suggestions for Parents to Prevent Cyber Bullying

Many parents assume that, if they just speak with their children about
respectful treatment of others, they will have done enough to prevent cyber

bullying. After years of research, prevention experts have learned that adults cannot give a message one time and expect that children have received it and incorporate it into their actions. Many prevention specialists use the immunization model as an example. A flu shot can be effective in preventing the flu, but needs to be repeated every year. The same holds true with messages about healthy behavior. Telling a child on one occasion not to use alcohol or other drugs will not be sufficient for him to navigate the teen years when underage drinking and drug use become more prevalent. Telling a child the golden rule on one occasion will not be sufficient to expect that she will always treat others as she would like to be treated.

It is, therefore, recommended that parents talk with their children regarding the dos and don'ts of each new piece of technology that enters the home (Franek, 2005/2006). Such discussions should include maintenance, safety, and forbidden uses. In addition, parents need to make sure they are supporting the age limit policies of various online sites. For example, the age limit for MySpace is 14, yet children regularly lie about their age to set up profiles at younger ages.

Because parents are seldom present in the online world of children and youth, setting up a home environment that lends itself to supervision is crucial. One of the most basic tips on Internet safety for families is to place the computer in a family room or kitchen where it can be easily viewed by adults in the home. This reasonable guideline becomes trickier as more families go wireless and laptop computers can travel from room to room and still access the Internet. Setting up family rules ahead of time that keep computers out of bedrooms will help prevent unmonitored online access.

Holding weekly family meetings encourages communication about any issue impacting the family. These weekly meetings are an ideal time to bring up the ground rules for use of new technology and to discuss potential inappropriate uses of such tools. Parents can define and explain cyber bullying at such family meetings and remind their children of the family rules as new technologies are introduced.

Not only must parents repeat and reinforce important messages in their discussions with their children, they also must help children apply these messages to new situations. This principle was in evidence in our efforts to address the new phenomenon of cyber bullying as part of the Olweus Bullying Prevention Program in Cobb County, Georgia, schools. Despite our efforts to encourage students to avoid engaging in or supporting bullying behavior, we discovered that some students didn't recognize their mean and harassing online behavior as bullying. This is an important lesson for parents. Parents need to help children make the transition in their learning by giving consistent messages about appropriate behavior and apply them to new situations and settings, including online environments. "Take time for training," was a favorite expression of psychologist Rudolph Dreikurs to parents in his audiences (Dreikurs & Stoltz, 1991). Parents need to look for opportunities every day to educate their children and communicate their values through discussions rather than lectures. Parents may find it helpful to ask their children to share new experiences with them so that they understand the challenges teens are facing as they move through the adolescent years.

Students Share Advice with Parents

In each of our focus groups, students were asked what adults could do to prevent cyber bullying. They had limited advice for educators, because the students perceived that most cyber bullying occurs after school hours. Some of the high school girls did have quite a bit of advice for parents, however. Here are some of their tips:

- Set age-appropriate guidelines.

  "I think in my case parents need to not let 11-year-old kids get on MySpace and stuff. I mean, I know that I started using the Internet at 13, but there wasn't MySpace and stuff then. They need to be a parent and take charge of what their kids do."
  "Tell kids not to put revealing information on their blogs and stuff."
  "A lot of parents say you can't have a blog but as long as they don't put anything personal on it I don't see a problem with it and then they would be more open with their parents and share more."

- Communicate about appropriate ways to deal with conflict.

  "I think parents need to talk to their kids more. Like in my family, when my brother and I fight, my parents stop us, but they don't talk to us about it, and they could just help us."

- Monitor their children's use of the Internet.

  "See what their kids are doing on the Internet. Limit their use."
  "I showed my Dad how to use the history to see where they are going on the Internet."
  "Some parents don't even know how much time their kids spend on the computer. They should at least talk to them about it and stuff."
  "I think they could help monitor it."
  "They should at least ask you what you are doing on the computer."

- Supervision, not snoopervision.

"[Parents should] not record everything, I hate it when they do that, because I have a friend whose parents do that. They like look at all her history and cookies and stuff."
"My mom does monitor me. Like my mom watched Oprah and it was on MySpace so then she came up and was standing behind me and I'm like, 'What are you doing?' and she says, 'I just want to make sure you are safe.'"

- Watch for warning signs.

"Usually you can tell if your kid is being weird, or keeping to themselves, or if their parent comes into the room and they like jump or are clicking to get rid of stuff."

- Don't blame the victim (or punish them for someone else's behavior).

"They might be scared to tell their parents [if they are cyber bullied] because they might say, I told you so, I told you not to have that blog."
"Parents shouldn't punish before you do something – that's just going to make the kid sneak around more. Talk with the kid more about what's right and what's wrong and what's normal."

- Educate themselves.

"They should have something for parents like a parent seminar or something that parents can go to about cyber bullying."

Explain the Challenges of Communicating Online

Parents may wish to begin by explaining to children that communicating online is prone to miscommunication because of the lack of nonverbal cues. Individuals readily use nonverbal cues in day-to-day conversation to determine if someone is being friendly, teasing playfully, or angry. Emoticons (smiley and frowny faces used in e-mails and instant messaging – ex: ☺ ☹) were developed to help users determine the emotional meaning behind messages. Parents need to explain to their children that it is more difficult to communicate accurately without nonverbal cues, and that they need to be careful to avoid sarcasm or other such emotions that can lead to hurt feelings. It is helpful to teach children to make use of emoticons so that misunderstandings can be avoided. Children should also consider whether the person on the other end of a cyber message will know that they are joking before they hit the send button.

Parents need to regularly communicate to their children that it is not acceptable to harass, spread gossip, or make mean or disparaging comments toward others online. Parents can also discuss with their children the importance of taking time to "cool down" if they are upset or angry with a friend or classmate before sending or posting a message online. Once an angry message has been sent, it may be forwarded to classmates or viewed by others and escalate a conflict. It is best to talk face-to-face with a friend or peer if they are having a disagreement. It is possible to retrieve an e-mail message, but only if the recipient has not yet opened it. This option may be a life-saver for users who experience an immediate feeling of regret after sending a negative or nasty e-mail. However, once the recipient has opened the message, it cannot be retrieved. This option came in handy to one parent we interviewed. When she realized her 11-year-old daughter had forwarded a threatening chain e-mail to another classmate, the mother was able to use this option to retrieve the message before it was viewed.

We Are Not Invisible Online

The phenomenon of "disinhibition" was discussed in detail in Chapter 3. Disinhibition is a term used to describe how people in cyberspace say and do things they wouldn't normally do face-to-face because they feel anonymous. Using an anonymous screen name or setting up a Web site anonymously may allow the user to believe he or she will not be held responsible for posting mean or offensive comments online. Parents should communicate to their children that they are not, in fact, invisible online. Any communications posted online or sent electronically can usually be traced back to the individual who originally posted or sent the message. Granted, not all communications will be deemed worthy of the effort; however, threats of violence, harassment, stalking, defamation, extortion, and posting pornographic images should be traced and many police departments have a high-tech crimes unit that will assist in such instances. Because parents can be held liable for a child's actions in many states, parents should discuss with their children that their actions could harm the entire family, as well as the children they are targeting.

Protect Passwords

Parents should discuss with their children the importance of protecting their passwords to their social networking sites, instant message programs, and even to their online gaming accounts. A student who sends instant messages can easily pose as another individual if he or she is aware of an individual's screen name and password. In addition, teens have been known to alter their peers' social networking sites when their passwords are known. Unfortunately, a peer who is friendly one day may turn on a classmate the next day, or may just suffer from indiscretion, so passwords should always be kept private. Parents, however, need to know their children's passwords, screen names, and account information should an emergency arise or if abuse needs to be reported.

Filtering Versus Monitoring

Parents have always had the difficult challenge of supervising their children, yet gradually allowing them more freedom as they become older and show more responsibility. Unfortunately, with the advent of the Internet, many parents assume that, if their child is home on the computer, he or she is safe. Thus, they allow their child complete freedom on the Internet. Making use of filtering or blocking sites that screen material is one way of preventing children, who are naturally curious, from stumbling into sites that could be risky or harmful to them. Setting parental controls on a "kid or teen setting" still allows children to visit most sites of interest, but provides protection from violent, pornographic, or otherwise inappropriate sites. Sometimes a favorite site will be mistakenly blocked because of the terms used in the description of the site. In such instances, parents can set the parental controls to allow access to individual sites that they feel are appropriate and that their children routinely use. John Halligan, who wrote the foreword to our book, recommends that parents let their children know upfront that monitoring software has been installed to ensure that the family's safety rules are followed and that inappropriate material or activity is not "pushed" on to the family's computer (J. Halligan, personal communication, January 17, 2007).

In cases where parents have reason to believe that their children have abused their online privileges or have abused others, they can install tracking software that records every site a child visits and every keystroke a child makes. Spectorsoft and IamBigBrother are examples of such tracking software. Keep in mind, however, that these programs communicate a lack of trust between the parent and child. As Larry Magid and Anne Collier (2007), the directors of BlogSafety.com, write in their book *MySpace Unraveled*, these tools should only be used as a last resort.

Parents also can check the history of the Web sites visited online if they have reason to believe that their children are accessing inappropriate Web sites. The toolbar has a view key that allows the user to view the recent

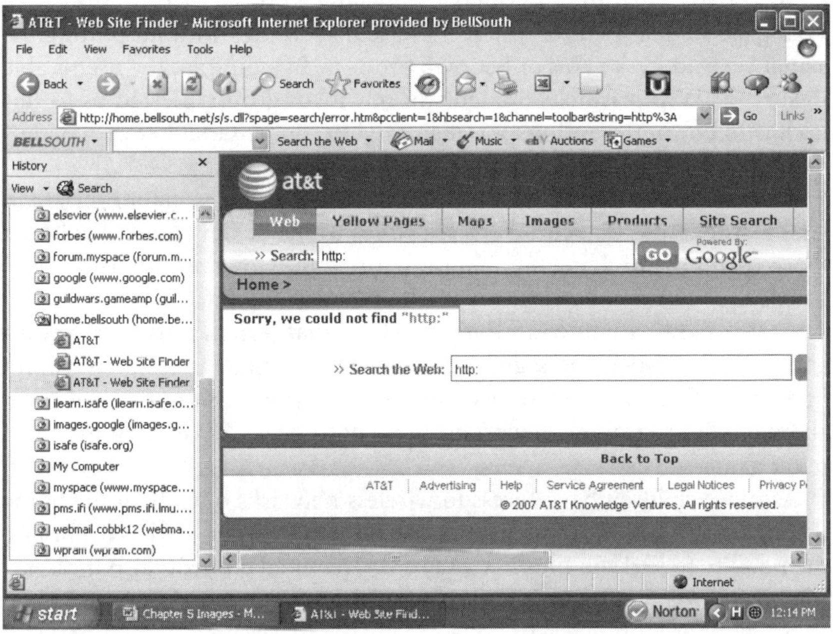

Figure 5.1 Computer screen with history displayed

history, or the user can press the control key and the "H" key simultane-
ously to display the history on most computers. Figure 5.1 shows a screen
shot of a computer with the history displayed on the left side of the
screen.

Parents need to remember that filters, tracking software, and other
checks on children's online activity should always be accompanied by
parental education, guidelines, and open communication.

As children age, filtering becomes less useful than monitoring the
computer. Filtering or blocking software allows many parents (and educators) to believe that their computer is completely safe, but, by the time
children enter the teen years, many learn ways to get around filters and
blocking software. Nothing takes the place of putting the computer in a
supervised area such as a family room and, more importantly, reaching a
consensus in a family regarding what types of sites are off-limits and why.
Despite having filtering software that blocks pornographic material on a
home computer, a child can go to a proxy server site that advertises "anonymous surfing" and access pornography if he wants to test the limits. A
proxy server is a third-party site that shields the real IP address from view.
Biersdorfer (2006) writes in his article "How to digitally hide (somewhat)

in plain sight," that the site works by opening a browser within the actual Web page so that the user can visit blocked Web sites without putting the actual Web address in his or her own browser. By doing so, the user is able to surf the Web privately. Students in our focus groups alerted us to this trick, and one of the authors was dismayed to confirm that her own parental blocks could be bypassed quite easily.

Thus, communicating with a teenager about why it is inappropriate to view pornography or send mean messages to his or her peers may be far more useful than relying on a filtering program. However, filters do have benefits. They help prevent children from stumbling into sites innocently. They also allow parents to set the time of day that certain features are available (such as instant messaging and online gaming) so that parents don't have to nag their children to get off of the computer in the evening or worry about children sneaking downstairs at night to play a favorite online computer game.

As more children have access to wireless networks outside of the home through mobile devices such as portable game players and cell phones, their ability to surf the Internet away from parental controls also increases (Olsen, 2006a, 2006b). In addition, tech-savvy teens can choose to log on to a neighbor's unsecured wireless network to circumvent the parental controls at home or log on at free Internet cafes. Parents should pay attention to the capabilities of the devices that they purchase for their children and take time to establish ground rules about acceptable and unacceptable uses of the wireless Internet devices they bring into their home.

Finally, parents need to explain to their children that they want to know if someone sends them inappropriate material or messages. This way, the parent and child can address the situation together before it escalates. Reassuring children that they will not be disciplined for someone else's abusive comments or actions will allow them to feel safe contacting their parents if they view something inappropriate.

Monitor Your Child's Reputation Online

It is important for parents to explain to their children that, if they choose to use a social networking site, anyone can view their entries. Young people often assume that only their friends will view their entries, but, as evidenced from media accounts, Internet predators routinely prey on victims they have contacted through social networking sites. Parents may find it helpful to explain to their children that, if everyone else can read their MySpace profiles, it is reasonable that the parents will too. Parry Aftab with WiredSafety.org recommends that parents review their guidelines with their children about safe profiles, and then tell them that they plan to visit their site in the near future to see if it complies with these guidelines (Reese, 2006). This will give a child the chance to correct any personal or inappropriate information that was shared on the site. As David Walsh, psychologist and President of the National Institute on Media and the Family, points out, teenagers' brains are not fully developed, especially in the prefrontal cortex area that assesses risks and considers consequences. That is why teens often feel that dangerous situations such as online predators contacting them "won't happen to me." He clarifies that our job as parents is to act as a "surrogate prefrontal cortex" through setting clear expectations and consequences (Walsh, 2004). That image is helpful in understanding why parents need to understand new cyber technologies. The prefrontal cortex area of the brain is shown in Figure 5.2.

Parents and children need to discuss the potential repercussions of posting negative comments on other individuals' Web sites and how this could also affect their online reputation. Students in our focus groups shared many stories of users writing nasty comments to one another on their social networking sites.

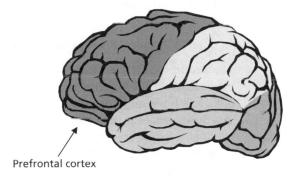

Prefrontal cortex

Figure 5.2 Prefrontal cortex

"Blogging sites like Xanga often have mean comments posted." – *middle school female*

"In my neighborhood there was like this one kid and we all got pissed off at him and he had a Xanga . . . so we left a bunch of stuff on his Xanga." – *high school boy*

"Some people shut their sites down because of people saying things on their sites or getting into them and messing them up." – *high school female*

"There is a teacher we didn't like . . . so we kind of made fun of that teacher . . . we have a Facebook blog of that teacher." – *high school male*

Blogging is encouraged on many sites and users often write journal-like entries about their day. Students who share their secrets or emotional state may be ridiculed or targeted with nasty comments. Conflicts among peers that are aired in a blog can escalate into confrontations at school. Thus, youth need to be advised to avoid sharing very personal information that could be used against them or their classmates in cyber bullying situations.

Another repercussion that may significantly affect high school and college students is that an increasing number of college admissions representatives and employers search prospective candidates' names online to learn more about them (Hass, 2006). Do teens really want a college admissions counselor reading about their sexual escapades or drinking binges? Would a profanity-laced blog entry help their chances of being selected by a potential employer? An employer or college representative who views a personal profile that shows a lack of discretion may be quick to choose another applicant. Parents should help their sons and daughters recognize how entries posted today may affect their reputation and future in life-changing ways.

Resources for Parents

Monitoring a child's reputation on the Internet is an important new role for parents. While it is challenging to parent in a world of rapidly evolving technology, it is a requirement to be a vigilant parent today. The good news is that the Internet can be a parent's friend in this area as well. Many Web sites exist that provide great learning tools for parents attempting to learn more about monitoring their child's Internet use. Netsmartz.org, WiredSafety. org, i-SAFE.org, and iKeepSafe.org provide excellent guidelines for parents on how to supervise their children on the Internet. The Stop Bullying Now Campaign provided through the Department of Health and Human Resources, Health Resources and Services Administration also has helpful tips for parents on bullying and cyber bullying prevention. The following Web sites provide helpful information on Internet safety and/or cyber bullying, and the list includes our own Web site, www.cyberbullyhelp.com.

- NetSmartz (www.netsmartz.org)
- i-SAFE Inc. (www.isafe.org)
- iKeepSafe Internet Safety (www.ikeepsafe.org)
- WiredSafety (www.wiredsafety.org)
- Stop Bullying Now (www.stopbullyingnow.hrsa.gov)
- Cyber Bully Help (www.cyberbullyhelp.com)

Parents should "google" their children's names occasionally (as well as their own) to see what is posted online about family members. Parents can simply go to the google.com search engine site, insert their child's first and last name in quotes, and search for what is posted online about them. Obviously this works better if a child's name is not extremely common.

Parents may also need to check for common misspellings of a child's name as well as their screen names. In addition, parents can use the google.com/ alert function to set up regular searches of their children's names online. Google will notify a parent by e-mail every time a child's name appears online. Adults would be wise to monitor their own online information as well. It is amazing and even frightening to learn how much personal information can be found with a few clicks on a search engine.

Allow Children to Be the Experts

Lastly, remember that children can be an important source of information in understanding the way that students at their school are interacting online. Parents will find it helpful in keeping the lines of communication open if they allow their children to be the "experts" on occasion. Youth are often happy to show adults around the popular sites where their classmates are spending time online. It takes courage to admit that children may have more information about the latest technology than adults, but it is also a wonderful opportunity for parents to build a positive relationship with their children by letting them be the teacher for a change.

Summary

Although parents are beginning to take a more active role in communicating personal safety guidelines to their children owing to their fear of online predators, most parents are less aware of the problem of cyber bullying and have yet to give their children ground rules for communicating online. Rather than forbidding Internet use, parents need to make sure their children understand that it is not acceptable to harass, spread gossip, or make mean or disparaging comments toward others online or through other digital devices. Parents should also set developmentally appropriate guidelines for introducing various technologies to their children.

In addition, parents need to help children understand the steps they can take if they are cyber bullied or witness a peer being cyber bullied. Empowering the bystanders to speak out against such actions will be one of the most effective strategies in reducing cyber bullying that parents and educators can pursue.

Note

1. The names of all individuals described in the real-life cyber bullying incidents have been changed to protect their identity.

6

What Educators Can Do

∽

"I feel really bad for him because he already told my mom he didn't want
to go to school because he didn't think he was going to make any friends,
and now he feels left out of everything."
                    (sister of a 15-year-old boy who was cyber bullied)

Just one year ago, one of the authors of this book was asked by an area
superintendent to talk about cyber bullying at a principal's meeting that
included her child's former principal. When asked by the principal why
she was joining their group, she responded, "I am here to talk about cyber
bullying." The principal's response? "What is cyber bullying?"

Since that time, the topic of cyber bullying has been frequently featured
in the media. But, while the topic of Internet safety is discussed regularly
in schools and by parents, the issue of cyber bullying still receives much
less attention. Is this because most adults, like the principal mentioned
above, are largely unaware of the phenomenon, its prevalence, and its possible consequences? Or because it is perceived as an issue that is relevant
to home environments, but not schools? In this chapter, we will look at
whether cyber bullying is, in fact, affecting the school environment. We
also will look at how educators can intervene, provide resources to families,
and help prevent cyber bullying. Our focus groups and individual interviews with students and parents suggest there are few educators who discuss
cyber bullying in the classroom. We authors hope that this chapter will
encourage educators to take steps to prevent and intervene in cyber bullying behavior among their students.

Is Cyber Bullying a Problem for Schools?

As discussed in Chapter 4, findings from our anonymous survey of students suggested that cyber bullying is an issue for many students, with 18%
reporting that they had been cyber bullied at least once in the previous two
months (and 6% having been cyber bullied 2–3 times a month or more

often), and 11% admitting that they had cyber bullied others at least once (and 2% admitting to doing so at least 2–3 times a month; Kowalski & Limber, 2006). Although most children are not bullied on the school premises, half of those who had been cyber bullied noted that they had been targeted by another student from school.

These survey findings were further supported by responses from middle and high school students in a series of focus groups that we conducted to better understand the extent of the problem and its effects (if any) on the school environment. While some students didn't feel that cyber bullying was a concern, others disagreed.

Their responses varied greatly depending on whether they personally knew someone who had been cyber bullied. Some sample responses are included below.

Interviewer: Is cyber bullying a problem at your school?
"No." – *high school male*
"Not really." – *middle school girl*
"I think it is a problem but people keep it to themselves." – *high school female*
"Yeah – because it happens a lot." – *middle school male*
"Yes. It is a problem specifically at this school." – *high school female*
"I remember when I first started using the Internet I didn't know anyone who got cyber bullied, and now it's really bad, it's getting a lot worse as time progresses. I feel like it's getting worse among young people, like young teenagers, like middle school." – *high school female*
"Yeah, it's getting a lot worse – even among elementary school kids." – *high school female*
"I think it bleeds into the school." – *high school male*

Examples of the Cyber Bullying

When students were also asked if they knew anyone who had been affected by cyber bullying, high school girls were particularly able to provide examples:

"My best friend in middle school, she had a Xanga and someone posted this horrible one about her, it was dedicated to her."
"I have heard of people knowing someone's password and going in and changing their MySpace."
"I only know it between people who know each other. Not like a stranger, so like if I didn't like her I might post something about her."

"I've heard of people going into chat rooms and picking on one person."

"I know someone who posted pictures of different people and they were just making fun of them."

"This one girl had the password to her MySpace or Facebook [stolen] and they put up all these bad pictures and stuff on it. Her parents found it and were very mad and they called the police about it."

"My brother has a MySpace and it has gotten really bad. The kids are really picking on him on MySpace. He just turned 11. I think it is ridiculous. They don't even know him."

"I know someone who got mean text messages."

"At my old school there was some kind of comment thing where all these kids ganged up on her. It wasn't really a blog site, just a comment website."

Does Cyber Bullying Affect Students?

While some students in our focus groups indicated that receiving mean online comments was no big deal and should just be ignored, many others were aware of students who were affected more negatively by cyber bullying. Below are some of the students' perceptions of the effects of cyber bullying on themselves and their classmates.

"[It] makes them think less of themselves. Because whenever someone is mad they say things they shouldn't and then they [the targets] think less of themselves." *middle school male*

"[It] makes me really mad. It's personal – to me and her – and I got a really bad temper, so . . . it doesn't affect my schoolwork but when I see his name come up I really want to go get him." – *high school male* (responding to how he feels when he sees comments from a classmate who has targeted him and his girlfriend)

"She would cry a lot. They said mean stuff and she couldn't get it shut down because she didn't have the password. She was really upset about it for awhile." – *high school female*

"She thought the girls who did it were her friends, so she lost those friendships." – *high school female*

"The stuff [the cyber bullies] said really affected [her]. I don't know how I could ever say something like that. It was just kind of ridiculous. It made [her] be mean to people for awhile. [She] just didn't want to do anything with anyone; [she] didn't want to deal with it. It affected [her] mood, [her] relationships. It affected [her] academically. [She] stopped coming to school for a few days." – *high school female*

"She was afraid to walk around the school and was afraid everyone was going to gang up on her. The people that were [cyber] bullying her told other people so they all picked on her." – *middle school female*

As noted in Chapter 2, traditional forms of bullying can result in higher rates of anxiety, somatic complaints, depression, and suicidal ideation among students, and poorer academic performance. Although there currently is very little research on the effects of cyber bullying on children (as victims or bystanders; see Chapter 4), participants in our focus groups believed that cyber bullying behavior could have serious effects on children. In addition, those students who experience bullying at school *and* cyber bullying at home may be at particular risk. They may feel that they have no safe place left. Children cannot perform their best at school when they are fearful or believe that they don't belong.

How Much Cyber Bullying Takes Place at School?

It is possible that some educators are not aware of the problem of cyber bullying because it often takes place outside of the school day, and students may be reluctant to tell teachers or administrators. While cyber bullying can occur on campus through the use of school technology, students in our focus groups noted that using the school system's technology to cyber bully was somewhat rare. Students seemed puzzled when asked about being cyber bullied at school. "How would someone cyber bully you at school?" was a common question that we received. Their responses indicated that most cyber bullying occurs after school through the use of instant messages or posts on social networking sites. While students indicate it is sometimes possible to access instant messaging and social networking sites at school (despite their being blocked from the district server), for the most part students in the focus groups avoided using these functions at school. This may change as more students begin using cellular phones with Internet browsing and instant messaging capabilities, a trend we were beginning to see toward the end of our focus groups.

However, students did mention that text messaging at school was perhaps the one way that students might cyber bully each other at school. When asked if most students send text messages during the school day despite the school district's policy, many students laughed and said, "Yes, all day, every day." When we asked if they would tell an adult at school if they were being cyber bullied at school through text messaging, many students gave comments similar to this one:

"No, because we are not supposed to have our cell phones on at school or be text messaging. So you can't tell an adult that you are being text messaged with mean messages because you might get in trouble for having your cell phone on."

In addition, many students felt there was no reason to tell adults at the school about cyber bullying, because there would be little they could do. The following are sample responses when asked what adults at school could do to prevent cyber bullying:

"It's not here so you wouldn't tell people." – *high school female*
"I don't really think they can do much because it's at home, not at school, so I don't think they can do much." – *middle school male*
"Nothing." – *high school male*

Is Cyber Bullying Discussed at School?

In order to gain a sense of how much the issue of cyber bullying was discussed in the home or school environment, students were asked in the focus groups if they had heard the term cyber bullying prior to the group. For the most part, students indicated that it was rare for a parent or teacher to talk with them about cyber bullying. However, students from one of the middle schools that is implementing a bullying prevention program indicated that cyber bullying was discussed in the classroom.

During our focus groups, many students commented that they had seen news stories about Internet predators and that their parents or teachers had spoken with them about Internet safety. However, many students had not heard the term cyber bullying prior to the focus groups (although many of these students could give examples of cruel or harassing online behavior that they had witnessed or that their friends had experienced).

While some educators may insist that a child's online behavior is the responsibility of the parent, in reality educators frequently teach and encourage students' use of appropriate behavior and social skills through character education lessons, guidance lessons that teach conflict resolution, and health classes that teach refusal skills for drug prevention. While parents need to take primary responsibility for their child's online behavior, as technology has become such an integral part of the classroom environment educators should make appropriate online behavior part of their technology instruction as well.

What Can School Personnel Do to Prevent Cyber Bullying?

In fact, there are many preventive steps that educators can take to help reduce the number of incidents of cyber bullying that occur in school and out of school. Two of the authors of this book have spent significant time training educators in schools to implement a research-based bullying prevention effort known as the Olweus Bullying Prevention Program. This systemic approach to bullying prevention is discussed in Chapter 2 and has shown significant reductions in bullying behavior among students, but it takes a long-term commitment by the entire faculty to establish a climate that discourages bullying. Schools that already are implementing bullying prevention programs are at an advantage when combating cyber bullying. Educators, parents and students who are already working to address bullying behavior can include cyber bullying as part of their prevention focus. The core components of an effective bullying prevention program can easily be adapted to include segments on cyber bullying

Assess Cyber Bullying

An important first step in implementing an effective bullying prevention program is to thoroughly assess the problem. As discussed in Chapter 2, one good way to do this is by having students complete an anonymous questionnaire about bullying behavior at school. Including questions on cyber bullying will help educators gain insight into the amount of cyber bullying that is occurring among their students. A good measure should define cyber bullying and include questions about cyber bullying through various mediums, including instant messaging, e-mails, text messaging, blogs, and social networking sites such as MySpace and Facebook. Such surveys not only will allow administrators to see how common cyber bullying is, but also they will help administrators to know if it is occurring during the school day or after school, and which mediums are most prone to abuse. It will be useful to be able to examine students' responses by grade and gender. For example, if cyber bullying peaks among 7th grade girls, prevention strategies targeting 6th graders may be ideal. Good assessment will help the school administration to craft policies and strategies to prevent cyber bullying from happening at school, effectively address cyber bullying that does takes place on school grounds, and work with parents to prevent and address cyber bullying that takes place away from school.

Provide Staff Training on Cyber Bullying

Many educators already discuss the importance of Internet safety with their students, but they also need to talk with students about proper "netiquette" (online etiquette) that defines and discusses cyber bullying and cyber threats. To do so effectively, they likely will need some degree of training about cyber bullying and children's use of cyber technologies.

Although it is not necessary for the entire faculty to be experts on cyber bullying, they should all be familiar with the issue, and certain staff members (i.e., counselors, administrators, and media specialists) should be comfortable recognizing and responding to concerns about cyber bullying that affect their students and the school environment. Incorporating cyber bullying training into staff training on bullying prevention is one way that schools can educate their faculty on this important topic.

To fully understand the many ways that students use technology to bully and harass others, educators need training on the various popular forms of online communication that students use, such as instant messaging, social networking sites, and text messaging. MySpace and Facebook are becoming a cultural requirement among middle and high school students. Educators need to understand the appropriate uses of such technologies as well as the potential for abuse. Training should also include tips on preventing cyber bullying as well as how to intervene in a cyber bullying incident. The training should include a discussion of the school district's policies regarding bullying in general, and cyber bullying in particular. It also would be helpful if the training included resources for educators such as sample lesson plans on cyber bullying and Web sites for additional information. Such training would allow educators to partner with parents in providing guidelines for children on appropriate uses of technology.

Define Cyber Bullying

One of the first things that schools must do when addressing bullying is to have a clear definition of bullying behavior that is understood by students, administrators, faculty, and nonteaching staff. The same is true of cyber bullying. If schools wish to prevent cyber bullying, they need first to define it and talk about it so that students and faculty members are clear about what cyber bullying is and what it is not. The definition should include the various methods that students employ to cyber bully one another including e-mail, instant messages, text messaging, social networking sites, and blogs, as discussed in Chapter 3.

Educators and students should discuss why that behavior is hurtful to others (and sometimes unlawful) and what classmates can do to prevent the use of cyber bullying among their peers. Educators could include in such discussions the when, why, and how of reporting cyber bullying. Supporting documents could be sent home by the school so that parents can better understand cyber bullying and the school's policies on it, ways that they can help to prevent and address cyber bullying at home, and where to go for additional help, if needed.

Develop Clear Rules and Policies About Cyber Bullying

As we will describe in more detail in Chapter 7, schools should develop policies that specifically address cyber bullying. These policies may be incorporated under an existing "student use of technology" policy or as a separate entity. The policy should include provisions that prohibit using district technology to access, send, create, or post material or communications that are damaging, abusive, obscene, threatening, or demeaning to others. The policy should use clear language and discuss expectations of students and staff, as well as consequences for violations. The U.S. Department of Justice's (2006) Web site section on computer crime and intellectual property (www.usdoj.gov/criminal/cybercrime) provides a model acceptable-use policy that school administrators may wish to review as a starting point when drafting their own policy.

School districts should provide students and their parents with a copy of the policy that includes a definition of cyber bullying, examples of cyber bullying, and consequences of such actions. Sharing this information with students and parents at the beginning of the year will likely decrease violations. Although public schools will probably need to limit school-based consequences to abusing technology while on campus (owing to legal protections that exist for free speech), they also should include examples of cyber bullying that will be reported to the police. As discussed in detail in Chapter 7, government organizations (including schools) are very limited in their ability to censure speech that occurs off campus; however, private schools could conceivably have a policy that includes off-campus conduct as well. As always, schools should consult with their local attorney for guidance in drafting acceptable use policies. By developing a comprehensive and easily understood policy, students and parents will be clear in their expectations of the school district as well as their rights. It can be helpful for parents and students to sign and return a copy of the district's acceptable use of technology policy to ensure that it has been reviewed.

Encourage the Reporting of Cyber Bullying

Students need to know that there are supportive staff members available who they can turn to if they are experiencing bullying or cyber bullying behavior, and that these adults can help them problem solve to deal with the issue. Establishing a school-wide reporting system has proven helpful for students who wish to report bullying behavior but are uncertain how to do so. Many schools make available, at various drop-off boxes around the school, forms that students can complete (anonymously or not) to report bullying. Including a section on cyber bullying in these forms will allow students a mechanism for reporting cyber bullying as well as other forms of bullying or troubling behavior. Students can be instructed to describe the cyber bullying incident and, where applicable, provide a Web site address if they are aware of a classmate being ridiculed or humiliated online. The sample form below may be used to report bullying behavior at school (Figure 6.1).

Share Resources with Parents

Because most cyber bullying occurs outside of the school day, parents often are the first to hear about cyber bullying from their children. Students in our focus groups indicated they would be more likely to tell a parent than an adult at school if they experienced cyber bullying. Because of this, parents need to be aware of strategies for preventing and addressing cyber bullying. Schools can assist parents by sending parent newsletters home with information on cyber bullying and by providing seminars for them on the issue. Parents need to know about legal issues that might arise if their child harasses or threatens another online. They also could benefit from tips on how to educate themselves (and their children) about safe use of the Internet. As discussed in Chapter 5, there are many helpful Web sites that parents can use to teach their children to safely navigate the Internet, such as WiredSafety.org, Netsmartz.org, iKeepSafe.org, and i-SAFE.org. Such Web sites also provide parents with suggestions for how to monitor their children's online behavior. The guidance office at a particular school may be the best resource for making such information available to parents. Parent letters or newsletters should include the following information for parents:

- Appropriate online netiquette
- Guidelines for Internet safety
- Definition of cyber bullying
- Examples of cyber bullying
- How to report cyber bullying at school
- Tips on responding to cyber bullying (such as ignoring, blocking, or warning)
- Safe use of social networking sites and how to report abuse to such sites
- When to notify the police
- Possible parental liability for youth online behavior
- Who to contact for more information or assistance.

Following is an example where a principal shared tips and resources with parents after becoming concerned about some of his students' online behavior. After one of the authors provided a training session around the

Middle School
Bullying/Cyber Bullying Report Form

(Please return to any staff member or to one of the drop boxes located in the counselors' office)

Name: _____ Team: _____

Date: _____ Homeroom Teacher _____

What happened or is happening?

_____
_____
_____
_____
_____

How long has this been happening?
When and where is this happening? (Include Web site or printed evidence if applicable)

_____

Did anyone see this happen? _____
Have you reported this situation? Yes/No
If so, to whom? _____

_____

How would you like to be contacted? (please check the box(es) that apply and fill-in the proper contact information, if necessary)

❑ Home phone: _____
❑ e-mail: _____
❑ I would like to speak with a school counselor
❑ I would like to speak with a school administrator
❑ I would prefer to not be contacted

Thank you for your report. Empowered Students like you are making a difference at _____ Middle School!

Figure 6.1 Sample reporting form

issue of bullying and cyber bullying to faculty at a middle school, the principal did some searching to see what students at his school were posting on a popular social networking site. He was dismayed to see the amount of personal information students shared online, as well as some photographs of inappropriate behavior. This administrator responded in a positive manner by working with his guidance department to notify parents of his concerns about what students were posting online, and to send home tips for parents on Internet safety and cyber bullying. While it is impossible for administrators to monitor all of their students' online behavior, occasional checking of sites that are popular among students can help determine if there are problem areas that need to be addressed with school staff and parents. As mentioned previously, parents have the primary responsibility for monitoring their child's online behavior, but educators can assist parents by encouraging them to take an active role in providing appropriate guidelines for a safe Internet experience. Communicating effectively with parents when problems arise, and providing parent workshops and "tip sheets" on cyber bullying and Internet safety, will prevent many problems from entering the school community. A sample letter that can be used when administrators are concerned about students' use of social networking sites is included below (Figure 6.2).

Spend Class Time on the Topic of Cyber Bullying

As mentioned previously, most students in our focus groups felt that educators could do little to address cyber bullying; however, one high school female had a helpful suggestion for educators:

> "Maybe introduce kids to cyber bullying at a younger age, talk to classes about it and signs of it so they'll know if it's going on and not be afraid to tell [their] parents and stuff." – *high school female*

This student already recognized the importance of spending class time to discuss bullying and cyber bullying. The importance of holding regular class meetings/discussions to address traditional bullying was noted in Chapter 2. It is important to incorporate cyber bullying and proper online communication into these classroom discussions to make sure that students understand that bullying is not acceptable in cyber space either.

Topics for classroom discussions on cyber bullying. What issues should be covered during classroom meetings on cyber bullying? Initially, teachers likely will want to ensure that children understand: (a) what cyber bullying is, (b) what the school's policies and rules are with regard to cyber

Dear Parents:

Our students' safety as well as their education is a primary concern of the _____ High School Community. It has been brought to our attention that many students are logging on to social networking sites such as _____. These web hosts, when used safely, offer young people and adults an opportunity to communicate with one another. However, when used inappropriately, these sites can become a hurtful or dangerous place for all students.

It has come to our attention that some students are using these sites in offensive and disrespectful ways. These sites are primarily accessed outside of school on home computers since the county's firewall prevents its access at school. Students are coming to school sharing what they have read about other students on these sites or are bringing in printed instant messages, Web sites and other material from home, which creates rumors and impacts the school milieu and learning environment. We are finding that students are creating negative profiles for their classmates and/or posting negative messages about other students and adults. We consider such incidents a form of cyber bullying. Cyber bullying is when someone uses the Internet or other mobile devices to send mean or harmful messages to harass and/or demean others. **Please talk with your child about cyber bullying and the importance of never posting something mean or hurtful about another person online.**

In addition, students are sharing personal identifiers that jeopardize their safety or another student's safety. After visiting several of these sites, the following pieces of personal information were found posted by students:

- Photos
- Date of birth
- Student's real name
- IM screen name
- Screen names with identifying information

Figure 6.2 Sample letter

- Home phone and cell phone numbers
- Personally identifiable journal entries
- School name
- School location
- Classmates' personal information

When students list personal information along with pictures of themselves, they are at risk for attracting the attention of online predators that may use this information to search for potential victims. Online predators may pose as teenagers or young adults in order to establish relationships with young people. Their goal is often to set up a face-to-face meeting, and it is easy to determine a home address once a student posts his or her phone number or last name and city. In addition, by posting their IM screen name or e-mail address, students increase their chances of being solicited sexually online or being sent unwanted pornographic material.

Please take time to review your family's safety guidelines for using the Internet wisely. Some helpful Web sites for Internet safety contracts and discussions with your student are:

www.netsmartz.org
www.isafe.org
www.ikeepsafe.org (for younger students)

Remember, just as we have rules and guidelines in the real world, we need to provide guidance to our children in the online world.

Principal _____

Figure 6.2 *Continued*

bullying,(c) what mechanisms there are at the school to report cyber bullying, and (d) how best to respond to cyber bullying (such as when to ignore, block, or report it). If the use of social networking sites is popular among students, teachers should discuss the "appropriate use guidelines" from such sites. Many students believe they have a right to free speech that allows them to say anything online. The site guidelines and steps for reporting abuse would help dispel this myth. The role of the bystander to cyber bullying should be discussed as well, so that students understand that witnessing cyber bullying and doing nothing is a harmful choice. Helping students to develop empathy for classmates who are targeted by cyber bullying is important, as students who taunt or abuse a classmate online do not witness the student's emotional response as they would with face-to-face bullying. Teachers can develop writing assignments where students take the perspective of someone who is experiencing bullying or cyber bullying behavior and discuss their reactions to the bullying behavior. Being able to take someone else's perspective is a cornerstone of empathy development and can assist students in their role as positive bystanders working to develop a caring school climate.

Establish a climate that encourages bystanders to speak out against bullying behavior. Feeling anonymous in cyber space appears to encourage some young people to develop unhealthy social norms for online behavior. The impulsivity of youth combined with a belief that "anything goes" online is a recipe for disaster if there are no competing positive social norms. Counteracting these faulty social norms is a critical role for educators and parents to ensure a positive online environment.

One effective way to build more positive social norms is through activities that focus on positive roles that bystanders can play to stop bullying. As discussed in Chapter 2, young people may assume a variety of roles in instances of bullying. When a bullying incident occurs, the majority of students assume roles as bystanders (e.g., as disengaged onlookers or possible defenders). Although many students are offended by cyber bullying and other forms of bullying, they often are not sure how to respond when they witness it. With adequate role-playing and class discussions, these students can be encouraged to report cyber bullying behaviors when they observe them. Students can also learn ways to support a classmate who is being cyber bullied, through positive comments, letters, and instant or e-mail messages. Discussing the various steps that bystanders can take when cyber bullying occurs is a great class discussion topic. Possibilities include:

- Don't view the mean material.
- Don't gossip or spread rumors online or talk about it at school.

- Support the victim – post or send positive messages!
- If you know the person, invite him/her to spend time with you.
- Tell an adult at home and at school.
- Print the evidence to share with an adult.
- Discourage student who is cyber bullying if it is safe to do so, and make it clear that you think their behavior is wrong.

Teach Students Online "Netiquette," Safe Blogging, and How to Monitor Their Online Reputation

Online netiquette skills are becoming vital as technology is increasingly being incorporated into most career paths. Many schools encourage teachers to keep blogs where class and homework assignments are posted for students to review. Students are asked to post assignments online. Providing tips on appropriate posting and online etiquette as part of incorporating more technology in the classroom is critical. As part of class discussions, teachers can help students set up class blogs where they can be taught appropriate online behavior. The students can choose whether the blogs will be public (for anyone's viewing) or private (solely for the viewing of and commenting by members of the class). As a class and with the teacher's facilitation, students can respond to comments made on the blog by their classmates and how those comments made them feel. There are Web sites available to help individuals and groups, such as a class, create blogs that might be used for this purpose.

School counselors need to teach classroom guidance lessons on the importance of keeping a positive online reputation as part of their lessons on careers and college. Such lessons should help students recognize how their personal profile on a social networking site can have a positive or negative impact on their future. Demonstrating how easy it is to search such sites and access personal information (without embarrassing anyone) will ensure that students learn that their postings are public information and, as such, may come back to haunt them in the future. Guidance counselors should make sure that students are aware that individuals have lost jobs, faced criminal charges, and been removed from college athletic teams as a result of personal information and offensive statements they have posted on social networking sites.

Train and Utilize Student Mentors

i-SAFE.org has excellent free resources for educators, including a mentoring program where students work with classmates or younger students to teach lessons on Cyber Bullying, Cyber Predators, Cyber Security, and

Intellectual Property. The i-Mentor Network targets middle and high school students and provides students with simple instructions on how to plan and perform outreach activities and events. Students begin by viewing the i-Mentor training videos. After completing the certified mentor training video and its components, the students may plan various outreach activities for their school and community. Making use of such youth driven strategies will ensure that students promote positive peer pressure to reduce all forms of bullying.

Use Students as Experts

Many schools recognize the power of youth leadership in developing a climate that is inclusive and supportive of others. Young people regularly serve as peer helpers, peer mediators, and as school ambassadors where they develop skills that will serve them for a lifetime. Students also are able to serve as mentors to others by teaching skills and modeling healthy behavior. In many school districts, students have taught lessons on drug prevention, postponing sexual involvement, and media literacy, to name just a few. Making use of students' expertise in the area of Internet safety and cyber bullying can send a strong message to classmates and younger students. The peer group often has more legitimacy than the teacher in addressing social issues, so making use of student leaders to teach lessons on Internet safety and cyber bullying is a great prevention strategy. As mentioned previously, i-SAFE America's Youth Mentor Program provides materials and lessons that students can use to reach out to their classmates and younger students. Students are also a great source of information on how best to address the "hotspots" of bullying or cyber bullying that occur at an individual school. We have learned that the popularity of sites among students changes rapidly, and youth are often the first group to embrace a new technology. Thus, educators need regular input from young people on popular Internet sites and new technologies that have been embraced by their student population.

Community/School Partnerships

While we have provided a variety of steps that educators can take to prevent cyber bullying, youth organizations also have an important role to play in the prevention of cyber bullying (and all forms of bullying). Many students engage in afterschool programs and activities that make use of computers and technology, and social skill development is often a goal of the many youth organizations in the community. These organizations can assist educators and parents by reinforcing the message of appropriate use of technology, netiquette, and personal safety by developing and implementing online safety/netiquette guidelines, lessons, group activities, and peer-to-peer mentoring.

A Guide to Social Networking Sites for Educators

Although we have referred to social networking sites throughout this book, it is critical that educators take time to familiarize themselves with one of the biggest social phenomena to affect youth and young adults in America. According to the Pew Internet & American Family Life Project, over 55% of American teens between the ages of 12 and 17 use online social networking sites (Lenhart & Madden, 2007). Individual entries on social networking sites are similar to a yearbook profile, but with so many communication features they give young people a way to "hang out together" in cyberspace. Depending on the site, there are features similar to e-mail, bulletin boards to post messages to friends, and blogging features that allow people to post diary-like entries about their day. While adults still communicate online largely through e-mail, teens communicate primarily through instant messaging and through the tools on MySpace, Facebook, or other similar sites. At the time of writing, MySpace was by far the most popular; however, Facebook was growing in popularity among students and appeared to be the preferred choice among many private school students (Jenkins, 2006).

While Facebook has, until recently, been limited to certain professional, student, and alumni populations, anyone can set up a MySpace account for free. This means that some (mostly younger) adults are using MySpace, but the popularity among high school students is enormous. Adults who are unfamiliar with these sites and work with youth would be wise to visit them in order to better understand their use by teens. Young people use these sites as a way to explore and define who they are. Many are quite comfortable (and in fact enjoy) sharing their most private thoughts and feelings online. Of course, as youth share personal information without discrimination, they can be ripe for exploitation by predators or victimization by classmates.

Social networking sites are not without merit, however, and it important to accept the reality that such sites have become the teen hotspot in a "cyber neighborhood" similar to the teen hangouts many of us frequented as youth. As young people have less opportunity to hang out in the real world because of their heavily scheduled extracurricular activities or because of safety concerns, youth have carved out a way to still interact, explore their identity, and share the subtleties of youth culture. Such interactions have always occurred; the difference is that adults were available to provide some supervision when the local teen hangout was a pizza place or bowling alley. Socializing primarily online, away from the eyes of any responsible adult, can lead to the problems that we currently face, i.e., Internet predators, cyber bullying, and cyber threats. The best solution lies in finding ways to make such sites safer through a combination of site-based strategies (tips on safe use and how to report abuse), and through increased supervision and sensible guidelines for use communicated by parents, educators, and the community at large.

Obviously bullying has always taken place, but the cyber bullying that occurs on social networking sites has the possibility to be more disruptive to the school day in that a majority of the school population may either witness the incident and/or rapidly spread gossip and rumors to classmates regarding the attack. Having so many classmates aware of their humiliation, combined with the victimization occurring outside of the school day (typically a safer time of day for a bullied student), can lead to the bullied students feeling they have no safe place to go and nowhere to turn. Thus, educators must play a role in addressing students' use of social networking sites whether these sites are banned from the school district server or not. A recent e-mail poll of educators, administrators, and school board members represented at the National School Boards Association annual Technology+Learning Conference indicated that only 35% of the respondents said their districts had policies to address the use of social networking sites, with 50% indicating their districts had no policies and 15% indicating they were unsure if they had policies ("Social networking sites confound schools," 2007).

Regardless of the accessibility from school, the use of such sites at home will impact the learning environment when they are used to bully and harass classmates. In addition, many students are accessing these sites at school through the use of personal digital assistants (PDAs) or cellular phones with Internet capabilities. Communicating with students about the proper use of social networking sites, how to report problems, and how to assist a victimized classmate are new lessons that proactive educators will begin addressing in the classroom.

What Can School Personnel Do to Intervene Effectively in Cyber Bullying Incidents?

Although prevention efforts will often decrease the likelihood that students will be involved in cyber bullying incidents, school personnel will, undoubtedly, be faced with periodic instances of cyber bullying. In this section, we will discuss how educators can best respond when a cyber bullying incident comes to their attention.

Notify Parents of All Involved Children (When Known)

Based on the content and severity of the messages, the parent of the student who has been victimized may wish to initiate contact with the parent of the student engaging in the cyber bullying behavior. Chapter 5 contains tips for parents on contacting other parents. If, however, the cyber bullying appears to be more serious in nature or disruptive to the school environment because it has occurred repeatedly or has been viewed by many students (such as a derogatory Web site), the parents of the targeted student may need the assistance of the school counselor or an administrator at their child's school. In some situations, it will be important for the school administration to notify the parents of the parties involved. In order to do this effectively, it is important for educators to have evidence of the cyber bullying. This evidence can be obtained from the parents of targeted students, or through actual viewing of a Web site. Web sites can be saved by hitting the print screen button on a computer and saving it as a file. If a student or adult recognizes the phone number, the sender of a text message can be identified and should be documented with the date and time, to indicate if the messages are being sent during the school day. (The phone company can trace a phone number if a student is not sure who is targeting him or her.) If the evidence confirms that those responsible are all in attendance at the same school, and it has created a disruption in the school environment, it makes sense for the administration to notify the parents of the parties involved.

Many issues come into play when a cyber bullying incident interrupts a school day. The cyber bullying may be taking place at school, which provides for a much clearer response by the administration. Most school districts now have policies around the misuse of school technology that can be followed when cyber bullying occurs on campus. Far more common, however, is a cyber bullying incident that occurs outside of the school day but causes some disruption in the learning environment because the students involved attend school together. In such situations, the educator may be in the role of providing suggestions, support, and resources to the family of the targeted student as well as the family of the student engaged in cyber bullying behavior.

Provide Suggestions on Various Response Options

If the cyber bullying behavior is a minor incident (calling someone a mean name) between two students that occurred on only one or two occasions, typically the best course of action is for the targeted student to ignore the behavior. A child who cyber bullies wants to see a reaction from the targeted student, and, if the comments are ignored, he or she may stop. Many technologies allow users to block other specific users. Instant messages and cellular phones have blocking features, e-mails have filters, and social networking sites allow users to block individuals from commenting or posting on their site. These steps will often be sufficient to address minor incidents of cyber bullying. Educators may be able to assist students and parents by providing training on how to use the blocking and warning functions of various technologies. It is still important to save the evidence in case the cyber bullying continues despite ignoring or blocking the user. In the following sections we will discuss steps to take if the cyber bullying is persistent or more severe.

Provide Resources/Tips on the Removal of Offensive Material

Most social networking sites have user agreements that prohibit cyber bullying, cyber threats, impersonation, and other dangerous behaviors. Educators can assist students and parents by locating the various user policies on such social networking sites as MySpace that explain how to report abuse or threats. MySpace has a frequently asked questions (FAQ) section that provides links to safety tips, as well as links to how to report identity theft, underage use, cyber bullying, and copyright violations. Students, parents, and educators can use the site procedures to report behavior that violates these user agreements.

The school can be a valuable resource to the parents by letting them know the various steps they can take to have the material removed. Sites such as MySpace, Xanga, and Facebook will routinely shut down a site if it is in violation of their use policies because it includes threats and harassment of others. Educators can also inform students that the site they have spent hours developing will no longer be accessible if they violate such guidelines.

Contact the Police

Although laws vary based on jurisdiction, serious allegations such as threats of physical harm, sexual harassment, posting nude or compromising photographs, extortion or stalking behavior should be reported to the police immediately, and the police will conduct their own investigation (Willard, 2005b). If a police report is being made, school administrators should consult with law enforcement to determine the appropriateness of the school contacting the parents of the parties involved. Law enforcement may not want the parents of the alleged perpetrator to be contacted in case evidence of the illegal behavior may be destroyed.

Share Concerns with the School Community

In many instances, simply providing referral resources and sending home a tip sheet on responding to cyber bullying will be an effective intervention for the family of the victim who has been targeted off campus. It is also worthwhile to send out a communication to all parents at a school or the parents of a particular grade level explaining that cyber bullying behavior has occurred among students at the school and inviting parents to partner with the school in monitoring students' use of technology.

Warn Parents of Children Who Have Been Threatened

One of the individual interviews conducted in preparation for this book involved a parent who was not notified by the school when her child was cyber bullied online. Even though school administrators were contacted by a parent regarding negative postings on a Web site that were threatening in nature, the administration did not notify the parents of the other targeted students, and they remained unaware that their child had been threatened. School personnel should always warn the parents of a child who has been threatened online if they have been made aware of the threats. The following comments from our interview with this parent illustrate the frustration she felt when learning that the school failed to notify her of the cyber bullying. According to the mother, a student at her daughter's school posted a picture of the school on a social networking site with the word "hell" written on it and the student threatened to go out with a bang. She reportedly included a list of female classmates that she did not like.

> *Interviewer:* What was your reaction when you learned of the cyber bullying targeting your daughter?
> *Parent:* Extreme anger that I wasn't notified by the school, because the parent who brought it to my attention had been there to see the principal earlier in the day, to bring it to her attention and [the principal's] initial reaction was that she couldn't believe she was being bothered by this "yet again" because there had been another incident regarding this particular Web site a few months prior. My second reaction was fear, that what did this mean for my daughter, having my daughter on this list? What do we do now, what are our rights as a parent, where do we turn – because we had never dealt with this before?

This parent filed a police report on her own, not knowing what else to do. It would have been so much better if the school had reacted with concern, and supported the parents in finding the appropriate resources to address the situation. The parents were unable to meet with the principal the next day, but they did meet with an assistant administrator, who was unaware of the details of the incident. They also took their concerns to the superintendent's office.

> *Interviewer:* Did the assistant principal have any actions she could recommend?
>
> *Parent:* Not initially. She brought in the school resource officer, who happened to be at the school at the time. He shed some light on it and said it had happened before, but since it didn't happen on school property using school equipment there was nothing they could do. [The assistant principal] indicated she would contact the district office, but she was just so blind sided [since the principal had given her few details] by it she didn't really know what to do. We didn't feel like there were going to be any actions or any action quick enough for the kids on the list, so I took it upon myself to take it to the superintendent's office. The superintendent for our area took it very seriously and got the legal team involved. It was only then that other parents from the school were notified.
>
> *Interviewer:* Were there statements [on the Web site] that made you concerned for the students' safety?
>
> *Parent:* Yes. She put a picture of the middle school on the Web site with the word "Hell!" written in red and said she was tired of these girls thinking they were all that, she would take care of it, she would go out with a bang . . . The police thought it was threatening enough to pursue an investigation.

Put yourself in the place of this mother for a moment. It is extremely distressing for a parent to view threatening messages targeting their son or daughter. In fact, some of our interviews indicated that the parents were more distraught over the cyber bullying and threats than the child who was being targeted. In any case, parents will likely be very concerned about threats and harassment toward their child, and they need to know that the school will assist and support them as they attempt to deal with the situation, even if the messages are posted at a home computer outside of the school day. When this parent felt that the school was not responsive, she went a step further to the school district office. Fortunately, the district superintendent for her area was concerned and demonstrated a commitment to addressing the incident and notified the other parties involved. A great deal of fear, frustration, and anger on the part of the parents could have been alleviated if the principal at the school had been more proactive initially, by notifying the parents of the targeted students, and contacting law enforcement about the threatening statements.

Parents of students who engage in cyber bullying behavior also need to be informed by the school administration of their child's actions as soon as possible. While it is true that some parents may view cyber bullying as insignificant or normal teenage behavior, many parents will be distressed to learn that their son or daughter has engaged in such negative behavior and will appreciate being notified. Such notification allows them to take steps to monitor their child's online behavior more closely. The parents of students who engage in cyber bullying may need resources on how to talk with their child about appropriate online use, and suggestions of how to monitor their child's online presence. Schools can refer them to such Web sites as www.stopbullyingnow.hrsa.gov, www.cyberbully.org, www.netsmartz.org, www.ikeepsafe.org, www.wiredsafety.org, and our own Web site, www.cyberbullyhelp.com, to learn more about monitoring their child.

On occasion, the statements might be severe enough to warrant a referral to a therapist for a consultation. Students who post statements that express a desire to hurt themselves or others (cyber threats) should be referred for a psychological assessment to determine if they are suicidal or homicidal. The school counselor may work with the administration to make such referrals. This will be discussed further in our section on appropriate referrals to mental health resources.

School Discipline for Cyber Bullying – A Delicate Issue

Parents of the victim of cyber bullying often want to know if there will be consequences for the students who bullied their child. If a student has violated the school's acceptable use of technology policy by using school-based technology to cyber bully another student, then the school should provide consequences for the cyber bullying behavior and advise the parents of the targeted student that the policy is being followed. If the student used their own technology (such as a cellular phone) but sent the messages while at school, his or her behavior may also warrant school-imposed consequences. This is why it is important to have evidence of the date and time that messages were sent. Many school districts ban the use of cellular phones during the school day, but then look the other way when students text message during the day. A policy that is regularly ignored by administration is ripe for abuse by students. Setting a clear policy on the possession and use of mobile phones accompanied by consequences for violators is critical if schools wish to limit their disruption of the learning environment.

It becomes especially challenging for the school, however, when the cyber bullying behavior occurs outside of the school day on home computers or cellular phones. While many administrators believe that they should be able to discipline students for cyber bullying behaviors that disrupt the school day, the standard for doing so is high. The cyber bullying must include severe or substantial threat of disruption to the learning environment, and "point of view" speech is usually protected under the first amendment (Willard, 2005b). Even if a student posts or electronically communicates outrageous comments about a classmate or teacher, if it occurs on a home computer it may be protected speech. Public schools may be legally challenged if they impose consequences on students' right to free speech. Some public schools that have suspended students for derogatory comments that they have posted from their home computer have reportedly been sued, according to Parry Aftab. "On a regular basis, schools are sued when they take disciplinary action for flaming a teacher or cyber bullying a kid" (Kennedy, 2006).

Private schools have more leeway to discipline for such infractions because they are not a government entity. Public schools *may* be able to discipline for cyber bullying if they have required students to sign a student behavior code that lists cyber bullying behaviors as inappropriate even if they occur outside of school. The best course of action for administrators is to consult with an attorney before disciplining students for cyber bullying behavior that has taken place outside of the school day, but still assist the family of the targeted student by providing support and referrals where appropriate. See Chapter 7 for a more detailed analysis of legal issues related to cyber bullying.

When counselors or administrators learn that one of their students has been a target of cyber bullying, they should look for evidence of traditional bullying that has occurred at school alongside of the cyber bullying behaviors. Schools that have implemented policies against bullying can impose consequences for bullying behavior occurring at school that has accompanied the cyber bullying behavior outside of school. If this is the case, schools should follow their district policy and guidelines for responding to the traditional bullying, but take sufficient time to determine the full extent of the bullying, both cyber bullying and traditional bullying. The perpetrator(s) and victim(s) should be interviewed individually, with a strong message against further retaliation on either side.

If the Target is a Faculty Member

Students have also been known to target faculty members through Web sites. A male high school student in one of our focus groups shared the following comments:

"There is a teacher we didn't like . . . so we kind of made fun of that teacher . . . we made a facebook blog about them."

The steps that we discussed previously in terms of response options and removal of offensive material are still relevant when a student or students target a faculty member; however, the school administration may need to take time to carefully assess the motivation of the students. There are a variety of reasons why students may target a particular teacher. However, there is always a possibility that the student or students are retaliating to perceived bullying behavior on the part of the adult faculty member (Willard, 2006). If such motivation appears plausible, the administration may need to take steps to address the situation

Threat Assessment

A couple of years ago, a mother called the student assistance office of one of the authors to seek guidance about some statements her daughter had posted on her blog, which was on a social networking site. On this blog, her daughter asked others to comment on whether or not she should kill herself. The author recommended that the daughter see a therapist immediately and explained the process by which she could arrange for an assessment of her daughter. "Has anyone responded to what she wrote?" the author asked her mother. "No," her mother responded with anguish in her voice. The daughter was seen for an assessment and hospitalized the same day for being actively suicidal. The author realized at that time that school personnel were entering into a new era where adults would have avenues for much deeper glimpses into young people's private psyches – whether they liked it or not.

Many school districts utilize a suicide/homicide protocol to guide educators on intervening with a student who has made statements regarding hurting himself or others. It is recommended that school districts engage in threat analysis for any reports of cyber bullying that allude to suicide or homicide (Willard, 2006). The student assistance office mentioned previously has a staff member at a central office "on call" daily to assist the counselors in determining whether to send a student for an assessment for risky behavior. Several years ago, the on-call counselors began to notice that more and more students were coming to their attention as a result of threats that students had sent by e-mail, instant message, or online posting to a social networking site. It is recommended that educators respond to online threats just as they would with a spoken or written threat by including online threats in their threat assessment procedures and taking the appropriate disciplinary, referral, or police report action as indicated.

Referrals to Mental Health Resources

The student who has engaged in cyber bullying acts should be carefully assessed to determine what dynamics are occurring in his or her home and school life that may have influenced his or her actions. Willard (2006) suggests that counselors and administrators look at the cyber bullying content as well as the student's overall relationships to determine if they are dealing with "put down" material generated by a power oriented bully/ wannabee, or at "get back" material generated by a frustrated victim. Preliminary data suggest that a fair percentage of students who engage in cyber bullying may be bully/victims or passive victims who are retaliating online (Kowalski & Limber, 2006). If the student has been bullied at school and is reacting to such actions by making cyber threats or cyber bullying others, he or she needs help and support in dealing with the bullying. The administrator, school counselor, parent, and child should work together to develop a safety plan or other strategies for the student that reduce the instances of the child being bullied at school. The student's level of social skills should also be assessed and resources or referrals offered to a student who is limited in these skills. Often the school counselor is the appropriate person to meet with the student and his or her parents to make recommendations of outside assistance. The cyber bullying incident may, in fact, be an opportunity to provide the student with much needed resources and referrals to deal with social and behavioral issues that are affecting the student's performance at school. It is imperative, however, that students who are bullied at school are given assistance and support to eliminate the school bullying, rather than implying they are to blame for the bullying.

Informal Resolution/Accountability Circles

Mediation is typically discouraged in dealing with traditional bullying behaviors. The imbalance of power is such that calling together a victim and a perpetrator, and asking them to work together to solve the conflict can seem like a revictimization to the targeted student. A helpful analogy is to think about bringing a child abuser and his/her victim together and telling them both, "We are going to resolve this abuse through mediation." The child would not be powerful enough or safe enough in this environment when the abuser was facing him or her, and might go along with whatever the abuser (or person engaging in bullying) said. That is why the Olweus Bullying Prevention Program (and indeed most bullying prevention programs, as well as the HRSA's National Bullying Prevention Campaign) strongly recommends that children who bully and children who are bullied be interviewed individually and a safety plan be developed for students who are being bullied at school that includes increased supervision by adults, consequences for the bully, and clear avenues for the victim to ask for help and report further victimization (Olweus et al., 2007). Scheduling changes may be necessary (preferably moving the child who bullies) to ensure that the targeted child is not further victimized.

Because schools are frequently limited in the consequences they can give in cases of cyber bullying, we are interested in positive alternatives to civil lawsuits or criminal prosecution that schools can recommend to parents. In some cases of bullying, there may be benefit in borrowing from a model of intervention developed by the legal system that is called "restorative justice," which has been defined as:

> . . . a theory of criminal justice that focuses on crime as an act against another individual or community rather than the state. The victim plays a major role in the process and receives some type of restitution from the offender. Restorative justice takes many different forms, but all systems have some aspects in common. Victims have an opportunity to express the full impact of the crime upon their lives, to receive answers to any lingering questions about the incident, and to participate in holding the offender accountable for his or her actions. Offenders can tell their story of why the crime occurred and how it has affected their lives. They are given an opportunity to make things right with the victim to the degree possible through some form of compensation. (word IQ, 17 July, 2006)

This type of intervention involves bringing victims and *remorseful* perpetrators together *willingly*, with a scripted process where the victims are able to share the impact of the perpetrators' actions on their lives, and the perpetrators have an opportunity to apologize for their actions and repair the harm done. Much training is required to properly administer restorative justice programs in the legal system, and much preparation background work is necessary. Although a full restorative justice program may be too time consuming for most school administrators, one of the authors has successfully used what we call an "accountability circle" in the school setting after attending a training program on restorative justice. The accountability circle blends some of the principles of restorative justice with those of mediation. We believe that school counselors and administrators (with training) can use these principles to intervene in more serious cases of cyber bullying (as well as other school incidents) when the parents of the parties involved are willing, when the targeted student is willing and emotionally prepared, and when the student who engaged in the cyber bullying behavior (and his or her parents) have demonstrated some remorse.

Burssens and Vettenburg (2006) write about a similar form of restorative justice called "restorative group conferencing" that has been used successfully in a number of countries. They indicate that it should be reserved for more serious offenses at school owing to the time involved, and their research investigated the use of restorative school conferencing with incidents of serious theft, extortion, physical intimidation of a teacher, bullying among students, and a serious fight where students were injured. Their research suggested that the restorative group conferences were judged as very positive and that the process "eased or even eliminated tensions within a class or school" (p. 12). Before pursuing such strategies, school administration needs to understand that the focus of the accountability circle is on repairing the harm done, rather than on punitive consequences. Schools interested in learning more about restorative justice practices may wish to visit: www.restorativejustice.org. Without this type of intervention, schools may be left giving parents the only options of pressing criminal charges or civil lawsuits as a response to the cyber bullying that occurs off school grounds.

Steps in setting up accountability circles. Typically the school counselor or other student assistance professional is the appropriate person to arrange for an accountability circle for the parties involved. The school counselor acts as the facilitator in such a scenario. He or she should contact the parents of the victim as well as the perpetrator to make sure that they seem willing and capable of making the meeting a constructive experience. The victim should always have the right to refuse attendance at the meeting or to say that the meeting should not take place. It is possible to do an accountability circle with the victim's parents rather than the victim herself, as was done in the McClain case described in Chapter 5. While Mrs McClain's daughter, Brandy, did not wish to attend the meeting, she was agreeable to her parents attending. Her parents felt strongly that they wanted to meet with the perpetrator and her parents. All parties should be made aware that the meeting is voluntary and can end at any time if the agreed upon guidelines are not followed by the parties involved. The facilitator should explain to the victim (if participating) and his or her parents that they will have an opportunity to explain how the incident impacted them individually and as a family, and what, if any, actions they would like to see occur to resolve the situation. The parents of the offender will also have an opportunity to share how the incident impacted them and to express remorse for their child's actions. The perpetrator will have the opportunity to share their remorse and any circumstances surrounding their behavior. After the facilitator summarizes the experiences of the parties involved, they agree on the steps necessary to repair the harm. The restitution steps are written down and signed by all the parties in attendance with targeted dates identified and responsibility for monitoring identified. A sample facilitator's script for use with an accountability circle is included in Box 6.1.

A successful accountability circle can provide a genuine learning experience for all of the parties involved and works to heal the relationships that

Box 6.1	Accountability script

Questions for student offender:

- What happened?
- What were you thinking at the time?
- What have you thought about since the incident?
- Who do you think has been affected by your actions?
- How have they been affected?

Questions for the student who was harmed:
(*These questions can also be asked of the parents of the parties involved.*)

- What was your reaction when you first saw the Web site/messages/etc.?
- How do you feel about what happened?
- What has been the hardest thing for you?
- How did your family and friends react when they heard about the incident?

Summarize and follow up with:

- What are the main issues?
- What do you want as a result of this meeting?

Resolution/signed agreement to include:

- Restitution and/or counseling
- Safety issues
- Retaliation issues
- Follow-up meetings if needed

have been harmed as a result of the incident. The student who has been cyber bullied (and his or her parents) has the opportunity to fully describe his or her experience and make an assertive request for a remedy to the situation. The student who has engaged in cyber bullying behavior has the opportunity to become more empathetic, gain a new perspective on his or her behavior, and make amends for such behavior. The result is that the participants gain new competencies and the school environment becomes safer as students take responsibility for their actions.

Summary

As bullying over the Internet becomes more commonplace, educators must become equally prepared to address this new form of bullying. To avoid dealing with such instances is to ignore a significant form of social interaction among our students. Educators have always been in the business of instructing children on appropriate behavior, and the appropriate use of technology should not be an exception. Because we live in an information society where students must have advanced skills in technology to compete, and where an increasing amount of socializing will take place using the tools of technology, educators must familiarize themselves with strategies for the prevention and intervention of cyber bullying behavior in order to ensure that civility is consistently taught in all forms of social interaction, be they face-to-face or online.

7

Laws and Policies

〜

As we noted earlier, attention to bullying among students exploded in the American media in the wake of the tragic shootings at Columbine High School. After 1999, there also was a flurry of state legislation related to bullying, as 30 states passed laws addressing bullying within a span of less than eight years (Alley & Limber, in press). At the same time, several widely publicized lawsuits have raised concerns among many educators about their legal options and responsibilities to prevent and address bullying in their schools.

With the advent of cyber technologies, there has been a whirlwind of recent media attention to cyber bullying and harassment, and a resulting uncertainty by many educators about how to meet ethical and legal duties to protect students from cyber bullying without infringing on their rights under the U.S. Constitution. In this chapter, we will discuss emerging state laws addressing bullying in general, and cyber bullying in particular. We also will summarize current case law, with an eye to answering three primary questions: (1) When may school personnel be held liable (under federal or state laws) for failing to address cyber bullying? (2) Under what circumstances can school personnel address cyber bullying without fear of violating students' First Amendment rights to freedom of speech and expression? (3) Under what circumstances can school personnel monitor or search student Internet records without fear of violating students' constitutional protections against illegal searches and seizures? Finally, we will address the development of school policies on cyber bullying, in light of emerging law.

Before addressing these issues, several words of caution are in order. First, this chapter is limited in its legal analysis to the American public school context. Unfortunately, a review of international laws and policies was beyond the scope of this book. Second, although this chapter describes current state laws relating to cyber bullying and describes the likely application of existing case law to instances of cyber bullying within American public schools, it is not intended to substitute in any way for the advice of local counsel, who are in a position to assess local laws and policies and the rapidly changing legal landscape. We strongly advise school administrators to consult with their district's attorney on these issues.

State Laws and Their Relevance to Cyber Bullying

One important first step in considering legal obligations to address cyber bullying is for school personnel to become familiar with relevant state laws addressing bullying. At the time of writing, 30 states had laws related to bullying and at least 10 others were considering legislation (Alley & Limber, in press). These statutes vary quite a bit in their definitions of bullying and in their specific requirements, but all either require or encourage state or local officials to establish policies against bullying among students in public schools.

At the time of writing, only five state laws (Arkansas, Idaho, Iowa, South Carolina, and Washington) explicitly addressed bullying through electronic communications. Several other states have considered such bills.

Arkansas law (Act 115, 2007) includes electronic acts in its definition of bullying (see Table 7.1). It defines "electronic act" as "a communication or image transmitted by means of an electronic device, including without limitation a telephone, wireless phone or other wireless communications device, computer, or pager." The legislation requires school boards to develop policies to prohibit bullying in a variety of locations on school grounds (including on school equipment), and at school-sponsored or school-sanctioned events, but it also prohibits bullying:

> ... by an electronic act that results in the substantial disruption of the orderly operation of the school or educational environment ... whether or not the electronic act originated on school property or with school equipment, if the electronic act is directed specifically at students or school personnel and maliciously intended for the purpose of disrupting school, and has a high likelihood of succeeding in that purpose.

Idaho law (Idaho Code, 2006) defines bullying as:

> any intentional gesture, or any intentional written, verbal or physical act or threat by a student that: (a) A reasonable person under the circumstances

Table 7.1
State laws on cyber bullying (current as of February 6, 2007)

State laws explicitly addressing cyber bullying

Arkansas   Arkansas law (Act 115, 2007) defines bullying as ". . . the intentional harassment, intimidation, humiliation, ridicule, defamation, or threat or incitement of violence by a student against another student or public school employee by a written, verbal, electronic, or physical act that causes or creates a clear and present danger of: (i) Physical harm to a public school employee or student or damage to the public school employee's or student's property; (ii) Substantial interference with a student's education or with a public school employee's role in education; (iii) A hostile educational environment for one (1) or more students or public school employees due to the severity, persistence, or pervasiveness of the act; or (iv) Substantial disruption of the orderly operation of the school or educational environment." The act further defines "electronic act" as "a communication or image transmitted by means of an electronic device, including without limitation a telephone, wireless phone or other wireless communications device, computer, or pager." The legislation requires school boards to develop policies to prohibit bullying in a variety of locations on school grounds (including on school equipment) or school-sponsored or school-sanctioned events, but it also prohibits bullying: "by an electronic act that results in the substantial disruption of the orderly operation of the school or educational environment . . . whether or not the electronic act originated on school property or with school equipment, if the electronic act is directed specifically at students or school personnel and maliciously intended for the purpose of disrupting school, and has a high likelihood of succeeding in that purpose."

Idaho   Idaho Code § 18-917A (2006; part of the state's penal code) defines bullying as "any intentional gesture, or any intentional written, verbal or physical act or threat by a student that: (a) A reasonable person under the circumstances should know will have the effect of:

Table 7.1

Continued

	(i) Harming a student; or (ii) Damaging a student's property; or (iii) Placing a student in reasonable fear of harm to his or her person; or (iv) Placing a student in reasonable fear of damage to his or her property; or (b) Is sufficiently severe, persistent or pervasive that it creates an intimidating, threatening or abusive educational environment for a student." The law further states: "An act of harassment, intimidation or bullying may also be committed through the use of a land line, car phone or wireless telephone or through the use of data or computer software that is accessed through a computer, computer system, or computer network."
Iowa	SF 61 (2007) defines harassment and bullying as "any electronic, written, verbal, or physical act or conduct toward a student which is based on any actual or perceived trait or characteristic of the student and which creates an objectively hostile school environment that meets one or more of the following conditions: "(1) Places the student in reasonable fear of harm to the student's person or property. (2) Has a substantially detrimental effect on the student's physical or mental health. (3) Has the effect of substantially interfering with a student's academic performance. (4) Has the effect of substantially interfering with the student's ability to participate in or benefit from the services, activities, or privileges provided by as school."
South Carolina	S.C. Code Ann. § 59-63-120 (2006) defines harassment, intimidation, or bullying as "a gesture, an electronic communication, or a written, verbal, physical, or sexual act that is reasonably perceived to have the effect of: (a) harming a student physically or emotionally or damaging a student's property, or placing a student in reasonable fear of personal harm or property damage; or (b) insulting or demeaning a student or group of students causing substantial disruption in, or substantial interference with, the orderly operation of the school."
Washington	SB 5288 (2007) requires school districts to adopt policies prohibiting "harassment, intimidation, or bullying of any student." The statute defines harassment, intimidation, or

Table 7.1

Continued

bullying as "any intentional electronic, written, verbal, or physical act, including but not limited to one shown to be motivated by any characteristic in RCW 9A.36.080(3), or other distinguishing characteristics, when the intentional electronic written, verbal, or physical act: (a) Physically harms a student or damages the student's property; or (b) Has the effect of substantially interfering with a student's education; or (c) Is so severe, persistent, or pervasive that it creates an intimidating or threatening educational environment; or (d) Has the effect of substantially disrupting the orderly operation of the school." The legislation requires the Washington state school directors association to develop a model policy "prohibiting acts of harassment, intimidation or bullying that are conducted via electronic means by a student while on school grounds and during the school day."

Other statutory definitions of bullying

Alaska	Alaska Stat. § 14.33.250 (2007) defines harassment, intimidation, or bullying as "an intentional written, oral, or physical act, when the act is undertaken with the intent of threatening, intimidating, harassing, or frightening the student, and (A) physically harms the student or damages the student's property; (B) has the effect of substantially interfering with the student's education; (C) is so severe, persistent, or pervasive that it creates an intimidating or threatening educational environment; or (D) has the effect of substantially disrupting the orderly operation of the school."
Colorado	C.R.S. 22-32-109.1 (2006) defines bullying as "any written or verbal expression, or physical act or gesture, or a pattern thereof, that is intended to cause distress upon one or more students in the school, on school grounds, in school vehicles, at a designated school bus stop, or at school activities or sanctioned events."
Connecticut	Conn. Gen. Stat. § 10-222d (2006) defines bullying as "any overt acts by a student or a group of students directed against another student with the intent to ridicule, humiliate or intimidate the other student while

Table 7.1

Continued

	on school grounds or at a school-sponsored activity which acts are repeated against the same student over time."
Georgia	O.C.G.A. § 20-2-751.4 (2006) defines bullying as "[a]ny willful attempt or threat to inflict injury on another person, when accompanied by an apparent present ability to do so; or . . . [a]ny intentional display of force such as would give the victim reason to fear or expect immediate bodily harm."
Indiana	Ind. Code Ann. § 20-33-8-0.2 (2006) defines bullying as "overt, repeated acts or gestures, including: (1) verbal or written communications transmitted; (2) physical acts committed; or (3) any other behaviors committed; by a student or group of students against another student with the intent to harass, ridicule, humiliate, intimidate, or harm the other student."
Louisiana	La. R.S. 17:416.13 (2006) defines harassment, intimidation, and bullying as "any intentional gesture or written, verbal, or physical act that: (a) A reasonable person under the circumstances should know will have the effect of harming a student or damaging his property or placing a student in reasonable fear of harm to his life or person or damage to his property; and (b) Is so severe, persistent, or pervasive that it creates an intimidating, threatening, or abusive educational environment for a student."
Maryland	Md. Education Code Ann. § 7-424 (2006) requires county boards to report incidents of "harassment or intimidation" which it defines as "conduct, including verbal conduct, that: (1) Creates a hostile educational environment by substantially interfering with a student's educational benefits, opportunities, or performance, or with a student's physical or psychological well-being and is: (i) Motivated by an actual or a perceived personal characteristic such as race, national origin, marital status, sex, sexual orientation, gender identity, religion, or disability; or (ii) Threatening or seriously intimidating; and (2) Occurs on school property, at a school activity or event, or on a school bus."

Table 7.1

Continued

Missouri	§ 160.775 R.S.Mo. (2007) requires school districts to adopt antibullying policies and defines bullying as "intimidation or harassment that causes a reasonable student to fear for his or her physical safety or property." The statute goes on to state that" [b]ullying may consist of physical actions, including gestures, or oral or written communication, and any threat of retaliation for reporting of such acts."
Nevada	Nev. Rev. Stat. Ann. § 388.135 (2006) prohibits harassment or intimidation "on the premises of any public school, at an activity sponsored by a public school or on any school bus." The statute defines harassment as "a willful act or course of conduct that is not otherwise authorized by law and is: 1. Highly offensive to a reasonable person; and 2. Intended to cause and actually causes another person to suffer serious emotional distress."
New Jersey	N.J. Stat. § 18A:37-14 (2007) defines harassment, intimidation, or bullying as "any gesture or written, verbal or physical act that is reasonably perceived as being motivated either by any actual or perceived characteristic, such as race, color, religion, ancestry, national origin, gender, sexual orientation, gender identity and expression, or a mental, physical or sensory handicap, or by any other distinguishing characteristic, that takes place on school property, at any school-sponsored function or on a school bus and that: (a) a reasonable person should know, under the circumstances, will have the effect of harming a student or damaging the student's property, or placing a student in reasonable fear of harm to his person or damage to his property; or (b) has the effect of insulting or demeaning any student or group of students in such a way as to cause substantial disruption in, or substantial interference with, the orderly operation of the school."
Ohio	ORC Ann. 3313.666 (2006) requires school districts to establish policies "prohibiting harassment, intimidation, or bullying of any student on school property or at school-

Table 7.1

Continued

	sponsored events." The statute defines harassment, intimidation, or bullying as "any intentional written, verbal, or physical act that a student has exhibited toward another particular student more than once and the behavior both: (1) Causes mental or physical harm to the other student; and (2) Is sufficiently severe, persistent, or pervasive that it creates an intimidating, threatening, or abusive educational environment for the other student."
Oklahoma	70 Okl. St. § 24-100.3 (2006) defines harassment, intimidation, and bullying as any gesture, written or verbal expression, or physical act that a reasonable person should know will harm another student, damage another student's property, place another student in reasonable fear of harm to the student's person or damage to the student's property, or insult or demean any student or group of students in such a way as to disrupt or interfere with the school's educational mission or the education of any student." The statute goes on to state that "'[h]arassment, intimidation, and bullying' include, but are not limited to, a gesture or written, verbal, or physical act."
Oregon	ORS § 339.351 (2006) defines harassment, intimidation, or bullying as "any act that substantially interferes with a student's educational benefits, opportunities or performance, that takes place on or immediately adjacent to school grounds, at any school-sponsored activity, on school-provided transportation or at any official school bus stop, and that has the effect of: (1) Physically harming a student or damaging a student's property; (2) Knowingly placing a student in reasonable fear of physical harm to the student or damage to the student's property; or (3) Creating a hostile educational environment."
Rhode Island	R.I. Gen. Laws § 16-21-26 (2007) requires school districts to "adopt a policy prohibiting harassment, intimidation, or bullying at school." The statute defines harassment, intimidation, or bullying as "an intentional written, verbal or physical act or threat of a physical act that, under the

Table 7.1

Continued

	totality of circumstances: (i) A reasonable person should know will have the effect of: physically harming a student, damaging a student's property, placing a student in reasonable fear of harm to his or her person, or placing a student in reasonable fear of damage to his or her property; or (ii) Is sufficiently severe, persistent or pervasive that it creates an intimidating, threatening or abusive educational environment for a student."
Tennessee	Tenn. Code Ann. § 49 6 1015 (2006) defines harassment, intimidation or bullying as "any act that substantially interferes with a student's educational benefits, opportunities or performance, that takes place on school grounds, at any school-sponsored activity, on school-provided transportation, or at any official school bus stop, and that has the effect of: (1) Physically harming a student or damaging a student's property; (2) Knowingly placing a student in reasonable fear of physical harm to the student or damage to the student's property; or (3) Creating a hostile educational environment."
Texas	Tex. Educ. Code § 25.0341 (2006) defines bullying as "engaging in written or verbal expression or physical conduct that a school district board of trustees or the board's designee determines: (1) will have the effect of physically harming a student, damaging a student's property, or placing a student in reasonable fear of harm to the student's person or of damage to the student's property; or (2) is sufficiently severe, persistent, or pervasive enough that the action or threat creates an intimidating, threatening, or abusive educational environment for a student."
Vermont	16 V.S.A. § 11 (2006) defines bullying as "any overt act or combination of acts directed against a student by another student or group of students and which: (A) is repeated over time; (B) is intended to ridicule, humiliate, or intimidate the student; and (C) occurs during the school day on school property, on a school bus, or at a school-sponsored activity, or before or after the school day on a school bus or at a school-sponsored activity."

Table 7.1
Continued

West Virginia	W. Va. Code § 18-2C-2 (2006) defines harassment, intimidation, or bullying as "any intentional gesture, or any intentional written, verbal or physical act or threat that: (a) A reasonable person under the circumstances should know will have the effect of: (1) Harming a student; (2) Damaging a student's property; (3) Placing a student in reasonable fear of harm to his or her person; or (4) Placing a student in reasonable fear of damage to his or her property; or (b) Is sufficiently severe, persistent or pervasive that it creates an intimidating, threatening or abusive educational environment for a student."

> should know will have the effect of: (i) Harming a student; or (ii) Damaging a student's property; or (iii) Placing a student in reasonable fear of harm to his or her person; or (iv) Placing a student in reasonable fear of damage to his or her property; or (b) Is sufficiently severe, persistent or pervasive that it creates an intimidating, threatening or abusive educational environment for a student.

It further notes that:

> An act of harassment, intimidation or bullying may also be committed through the use of a land line, car phone or wireless telephone or through the use of data or computer software that is accessed through a computer, computer system, or computer network.

Idaho legislators did not specify that such acts must occur on school equipment or on school grounds.

The three remaining state laws addressing cyber bullying are more limiting in focusing on cyber bullying that takes place on school grounds or at school-sponsored events. Washington law (SB 5288, 2007) requires school districts to adopt policies prohibiting "harassment, intimidation, or bullying of any student." The statute defines harassment, intimidation, or bullying as:

any intentional electronic, written, verbal, or physical act, including but not limited to one shown to be motivated by any characteristic in RCW 9A.36.080(3), or other distinguishing characteristics, when the intentional electronic, written, verbal, or physical act: (a) Physically harms a student or damages the student's property; or (b) Has the effect of substantially interfering with a student's education; or (c) Is so severe, persistent, or pervasive that it creates an intimidating or threatening educational environment; or (d) Has the effect of substantially disrupting the orderly operation of the school.

The legislation requires the Washington state school directors association to develop a model policy "prohibiting acts of harassment, intimidation or bullying that are conducted via electronic means by a student while on school grounds and during the school day."

Iowa law (SF 61, 2007) that addresses harassment and bullying includes electronic communications, which it defines as "any communication involving the transmission of information by wire, radio, optical cable, electromagnetic, or other similar means" and notes that it includes but is not limited to "communication via electronic mail, internet-based communications, pager service, cell phones, and electronic text messaging." Legislators further require school board members to develop policies against harassment and bullying "in schools, on school property, and at any school function, or school-sponsored activity regardless of its location."

Finally, South Carolina law (S.C. Code Ann., 2006) defines harassment, intimidation or bullying[1] as:

a gesture, *an electronic communication*, or a written, verbal, physical, or sexual act that is reasonably perceived to have the effect of: (a) harming a student physically or emotionally or damaging a student's property, or placing a student in reasonable fear of personal harm or property damage; or (b) insulting or demeaning a student or group of students causing substantial disruption in, or substantial interference with, the orderly operation of the school. (emphasis added)

The legislation further notes that "school" means "in a classroom, on school premises, on a school bus or other school-related vehicle, at an official school bus stop, at a school-sponsored activity or event whether or not it is held on school premises, or at another program or function where the school is responsible for the child."

Of the remaining 25 states with laws addressing bullying, all but one (Georgia) arguably cover at least some instances of cyber bullying. Fifteen of these laws provide definitions of bullying, which may, to a greater or lesser extent, be interpreted to include various acts of cyber bullying. Eight

(Arizona, California, Illinois, Maine, Minnesota, New Hampshire, New York, Virginia) address bullying but fail to define the term, and two (Maryland and Nevada) address "harassment or intimidation" but not specifically bullying.[2] Georgia's bullying law (O.C.G.A., 2006) focuses only on conduct of a physical nature ("[a]ny willful attempt or threat to inflict injury on another person, when accompanied by an apparent present ability to do so"), and, therefore, likely does not include cases of cyber bullying (unless perhaps the perpetrator was in the victim's presence when the victim received the message).

A number of these state laws (e.g., Colorado, Connecticut, New Jersey, Oregon, Tennessee, and Vermont) address bullying in particular locations on school property or at school-sponsored events. For example, under Colorado law, bullying includes acts that take place "in the school, on school grounds, in school vehicles, at a designated school bus stop, or at school activities or sanctioned events" (C.R.S., 2006). Presumably, cyber bullying (or any form of bullying) that takes place outside of these areas (e.g., on a computer located in a home or community library) would not be covered under these state laws, although, as will be discussed below, educators' legal responsibility for off-campus bullying behavior is not entirely clear.

Litigation

Recent legal attention to bullying has not been limited to actions by state legislatures, however (Alley & Limber, in press). There also has been speculation about an increased focus within the courts on bullying, perhaps most visibly in the form of lawsuits filed by parents against schools for harm caused to their bullied children (e.g., Seper, 2005). For example, in 2004 the Anchorage School District in Alaska paid $4.5 million to settle a lawsuit filed by the family of a middle school student who had tried to commit suicide after he was bullied at school (Pesznecker, 2004). The following year, a New Jersey appellate court upheld a jury award for $50,000 to a high school student who had been physically and verbally abused by his peers who thought he was gay (Mikle, 2005).

High-profile news accounts notwithstanding, it is extremely difficult to document whether and how much bullying-related litigation may have actually increased in recent years (Alley & Limber, in press). Why? First, many, if not most, lawsuits that involve bullying are likely settled out of court, making court records of such litigation scarce and by no means representative. Second, there is no national system for counting and tracking the lawsuits related to incidents of school violence that do, in fact, make it to court. Third, the primary legal databases, on which lawyers and legal scholars rely, include only those court decisions that have been appealed. This means that cases that are decided at the trial court level and are not ultimately appealed are not represented in these databases. As a result, these databases may be skewed to overrepresent the "close" cases and underrepresent the "easy" cases, which are more likely to be settled out of court or not reach appeal.

Added to these general difficulties of tracking trends in bullying-related litigation are challenges of tracing legal developments related to cyber bullying, in particular. Cyber bullying is a relatively new phenomenon, and published case law relevant to cyber bullying is scant and still somewhat unclear, particularly as it relates to behavior that occurs off school grounds (see also Willard, 2006).

With these caveats in mind, we will turn to address several legal questions that are most relevant to school personnel concerned with cyber bullying, namely: (1) When might school personnel be liable for failing to address cyber bullying? (2) Under what circumstances can school personnel intervene to address cyber bullying without violating students' First Amendment rights to freedom of expression? and (3) Under what circumstances can school personnel monitor or search student Internet records without violating Fourth Amendment restrictions on illegal searches and seizures?

Under What Circumstances May School Personnel Be Held Liable for Failing to Address Cyber Bullying?

School personnel have a duty to protect students in their care and to ensure that there is no substantial interference with their rights to receive an education (Willard, 2006). School districts may be held liable for failing to stop bullying (and, specifically, cyber bullying) if personnel are found to have acted negligently or if they violate provisions of relevant federal or state statutes.

Statutory liability. Although there currently is no federal law against bullying per se, victims and their parents may, depending on the circumstances, sue for damages under a number of federal laws that prohibit harassment against protected classes of individuals (Alley & Limber, in press). The federal laws that are most often implicated in such cases relate to sexual- or gender-based harassment, racial harassment, and disability harassment.

Claims of sexual harassment or gender discrimination usually rely on Title IX of the Education Amendments Act of 1972. Under this federal

statute, "no person . . . shall, on the basis of sex, be excluded from participation in, be denied the benefits of, or be subjected to discrimination under
any education program or activity receiving Federal financial assistance"
(Education Amendments Act of 1972, 2006). In the case of *Davis v. Monroe
County Board of Education* (1999), the U.S. Supreme Court ruled that,
under Title IX, schools and school districts (but not individual school
personnel) may be liable for student-on-student sexual harassment when
it can be shown that the school or district acted with "deliberate indifference" toward harassment that was "so severe, pervasive, and objectively
offensive" (p. 650) that it denies victims equal access to education. In order
to prove that a school acted with "deliberate indifference," a court must
find that school personnel had actual knowledge of the harassment and
that their response was clearly unreasonable in light of the known circumstances. In addition, the court must find that there has been a significant
impact of the harassment on the student's access to education, as evidenced
by more than "a mere decline in grades" (p. 652). Finally, the Supreme
Court distinguished acts of harassment from common forms of bullying,
noting that:

> It is not enough to show . . . that a student has been "teased," or "called . . . off-
> ensive names[.]" Comparisons to an "overweight child who skips gym class
> because the other children tease her about her size," the student "who refuses
> to wear glasses to avoid the taunts of 'four-eyes,'" and "the child who refuses
> to go to school because the school bully calls him a 'scardy-cat' at recess,"
> are inapposite and misleading. (p. 652)

Subsequent lower court rulings have applied the *Davis* standard to other
forms of peer harassment, in addition to sexual harassment. There are, for
example, two other contexts, in addition to peer sexual harassment, in
which victims may sue under Title IX (Alley & Limber, in press). The first
involves nonsexual harassment of female students based on their gender
(e.g., gender-based name calling). The second involves harassment of students based on perceived sexual orientation or a "failure to meet gender
stereotypes" (although many courts have not found that Title IX prohibits
sexual orientation harassment; Alley & Limber, in press).

The *Davis* standard has also been applied to claims of racial harassment.
Under Title IV of the Civil Rights Act of 1964, "[n]o person . . . shall, on
the ground of race, color, or national origin, be excluded from participation in, be denied the benefits of, or be subjected to discrimination under
any program or activity receiving Federal financial assistance." Students
may sue a school or school district for peer racial harassment under Title
IV. However, in order to be successful, they must show that the school or

district acted with deliberate indifference toward harassment that is so severe, pervasive, and objectively offensive that it deprives the victim of access to educational opportunities.

Students or their parents also may bring claims against a school or school district for peer harassment that is based on the physical or mental disability of the victim (Alley & Limber, in press). Typically, such claims are brought under Section 504 of the Rehabilitation Act of 1973 and Title II of the Americans with Disabilities Act of 1990 (ADA; 2006), which have similar provisions. Section 504 provides that "[n]o otherwise qualified individual with a disability . . . shall, solely by reason of her or his disability, be excluded from the participation in, be denied the benefits of, or be subjected to discrimination under any program or activity receiving Federal financial assistance."

Similarly, Title II of the ADA states that: "[n]o qualified individual with a disability shall, by reason of such disability, be excluded from participation in or be denied the benefits of the services, programs or activities of a public entity, or be subjected to discrimination by any such entity." Courts that have considered claims based on Section 504 and Title II frequently rely on the *Davis* standard, reasoning that a school district or school may be liable for student harassment of another student based on the victim's disability when the school or district acted with deliberate indifference to harassment that was so severe, pervasive, and objectively offensive that it denied the victim equal access to educational resources and opportunities (Alley & Limber, in press; see e.g., *K.M. v. Hyde Park Central School District*, 2005). Although courts have varied in their findings of what types of harassment (e.g., physical violence, name calling) are sufficient to meet the *Davis* standard, at least some have found that nonphysical acts, such as verbal taunting or social isolation of developmentally disabled victims, may in fact be sufficiently severe to qualify under *Davis* (e.g., *K.M. v. Hyde Park Central School District*, 2005).

Under what conditions may individuals (e.g., teachers, principals, or other school staff) be held liable under federal law in cases of student-on-student harassment? As mentioned earlier, only school districts or schools – and not individual staff members – may be held liable for sexual harassment under Title IX or racial harassment under Title IV. It is less clear whether individuals may be held liable for student-on-student disability harassment under Section 504 or Title II. Some jurisdictions have allowed these claims, whereas others have not (Alley & Limber, in press).

There is at least one other federal statute that may allow students and their parents to bring claims against individual school personnel under federal law. Section 1983 of the Civil Rights Act is a federal law that allows citizens to bring lawsuits to collect damages against state officials, including school teachers, administrators, and other district employees, who deprived them of their rights under federal law. Although the federal rights that are involved vary, in litigation related to instances of harassment or bullying, the federal right in question is often the Fourteenth Amendment to the U.S. Constitution. There are two clauses of the Fourteenth Amendment that are relevant (Alley & Limber, in press). The first, known as the due process clause, states that "[n]o State shall . . . deprive any person of life, liberty, or property, without due process of law." Courts have found that due process rights may be violated when state officials engage in conduct of such an egregious nature as to be conscious-shocking (*County of Sacramento v. Lewis*, 1998), but as Alley and Limber (in press) point out, "they have been reluctant to impose liability on state officials for failing to prevent a person, such as a school child, from being injured by a third party, such as another school child" (see *DeShaney v. Winnebago County Department of Social Services*, 1989). In cases involving school violence, some courts have set an even higher bar and have required deliberate indifference on the part of school personnel in order to find them liable for peer-on-peer harassment or attacks under Section 1983 (see e.g., *Stevenson v. Martin County Board of Education*, 2001).

The second clause of the Fourteenth Amendment, commonly referred to as the equal protection clause, also is occasionally relied on in lawsuits related to harassment of students by other students. The equal protection clause states that "[n]o State shall . . . deny to any person . . . the equal protection of the laws." In order to be successful, a litigant must show that a defendant (e.g., a school teacher) discriminated against them as a member of an identifiable class and that the discrimination was intentional (see *Flores v. Morgan Hill Unified School District*, 2003). This discrimination may be based on a number of class characteristics, including gender, race, disability, and religion. In the case of student harassment at school, students (or parents on their behalf) bringing the suit must show that a school official treated them differently than other students, as would be the case if a principal failed to enforce a school's antiharassment policy to prevent students from harassing gay students, even though the principal enforced the policy to protect the rest of the student body (Alley & Limber, in press).

As Alley and Limber (in press) note, "there are numerous high hurdles for litigants bringing lawsuits in federal court" for injuries arising out of school bullying or peer-on-peer harassment. Some have succeeded, particularly where a victim has suffered severely and school officials knew of a pattern of harassment against the victim but took no action. However, many victims of bullying are unable to bring suit under federal law because they are not a member of a protected class.

In such cases, they may choose, instead, to file suit under any number of state laws that address concerns such as intentional infliction of emotional distress, negligence, and privacy violations, as well as under various provisions of state education codes. Perhaps the most common suits involve claims that school personnel acted negligently to prevent or address bullying.

Negligence. Negligence is "the failure to exercise the standard of care that a reasonably prudent person would have exercised in a similar situation" (*Black's Law Dictionary*, 2004, p. 1061). It may involve: (a) doing something that a reasonable person would not have done under similar circumstance, or (b) failing to do what a reasonable person would have done under similar circumstances.

Claims of negligence are based on state laws related to the conditions under which liability may be imposed on public officials. As Willard (2006) notes, some states have immunity laws that protect school officials against negligence claims, whereas others do not. As a result, there may be considerable variation from state to state in the manner in which negligence claims are decided.

Generally, an individual bringing a claim of negligence against school personnel must show: (a) a legal duty (e.g., a duty to anticipate foreseeable dangers for students in their care and a duty to take necessary precautions against these dangers), (b) a breach of that duty (failure to use reasonable care in the context of a foreseeable risk), (c) proximate cause (the breach of the duty was a substantial factor in leading to injury or harm), and (d) actual injuries, loss, or damages (Willard, 2006). Willard examined these elements within the context of school personnel's duty to protect students from possible harms caused by using cyber technologies at school.

Do school administrators have a duty to protect the safety of students who use the Internet at school through the district's system? Willard concludes, "Yes, clearly" (p. 69). School personnel have a general duty to provide safe schools and adequate supervision of students within their care. A more specific duty is outlined in The Children's Internet Protection Act (CIPA; 2007). CIPA is a federal law enacted to address concerns about access to offensive content over the Internet on school and library computers. The law imposes certain requirements on any school or library that receives funding support for Internet access or internal connections from the "E-rate" program, a program that makes certain technology more affordable for eligible schools and libraries. Among CIPA's requirements are that schools adopt and implement a policy addressing the safety and security of minors when using e-mail, chat rooms, and other forms of direct electronic communications.

Willard (2006) argues that not only do school personnel have a duty to protect the safety of students who use the Internet while at school, but they have a similar duty in cases where districts provide students with the ability to access the school's Internet system while off campus, where schools allow students to take home district-owned computers, and where schools permit students to use cell phones or other mobile communication devices at school.

Not only do school officials have a *legal duty* to ensure the safety and security of students in such situations, but they also should be able to *foresee* that students may use cyber technologies to harm other students. Given the emerging evidence that students use such technologies to bully, threaten, and harass each other, and given the intense media attention to this issue, these behaviors should come as no surprise to school officials.

Provided that school officials have a legal duty to protect the safety and security of students and that they should be able to foresee misuse of cyber technologies to cause harm, a critical question in determining negligence becomes, "What is a *reasonable standard of care* that school personnel should be expected to provide in order to protect students?" Until courts address this issue directly, it will be difficult to answer this question. However, the standard is generally expressed as, "what a reasonably prudent person would do in similar circumstances" (Willard, 2006, p. 70).

We believe that reasonably prudent administrators should, at a minimum: (a) develop rules and policies that prohibit the use of district computers and other cyber technologies to bully or harass others; (b) establish policies and procedures that limit students' use of school Internet resources for nonacademic purposes; (c) educate students and staff about cyber bullying and the school's policies and procedures (see Chapter 5); (d) provide adequate supervision and monitoring of students (including their use of the Internet; see Chapter 6); (e) establish effective mechanisms for students and staff to report suspected cyber bullying or other misuse of cyber technologies (see Chapter 6); and (f) establish effective procedures to respond to reports (see Chapter 6; see also Willard, 2006, for similar recommendations for administrators). If they do so, we believe it unlikely that they would be successfully sued for negligence.

Under What Circumstances Can School Personnel Intervene to Address Cyber Bullying Without Fear of Violating Students' First Amendment Rights?

In their efforts to protect students from foreseeable harm, educators may, on occasion, infringe on students' rights under the U.S. Constitution, including First Amendment rights to freedom of speech and expression, and Fourth Amendment rights to be free from unreasonable searches and seizures. The U.S. Supreme Court has clearly held that "First Amendment rights . . . are available to teachers and students" and that students do not "shed their constitutional rights of speech or expression at the schoolhouse gate" (*Tinker v. Des Moines Independent Community School District*, 1969, p. 506). Nevertheless, the Court has also placed a number of limitations on this speech. Student speech is not protected by the Constitution (and, therefore, may be suppressed or punished) if it: (1) constitutes a threat; (2) is lewd, vulgar, or profane; (3) is (or appears to be) sponsored by the school; or (4) otherwise materially disrupts the schools or invades the rights of others. Even though the U.S. Supreme Court has not directly addressed cases involving First Amendment questions raised by "cyber speech," several seminal decisions likely would apply to such cases and will be discussed briefly below.

Speech involving a threat. In *Watts v. United States* (1969), the Supreme Court ruled that a true threat is not protected by the Constitution. Several years later, the Court clarified that, in order to constitute a threat, a statement must actually be threatening, and there also must be "proof that the speaker intended the statement to be taken as a threat" (*Rogers v. United States*, 1975, p. 48) even if there was no intent to carry it out. Presumably, based on these Supreme Court rulings, any student speech that is found to be a "true threat" (including messages sent through cyber space) may be regulated without fear of violating students' First Amendment rights.

Speech that is lewd, vulgar, or profane. In *Bethel School District v. Fraser* (1986), the Supreme Court ruled in favor of a school district that had suspended a high school student for giving a speech at school that was laced with sexual innuendos. The Court noted that "the First Amendment does not prevent the school officials from determining that . . . permit[ing] a vulgar and lewd speech . . . would undermine the school's basic educational mission" (p. 685). A concurring opinion clarified that the same speech likely would have been protected by the First Amendment if it had taken place outside of school grounds, however. Thus, arguably cyber speech that is lewd, vulgar, or profane may be regulated, at least if it takes place at school.

Speech that is school sponsored. Educators are entitled to control school-sponsored publications, theatrical productions, and other "expressive activities" that might be reasonably perceived to be sponsored by the school as long as educators' actions "are reasonably related to legitimate pedagogical concerns" (*Hazelwood School District v. Kuhlmeier*, 1988, p. 271). In the

Hazelwood case, a school principal decided to remove two articles from the student newspapers because he feared that the content (which included references to sexual activity and birth control) was inappropriate for younger readers and that it might raise privacy concerns for several individuals mentioned in the articles. The Court ruled that the newspaper was not a forum for public expression but rather was school-sponsored and that, as a result, administrators could legitimately make educationally related restrictions on student speech. It is likely that cyber speech that takes place at school and that appears to be sponsored by the school (e.g., a student sends electronic messages that contain the school's logo) may be legitimately regulated.

Speech that disrupts the school or rights of others. Speech that falls outside the purview of these cases (i.e., speech that does not constitute a threat; is not lewd, vulgar, or profane; and is not school-sponsored, or perceived to be school-sponsored) is protected by the First Amendment unless it is found to disrupt the school or rights of others. In *Tinker v. Des Moines Independent School District* (1969), the Supreme Court found that administrators had inappropriately disciplined students for wearing black armbands to protest against the Vietnam War, where there was no evidence that the wearing of the armbands had disrupted the work of the school or affected the rights of any individuals at the school. The Court ruled that student speech may not be restricted if there is "a mere desire to avoid the discomfort and unpleasantness that always accompanies an unpopular viewpoint" (p. 512). However, it *may* be suppressed if it "materially disrupts classwork or involves substantial disorder or invasion of the rights of others" (p. 512). The Court clarified that speech is not only protected in the classroom but also "in the cafeteria, or on the playing field, or on the campus during the authorized hours" (p. 512). The Court did not expressly address whether such speech would be protected off campus.

Off-campus speech. As noted above, although the Supreme Court has not directly addressed students' rights to express themselves through cyber space (e.g., through email or on Web pages accessed through school computers), the cases cited above arguably apply to forms of "cyber speech" that take place on a school's campus. It is somewhat less clear whether and to what degree school personnel can legitimately restrict student speech that takes place off campus (Chaker, 2007; Willard, 2006).

Although the standard in *Fraser* likely does *not* apply to off-campus lewd speech, the *Tinker* standard (requiring material disruption of classwork, substantial disorder, or invasion of others' rights) likely does apply. Several lower court rulings in cases involving cyber bullying or cyber threats toward other students and school personnel are relevant and may provide some insight to educators.

In *Coy v. Board of Education of the North Canton City Schools* (2002), a district court reviewed the case in which a student was suspended for four days after using a school computer to access a Web site that he had created at home on his personal computer. The Web site included profanity and insults, identified a group of students as "losers" and, according to the court, contained "a depressingly high number of spelling and grammatical errors" (p. 795). The judge ruled that the *Tinker* standard applied in this case but found that "no evidence suggests that Coy's acts in accessing the website had any effect upon the school district's ability to maintain discipline in the school" (p. 801).

The case of *J.S. v. Bethlehem Area School District* (2000) features an 8th grade student, J.S., who created a Web site entitled "Teacher Sux". The site, which was created off of school grounds, featured sexual and threatening comments about the student's algebra teacher, including a picture of her severed head dripping with blood, a picture of her morphing into Adolph Hitler, and the solicitation of funds to cover a hit man. J.S. also had encouraged other students to post derogatory comments on the site. In its decision, the court noted that "it is evident that the courts have allowed school officials to discipline students for conduct occurring off of school premises where it is established that the conduct materially and substantially interferes with the educational process" (p. 421). In applying the *Tinker* standard, the court found that the school district acted reasonably in holding an expulsion hearing for the student, as there was evidence that the targeted teacher had been seriously affected by the Web site. (She was unable to complete the school year and took a medical leave of absence for the following school year.)

In *Killion v. Franklin Regional School District* (2001), the court considered whether school administrators had violated a student's First Amendment rights after they suspended him for circulating an email list containing derogatory comments about the athletic director. The "top ten" list was emailed from the student's home computer to a number of friends. Although the student did not bring the list to school, another student did, and it was widely circulated. The court ruled that "although there is limited case law on the issue, courts considering speech that occurs off school grounds have concluded . . . that school officials' authority over off-campus expression is much more limited than expression on school grounds" (p. 454). In applying the *Tinker* standard, the court found that there was no evidence of disruption at the school caused by the list, and as a result, the student had been suspended inappropriately.

Currently pending before the U.S. Supreme Court is a case that, although unrelated to bullying, may directly answer the question of whether public school officials can suppress student speech that takes place off campus (*Frederick v. Juneau School Board*, 2006). A high school principal in Juneau, Alaska, suspended a student for unfurling a banner reading "Bong Hits 4 Jesus" on a sidewalk across the street from the school, where students had congregated to watch the Winter Olympics Torch Relay. The U. S. Court of Appeals for the Ninth Circuit concluded that there was no evidence that the presence of the banner, which was displayed off school grounds and during a noncurricular activity, interfered in any way with the school's basic educational mission. As one commentator (Chaker, 2007) noted, "the [Supreme] Court's decision in this case may have implications for other forms of off-campus speech, such as online postings" (p. D4).

When Can School Personnel Monitor or Search Student Internet Records?

In addition to examining under what conditions school personnel may suppress cyber speech or sanction students for engaging in it, it is important to determine whether and to what degree school personnel may monitor or search student Internet records for cyber bullying and other inappropriate speech. School personnel may attempt to address cyber bullying through monitoring and searching of students' Internet records on campus. Under what conditions are such actions permissible, and when may they violate Fourth Amendment prohibitions against unreasonable searches and seizures?

The Supreme Court, in the case of *New Jersey v. T.L.O.* (1985), considered whether school officials violated the rights of a high school girl when an assistant vice principal searched her purse and found marijuana and evidence of drug dealing. The Court ruled that teachers or other school officials may legitimately search a student if: (a) there are reasonable grounds for suspecting that the search will produce evidence that the student has violated (or is currently violating) a law or a school rule, and (b) the measures adopted in conducting the search are "reasonably related to the objectives of the search and not excessively intrusive in light of the age and sex of the student and the nature of the infraction" (p. 342).

In light of the Court's decision in *T.L.O.*, most schools have developed search and seizure policies for student desks and lockers. Typically, these policies note that students should expect limited privacy in the contents of their desks and lockers and they stipulate that general inspections may occur on a regular basis (Willard, 2006). More specific searches of individual desks or lockers may be conducted where school personnel have reasonable suspicion of the presence of items that are illegal or that may provide evidence of activities that are illegal or against school rules. As Willard (2006) notes, "these same standards can be applied in the context of analysis of Internet usage records and computer files" (p. 61).

School Policies Related to Cyber Bullying

As mentioned earlier in this chapter, more than half of all states in the U.S. have passed bullying laws that encourage or require schools to develop policies addressing bullying among students. Many administrators have created such policies even when not legally required to do so. With the recent attention to cyber bullying among students, administrators are increasingly grappling with whether and how to address cyber bullying and related behaviors within the school's bullying policies and within policies that govern acceptable uses of technology by students. We will discuss trends in the development of these policies and provide examples of language from actual and sample policies in the field. In establishing any such policies, administrators are again encouraged to consult legal counsel and be mindful of the need to protect students' First Amendment rights (as established by the U.S. Supreme Court in its *Tinker*, *Fraser*, and *Hazelwood* decisions) and Fourth Amendment rights (consistent with the Supreme Court's decision in *T.L.O.*) that were outlined earlier.

Bullying Policies

School bullying policies vary dramatically from district to district, as do sample/model policies on bullying that are developed by state departments of education or other state-level organizations (Alley & Limber, in press). These policies may include: statements prohibiting bullying behavior, definitions and examples of bullying, procedures for reporting and investigating suspected bullying, discipline for students involved in bullying, assistance for victims of bullying, and guidelines for training and prevention efforts. Where administrators have developed (or are considering the development of) policies addressing bullying, they should carefully consider the application of these policies to various forms of cyber bullying. Some bullying policies refer specifically to cyber bullying behavior, but most provide more general definitions of bullying which may, in many cases, be interpreted to include acts of cyber bullying.

In a review of 14 state model or sample policies developed by state departments of education and several other relevant state-level organizations (see Alley & Limber, in press, for more information about these policies), we noted only a handful that directly address cyber bullying. Massachusetts' sample policy ("Promoting civil rights," 2005) defines bullying as:

> any written or verbal expression, or physical acts or gestures, directed at another person(s) to intimidate, frighten, ridicule, humiliate, or cause harm to the other person, where the conduct is not related to the person's membership in a protected class (e.g., race, sex). Bullying may include, but is not limited to, repeated taunting, threats of harm, verbal or physical intimidation, *cyber-bullying through e-mails, instant messages, or websites*, pushing, kicking, hitting, spitting, or taking or damaging another's personal property. (emphasis added; p. 13)

Maine's School Management Association Sample Policy (2006) on bullying provides examples of conduct that may constitute bullying, including "threats of harm to a student, to his/her possessions, or to other individuals, whether transmitted verbally, in writing, *or through cyberspace*" (emphasis added). The New York State School Board Association's Sample Policy on Harassment, Hazing, and Bullying (2006) includes "intentional written, verbal, *or electronic communication* . . ." (emphasis added) in its definition.

More common are definitions that do not explicitly refer to cyber bullying or bullying through electronic communications, but may implicitly include these behaviors. For example, Ohio's sample policy addressing antiharassment and bullying (Ohio Resource Network for Safe and Drug Free Schools, n.d.) defines bullying as:

> any written, verbal or physical act taking place on or immediately adjacent to school grounds . . . that a reasonable person under the circumstances should know will have the effect of: (a) placing a student in reasonable fear of physical harm or damage to the student's property, (b) physically harming a student or damaging a student's property, (c) insulting or demeaning any student or group of students in such a way as to disrupt or interfere with the school's educational mission or the education of any student.

Most forms of cyber bullying that take place on campus involve written or verbal acts (with the possible exception of sending digital photos or graphics) and, therefore, likely would be included under this sample policy. However, it also is worth noting that most acts of cyber bullying also take place off campus, as opposed to "on or immediately adjacent to school grounds."

Policies Addressing Use of Technology by Students

Most schools have developed policies that address acceptable uses of technology by students and Internet safety and security issues. (As noted earlier, all schools that receive funding from the "E-rate" program are required to do so under the Children's Internet Protection Act [2001].) Within these policies, administrators should provide clear prohibitions against cyber bullying and related behavior and clarify procedures for monitoring or searching students' Internet records.

Prohibitions against use of cyber technology to cyber bully. Many schools have expressly prohibited cyber bullying and related behavior in their acceptable use policies. For example, in its administrative rules, Cobb County (GA) School District (2006) does not prohibit "cyber bullying" per se, but it prohibits students from using school technology resources to display or distribute *inappropriate material.*

> Inappropriate material does not serve an instructional or educational purpose and includes but is not limited to the following:
> * Is profane, vulgar, lewd, obscene, offensive, indecent, sexually explicit, pornographic or threatening;
> * Advocates illegal or dangerous acts;
> * Causes disruption to Cobb County School District, its employees or students;
> * Advocates violence;
> * Contains knowingly false, recklessly false, or defamatory information; or
> * Is otherwise harmful to minors as defined by the Children's Internet Protection Act.

As noted earlier, the U.S. Department of Justice (2006) provides a Model Acceptable Use Policy for Information Technology Resources in the Schools, which requires, in part, that students:

* *Respect and practice the principles of community.*
  * Communicate only in ways that are kind and respectful.
  * Report threatening or discomforting materials to a teacher.
  * Not intentionally access, transmit, copy, or create material that violates the school's code of conduct (such as messages that are pornographic, threatening, rude, discriminatory, or meant to harass).
  * Not intentionally access, transmit, copy, or create material that is illegal (such as obscenity, stolen materials, or illegal copies of copyrighted works).
  * Not use the resources to further other acts that are criminal or violate the school's code of conduct.

- Not send spam, chain letters, or other mass unsolicited mailings.
- Not buy, sell, advertise, or otherwise conduct business, unless approved as a school project.

In their acceptable use policies or behavior codes, some school districts also address use of technology off of school grounds. When doing so, they should be careful to be in compliance with the *Tinker* standard, which allows suppression of speech if there is material disruption to class work, substantial disorder, or invasion of others' rights. For example, in their Code of Behavior, Prince William (Virginia) Schools (2006) note that unacceptable uses of technology include:

> Use of technology off school property which has a material effect on the operation or general welfare of the School Division, impacts the integrity of the educational process, threatens the safety and welfare of students, staff, or school property, occurs when the student is under the school's authority *in loco parentis*, or otherwise invades the rights of students or staff.

Notification of students' privacy limits. In order to ensure that school policies do not violate students' Fourth Amendment rights (i.e., are in accordance with the *T.L.O.* standards) and to help deter improper use of school computers, administrators are advised to establish user policies that notify students about the limits of their privacy and the likelihood of routine monitoring of files. Willard (2006) recommends the following model policy language:

> Users have a limited expectation of privacy in the contents of their personal files, communication files, and record of web research activities on the district's Internet system. Routine maintenance and monitoring, utilizing both technical monitoring systems and staff monitoring, may lead to discovery that a user has violated district policy or the law. An individual search will be conducted if there is reasonable suspicion that a user has violated district policy or the law. Students' parents have the right to request to see the contents of their children's files and records. (p. 62)

Willard (2006) also recommends that administrators provide reminders on log-in screens and in school computer labs about students' limited expectations of privacy.

Conclusions

With the recent flurry of public interest in cyber bullying and the focus on the harms that it may cause, many school administrators are concerned about meeting their ethical and legal duties to protect students without infringing on their constitutionally protected rights. Some administrators are considering whether and how cyber bullying fits with their existing policies about bullying and/or the appropriate uses of school technology. Others, perhaps prompted by state laws that increasingly require district or school-wide policies on cyber bullying, are developing new policies that include attention to cyber bullying.

Whether developing new policies or refining existing policies about bullying, we encourage administrators to become well acquainted with current research on students' use of emerging technologies, the nature and prevalence of cyber bullying and other forms of bullying among children and youth, and best practices in preventing and addressing bullying; this research finds that bullying is best addressed through comprehensive school-wide efforts. As local policies will be most effective where they reflect unique assets and needs of the community, we encourage administrators to develop these policies through a process that involves input from all relevant stakeholders, including educators, parents, and students (see also Alley & Limber, in press). Finally, administrators (and their legal counsel) should be aware of the variety of state and federal laws that may be relevant to these policies.

As is often the case in any rapidly changing legal landscape, there remains some uncertainty about how U.S. law may be applied to forms of cyber speech, particularly those that occur away from school grounds. However, it appears clear that schools may, under certain circumstances, be held liable under state or federal laws for failing to address cyber bullying or harassment. Under many state laws, students (or parents on their behalf) may bring claims of negligence against school personnel for failing to use reasonable care to protect students from foreseeable harms caused by cyber bullying. Under a variety of federal laws, students who are members of protected classes may bring lawsuits against schools or school districts for injuries arising out of peer-on-peer harassment based on race, gender, or disability.

In their efforts to protect students from harms caused by cyber bullying, it appears that administrators may legitimately suppress cyber speech that takes place on school grounds under certain conditions: (a) If the speech constitutes a threat; (b) if it is lewd, vulgar, or profane; (c) where the speech is (or appears to be) sponsored by the school; or (d) when it materially disrupts the school or the rights of others. In addition, following precedent set in cases involving searches of school lockers and desks, it appears that students should expect limited privacy in the contents of their computers at school and that administrators may make general inspections of school computers and Internet accounts on a regular basis. More specific searches of computers or accounts may be conducted where school personnel have reasonable suspicion of the presence of content that is illegal or that may provide evidence of activities that are illegal or against school rules.

Lest our legal review leave readers with the inaccurate impression that administrators' primary goals should be to avoid liability, we conclude this chapter with a reminder that, in developing and enforcing sound policies that focus on the prevention of bullying (including cyber bullying), administrators will not only decrease the chances that legal action will be brought against schools and school districts but they will, more importantly, decrease the likelihood that children will continue to suffer from being bullied.

Notes

1. It is unfortunate that several states (at least nine, at the time of writing) equate bullying with harassment (Alley & Limber, in press). Although both involve an aggressive pattern of behavior, harassment involves discrimination against protected classes of persons. As Alley and Limber note, "[w]hile bullies may act aggressively toward their victim for any reason, or for no reason at all, perpetrators of harassment act in a discriminatory manner based on some characteristic of the victim." As will be discussed later in this chapter, prohibitions against harassment occur at the federal and state levels. The new wave of legislation on bullying currently exists at only the state level.
2. Maryland's Department of Education has, at times, suggested that bullying is included in this definition, see, for example, the Department's Harassment or Intimidation (Bullying) Reporting Form at http://www.marylandpublic-schools.org/nr/rdonlyres/0700b064-c2b3-41fc-a6cf-d3dae4969707/7243/harassmentorintimidationbullyingreportingform.pdf

8

Conclusion

ᔑ

Lauren, an 8th grade student, was startled when she was walking down the hall at school one morning and a male student said, "Hey Lauren, I saw your MySpace last night." Lauren was puzzled because she didn't have a "MySpace", and she wasn't really sure what one was. Fortunately, she had a close relationship with her school counselor and went to see her to get advice. The school counselor contacted Lauren's mother to let her know about the incident, and shared with her a link to the MySpace page that allows an individual to report a false profile. The counselor and parent were unable to locate the actual profile and were unsure what screen name was used for the profile since a search under Lauren's first and last name did not show any profile evidence.

Fortunately, the school administrators did not let such a roadblock stop them in addressing the situation. The counselor spoke to the boy who had made the remark to Lauren and asked for his help in locating the name of the profile. In addition, she asked Lauren to see if any of her friends knew anything about the profile. In fact, a friend of Lauren's overheard two classmates on the school bus admit to setting up the profile.

The administrator and counselor called the classmates in separately and explained the seriousness of impersonating another individual online, and gave them a warning that this was cyber bullying. They asked the students to remove the profile, and warned them against any retaliation toward Lauren. The counselor and administrator let the students know that they would be monitoring the situation with Lauren closely. They also contacted the parents of the students involved. While the students admitted to setting up the profile, they were initially quick to blame each other. The administration, however, emphasized the seriousness and cruelty of the incident, and one of the students was so affected by their conversation that she remarked, "I am going to apologize to Lauren right now!"

We have attempted to present a thorough overview of what we currently know about cyber bullying; where it is similar to and dissimilar from traditional forms of bullying; what strategies educators, parents, and community members can take to prevent cyber bullying; and how adults can intervene effectively when it occurs. As highlighted in Chapter 4, there are still many areas where questions remain that require further research, and, as noted in Chapter 7, relevant laws and policies are still evolving. These limitations, however, should not keep parents, educators, and other adults from responding to and addressing cyber bullying. As demonstrated in the above incident that actually occurred in a school where one of the authors consults, adults can be proactive in the face of limited information and limited school policies. A willingness of adults to monitor online behavior, teach social skills, and protect youth who are harassed at school or off campus, through traditional or cyber bullying, will enable adults to respond effectively to our children's desire to socialize online.

What We Know and What We Question

We have noted throughout this book that youth spend significant amounts of time online, and that the overwhelming majority (90%) of preteens and teens have Internet access (Ybarra et al., 2006). We also have discussed the many ways that young people bully others online, whether through instant messaging (the most common form of bullying among American children), e-mail, or postings on social networking sites such as MySpace. Youth are assuming others' identities through stolen passwords to e-mail or instant message accounts, and entire Web sites have been created to target classmates or teachers. Cyber bullying through the use of cellular phones and personal digital assistants (PDAs) is also occurring and is particularly challenging for parents and educators to monitor, because cellular phones and PDAs are by nature more private, and often readily accessible to the cyber bully. At the time of writing, Cingular had just announced plans to partner with MySpace to make it possible for users to access their MySpace profiles via a Cingular cell phone. This agreement links MySpace with the largest provider of cell phone service in the United States (Leith, 2006). It seems reasonable to expect that cyber bullying via cellular phone will increase as students find it easier to target their peers through posting comments on MySpace in addition to text messaging throughout the day.

As outlined in Chapters 3 and 4, our review of the research indicates that cyber bullying is a form of bullying behavior that is on the rise and peaks during middle school (Kowalski & Limber, 2006; Ybarra et al., 2006). It is important to recognize that, as with traditional bullying, young people are more likely to engage in cyber bullying if they believe that adults and bystanders are unlikely to intervene (Williams & Guerra, 2006). This same research indicates that students perceive adults as least likely to intervene in bullying that occurs over the Internet, which may help explain the increases we are observing in cyber bullying behavior.

The research also suggests that females are more likely than males to both engage in cyber bullying others and to be a target of cyber bullying behavior at certain grade levels (Kowalski & Limber, 2006; Ybarra et al., 2006), unlike some specific forms of traditional bullying behavior (e.g., physical bullying) and overall rates of traditional bullying. This is consistent with research showing that females are more likely than males to engage in indirect forms of aggression, as discussed in Chapter 4. However, fewer girls than boys reported engaging in the highest frequencies of cyber bullying (i.e., several times a week).

Though in its infancy, research on cyber bullying has spanned several countries. As discussed in Chapter 4, although the prevalence rates and methods of cyber bullying vary slightly from one country to another, most, if not all, developed countries are being forced to deal with this phenomenon. As attention to cyber bullying continues to increase, it will be important that researchers and policy-makers adopt an interdisciplinary and multicultural approach to the topic.

While we are learning more about cyber bullying, there is still much that is unknown about this new form of bullying. The research on traditional bullying presented in Chapter 2 provided a context for examining how cyber bullying is similar to and different from traditional bullying. The definition of traditional bullying that is widespread involves behavior that is repeated, intentionally aggressive and based on an imbalance of power. Cyber bullying often meets the definition of intentionally aggressive behavior. Although cyber bullying shares these characteristics, questions may be raised about the repetitiveness of actions online. Might repeated viewings of a one-time posting of an aggressive message constitute cyber bullying? This issue needs further clarification and research. Similarly, the nature of an online power imbalance also warrants further attention. We suspect that the Internet is such a powerful (and often anonymous) tool that the ability to reach vast audiences with a single mouse click frequently tilts the balance of power in the cyber bully's favor. Again, this is an issue that needs further exploration by researchers.

Chapter 2 also explained the myriad of harmful consequences that both perpetrators and victims of traditional bullying may experience. It is likely that cyber bullying could have effects on the instigators and targets similar to those observed with traditional bullying. We discussed in Chapter 4 that research by two of the authors suggests that children who experience cyber bullying or are provocative victims have higher rates of anxiety than students who bully or those who are not involved at all (Kowalski & Limber, 2006). Recent research has also confirmed that 2 out of 5 youths who are targets of Internet harassment experience emotional distress, particularly preadolescents (Ybarra et al., 2006). Our individual and focus group interviews suggest that at least some students avoid school, have their academic performance affected, and experience damaged relationships after enduring cyber bullying, but other young people emerge relatively unscathed from such incidents.

We noted in Chapter 4 that there is even less research available regarding the perpetrators of cyber bullying; however, the Kowalski and Limber (2006) study suggests that students who cyber bully have slightly lower self-esteem than those not involved in cyber bullying at all (although cyber victims and bully/victims appear to have still lower self-esteem than cyber bullies). We also noted in Chapter 4 that the perpetrators of cyber bullying share feelings of enjoyment, power and/or revenge as motivations for their actions (Kowalski & Witte, 2006). Such motives are obvious cause for concern and are deserving of further study.

How Can We Use This Information to Prevent Cyber Bullying?

As we have learned from the research on traditional bullying, when youth participate in activities with little or no adult supervision, bullying often thrives. Youths' use of technology is no exception, and we hope that this book will be a wakeup call to parents and educators that youth need more guidance, training, and supervision when utilizing the myriad of technologies that are increasingly embraced by young people. Such guidance also needs to be offered in a developmentally appropriate manner, recognizing that supervision of a 10-year-old will be different than supervision of a 16-year-old. Just as parents and educators provide developmentally appropriate supervision in children's activities at home and school, adults need to provide such supervision and guidance in children's online activities as well. The following conversation that took place during one of our middle school girls' focus groups demonstrates the range of involvement of parents in their children's online lives. The comments were made by 13- and 14-year-old students in the group.

> "If you have a MySpace, let your parents check it."
> "My mom doesn't know that I have a MySpace."
> "Noooooo!"
> "I don't tell my mom what goes on at school . . . for my mom to see my MySpace, well she would have a lot of questions."
> "My mom wouldn't approve of a lot of my friends. She wouldn't want them at my house because some of my friends have very big potty mouths."
> "I don't have any dirty comments on my MySpace."

Keep in mind that these are not 17-year-olds discussing their MySpace; the majority of these girls were 13 years of age. This is clearly an age where it would be developmentally appropriate for parents to provide guidance to a child setting up a personal profile online. Yet, only two of the focus group participants suggested that their MySpace would meet parental approval.[1]

We also recommend that parents educate themselves regarding each new piece of technology they consider purchasing for their children to use, and that they spend time discussing with their children acceptable and unacceptable uses of such technology and possible consequences for violations. Parents who learn to use the technology that their children operate will be better prepared to monitor its use. Staying in touch with popular youth technology will facilitate more communication between parent and child about such devices. Parents can educate themselves about various technologies by talking to salespersons, computer experts, and searching for information online. In addition, school and community organizations can assist by hosting frequent parent workshops on the Internet as well as other popular youth technologies. Such workshops on "technology and youth" should include both positive uses and potential abuses and would greatly assist parents in navigating the rapidly evolving world of technology.

In addition to supervision, adults need to teach youth how to communicate effectively online. Adults can make use of some of the key research findings described in this book in order to help shape the developmentally appropriate messages they give youth about Internet behavior. Because it appears that cyber bullying behavior peaks in middle school, prevention messages need to begin prior to middle school. Parents and educators of 9- and 10-year-olds (3rd and 4th grade) should begin providing messages about appropriate online behavior when communicating with others so that youth receive consistent messages beginning at early ages. We know that both males and females engage in cyber bullying and, therefore, prevention messages need to be given to everyone. Yet as we discussed in Chapter 4, there appears to be more cyber bullying as well as victimization among females at certain grade levels, at least in American populations. Therefore, it makes sense for community organizations targeting young females to specifically address this topic, e.g., Girl Scouts, Girls Inc., and Girls on the Run.

As discussed in Chapter 4, because cyber bullying can be a form of online retaliation by victims of traditional bullying, we encourage educators to do everything possible to address traditional bullying at school to avoid bully–victim conflicts escalating online. Incorporating research-based bullying prevention programs that also discuss cyber bullying is an important step in the prevention of cyber bullying in schools. While some schools may wish to incorporate curricula specific to cyber bullying, we recommend that such curricula tie into a comprehensive bullying prevention program that focuses on steps that bystanders can take to prevent or intervene in any form of bullying behavior among their peers. In addition to educating students about cyber bullying, teachers and administration need training regarding the seriousness of cyber bullying, and school districts should include cyber bullying in their acceptable use of technology polices and their bullying policies.

Youth who believe that cyber bullying is just a form of "online entertainment" need messages from their schools and communities that such behavior is, in fact, a form of bullying that is malicious and may have far-reaching consequences. Internet Service Providers, as well as Web sites popular among youth, often have acceptable use policies that provide guidelines for using their services, plus consequences for violation of the guidelines. Many of these youth-oriented Web sites include safety tips and guidelines for appropriate Net etiquette that parents can review with their children.

Young people also need to be aware that some forms of online bullying are considered criminal acts. While laws differ across countries and states, cyber bullying may meet the definition of libel, harassment, stalking, or even sexual exploitation in a given community. The myth of online anonymity is another issue presented in Chapter 3 that needs to be addressed in our prevention efforts. Youth who falsely believe that posting under a screen name protects their true identities may be more likely to abstain from cyber bullying if they realize that comments can still be traced back to their accounts. The media could also be a tool for prevention in addressing these myths by incorporating public service announcements targeting both parents and youth on the harmfulness of cyber bullying as well as the lack of true anonymity. Youth need to receive consistent messages from parents, educators, and community members (including members of the online community) that no one is invisible online, that cyber bullying is harmful and possibly criminal, and that harmful messages can often be traced back to the perpetrator.

How Can We Use this Information to Intervene in Cyber Bullying?

We have attempted to provide helpful tips for both parents and educators in responding to cyber bullying in Chapters 5 and 6 and to outline legal obligations of educators in Chapter 7. While a variety of actions are possible when dealing with cyber bullying, many educators and parents are unfamiliar with how to intervene (or are unsure of their legal obligations or limits in doing so) and do not begin to educate themselves until a child or student has been victimized. In addition, adults cannot intervene if they do not know that abuses are occurring. As mentioned throughout this book, participants in our focus groups indicate that students are reluctant to report cyber bullying because they lack confidence in adults' ability to provide assistance or intervene effectively without making matters worse. Punishing the victim by banning his or her use of technology or telling students that educators are not able to intervene in cyber bullying situations will result in a failure of young people to trust adults to respond in a helpful manner, thus discouraging their reporting of abuse. Adults need to encourage youth to report cyber bullying by frequently discussing cyber bullying, providing nonthreatening reporting mechanisms at school, and explaining and reassuring students that adults can be of assistance. Adults at home can respond proactively by reminding children that if they are bullied online they will be supported rather than punished for telling an adult. Adults who take time to familiarize themselves with the technologies that are popular with youth will be more likely to intervene quickly and calmly when cyber bullying occurs. In addition, school administrators should work closely with local law enforcement when cyber bullying and cyber threats become criminal in nature.

We noted in Chapter 5 that if the parents of a targeted student learn that the perpetrator of the cyber bullying is a student at their child's school, they may need to meet with school officials and request assistance in ending the abuse. Parents should be prepared to share evidence of the cyber bullying and also request investigation of any traditional bullying that may occur on campus. Educators need to support the targeted students and their parents by investigating and, where appropriate, having serious talks with the students engaged in cyber bullying behavior. They should also notify the parents of the student engaged in cyber bullying behavior if they have evidence to support the targeted student's claim. Of course, parents may also be able to contact the parents of the student engaged in cyber bullying on their own when it is not a fellow student, or when they wish to first attempt to end the cyber bullying without the school's involvement. However, such interactions may be emotionally charged and difficult to handle. Finally, student assistance team staff (administrators, counselors, psychologists, and social workers) may find a restorative justice model, as outlined in Chapter 6, useful in attempting to resolve cyber bullying situations in a manner that is beneficial to all parties.

In Chapters 5 and 6, we discussed how to report abuse posted or sent via text messages, e-mail, instant messages, and social networking sites, noting that many youth-oriented Web sites have links to report cyber bullying, and ISPs and cell phone providers are generally responsive to reports of cyber bullying over their networks. However, we recognize that new technologies and sites will continue to emerge that provide new opportunities for abuse. That is why we also recommend that adults use youth as resources, not only to mentor their peers on appropriate Internet use, but also to advise adults on the online activities that youth frequent.

Where Do We Go from Here?

Our narrow focus on cyber bullying was necessary to bring attention to this form of online abuse that has erupted quickly on our landscape. Yet it really must be part of a larger dialogue about media literacy that is occurring in the United States and in many countries globally. Much attention has been given to the role that television has played in shaping our culture over the past 50 years. The suggestions that experts in the field give to parents for helping their children to become media literate and to mitigate the negative messages viewed via the television are also applicable, to a degree, to the Internet. The challenge to date is that "surfing the Internet" is largely a solitary habit; however, making it more of a family or community experience will help parents, educators, and youth leaders deal with some of the current concerns we face. Consider these tips advocated by media literacy expert Ronald Slaby:

> Parents, teachers, and other adults can directly alter the effects of media violence on children and youth when they watch programs and movies with them while commenting critically on the depiction of violence and discussing nonviolent alternatives; they also can teach media literacy skills that

permit young viewers to "see through" the falseness of particular media presentations. (Slaby, 2002, p. 329)

In addition to watching television programs and movies with our children, it is time to "surf the Internet" with our children and teach the skills that are necessary to ensure that the use of the Internet is an educational and social enhancer, rather than a negative force in our children's lives. The 11th Annual Media Wise Video Game Report Card points out that "every child who engages in playing video games is undertaking a powerful, developmental experiment – the results of which we don't understand" (Walsh, Gentile, Walsh, & Bennett., 2006). The same could be said of the children who are spending vast amounts of time online, whether it is through social networking sites, online gaming, instant messaging, or text messaging. As multiple new ways to interact online become available, the challenge to adults in general and parents in particular is to become familiar with the myriad of new methods by which youth are engaged in online activities, and to actively participate in these new technologies. Parents and educators need to address the online experiences of children by communicating media guidelines and expectations for appropriate use, defining and explaining why certain activities are inappropriate, setting time limits, and using parental controls or district filters. As the Video Game Report Card suggests, adults also need to "watch what your kids watch, play what your kids play" (Walsh et al., 2006, p. 2). In the online world, Walsh's advice could be adapted to include, "Visit the sites your kids visit, use the technologies your kids use."

Rather than focusing on only the negative aspects of the Internet, parents and educators can find ways to engage youth in using popular technologies in meaningful ways. As we discussed in Chapter 5, an example of incorporating popular youth technology would be to teach youth how to use a social networking site to promote themselves in a positive manner that would appeal to prospective admissions counselors, employers and, of course, friends. Educators can develop lessons that teach students to appropriately post their opinions on blogging sites using topics that engage youth such as the environment, politics, and community service. There may be a few adults who could benefit from this type of training as well!

Engaging our youth in a variety of activities where they are "unplugged" will make it easier to limit their time online. Inviting children to participate in regular physical activity and creative outlets such as art and music will be more effective than simply nagging a child to turn off the computer.

Finally, through a concerted effort to engage in the media experience of our children, the lines of communication can be opened and greater understanding gained, not only of the harmful uses of technology, but the many benefits that await our children who use technology wisely.

Note

1. Since the current minimum age for MySpace is 14, it is also safe to assume that some of these students are violating the site policies by having a profile.

References

Act 115, 86th Gen. Assembly (Ar. 2007).

Aftab, P. (2006). http://www.wiredsafety.nct.

Agatston, P., & Carpenter, M. (2006). Electronic bullying survey. Unpublished manuscript.

Akwagyiram, A. (2005, May 12). Does "happy slapping" exist? Retrieved July 3, 2006, from http://news.bbc.co.uk/1/hi/uk/4539913.stm.

Alaska Stat. § 14.33.250 (2007).

Alley, R., & Limber, S. P. (in press). Bullying issues in schools: Legal issues for school personnel. In S. M. Swearer & D. Espelage (Eds.), *Bullying prevention and intervention: Realistic strategies for schools.* New York: Sage.

Americans with Disabilities Act of 1990, Title II, 42 U.S.C. § 12134 (2006).

Anderson, M., Kaufman, J., Simon, T. R., Barrios, L., Paulozzi, L., Ryan, G., Hamnond, R., Modzeleski, W., Feucht, T., Potter, L., & the School-Associated Violent Deaths Study Group (2001). School-associated violent deaths in the United States, 1994–1999. *Journal of the American Medical Association, 286,* 2695–2702.

Archive of CRN home page topics for discussion: On the fatal stabbing of a sixth-grade girl (2004, June 11). Retrieved November 13, 2006, from http://www.childresearch.net/cgi-bin/topics/column.pl?no=00215&page=1.

Arseneault, L., Walsh, E., Trzesniewski, K., Newcombe, R., Caspi, A., & Moffitt, T. E. (2006). Bullying victimization uniquely contributes to adjustment problems in young children: A nationally representative cohort study. *Pediatrics, 118,* 130–138.

Baldry, A. C. (2003). Bullying in schools and exposure to domestic violence. *Child Abuse & Neglect, 27,* 713–732.

Baldry, A. C. (2004). "What about bullying?" An experimental field study to understand students' attitudes towards bullying and victimization in Italian middle schools. *British Journal of Educational Psychology, 74,* 583–598.

Bargh, J. A., McKenna, K. Y. A., & Fitzsimons, G. M. (2002). Can you see the real me? Activation and expression of the "true self" on the Internet. *Journal of Social Issues, 58,* 33–48.

Becker, K., & Schmidt, M. H. (2005). When kids seek help on-line: Internet chat rooms and suicide. *Reclaiming Children and Youth, 13,* 229–230.

Beder, M. (2006, May 23). Free speech fight hits Kirkwood High. *St. Louis Post-Dispatch.* Retrieved July 3, 2006, from http://www.stltoday.com/stltoday/news/ Stories.nsf/education/story/CD0CE6B1B78A488D.

Belluck, P. (2006, July 2). Web postings worry summer camp directors. *The New York Times.* Retrieved July 3, 2006, from http://news.zdnet.com/2100-9588_22- 6087060.html.

Belsey, B. (2006). Cyber bullying: An emerging threat to the "always on" generation. Retrieved July 4, 2006, from http://www.cyberbullying.ca.

Beran, T., & Li, Q. (2005). Cyber-harassment: A study of a new method for an old behavior. *Journal of Educational Computing Research, 32,* 265–277.

Bethel School District v. Fraser, 478 U.S. 675 (1986).

Biersdorfer, J. D. (2006, August 21). How to digitally hide (somewhat) in plain sight. *The New York Times,* p. B-3.

Bjorkqvist, K., Lagerspetz, K. M. J., & Osterman, K. (1992). The development of direct and indirect aggressive strategies in males and females. In K. Bjorkqvist & P. Niemela (Eds.), *Of mice and women: Aspects of female aggression* (pp. 51– 64). San Diego, CA: Academic Press.

Black, S. (2003). An ongoing evaluation of the bullying prevention program in Philadelphia schools: Student survey and student observation data. Paper presented at the Safety in Numbers Conference, Atlanta, GA.

Black, S. A., & Jackson, E. (in press). Using bullying incident density to evaluate the Olweus Bullying Prevention Programme. *School Psychology International.*

Black's Law Dictionary (2004), 8th ed., B. A. Garner (Ed.). St. Paul, MN: West Group.

Blair, A., & Norfolk, A. (2004, September 25). Modern bullies are seeking victims through cyber space. *The Times (London),* Home news, 3.

Boulton, M. J. (1994). Understanding and preventing bullying in the junior school playground. In P. K. Smith & S. Sharp (Eds.), *School bullying* (pp. 132–159). London: Routledge.

Boulton, M. J., & Underwood, K. (1992). Bully victim problems among middle school children. *British Journal of Educational Psychology, 62,* 73–87.

Buhs, E. S., Ladd, G. W. & Herald, S. L. (2006). Peer exclusion and victimization: Processes that mediate the relation between peer group rejection and children's classroom engagement and achievement? *Journal of Educational Psychology, 98,* 1–13.

Bullycide memorial page: Cases of bullycide (n.d.). Retrieved September 16, 2006, from http://www.bullyonline.org/schoolbully/cases.htm.

Burssens,D., & Vettenburg, N. (2006). Restorative group conferencing at school: A constructive response to serious incidents. *Journal of School Violence, 5,* 5–16.

Byrne, B. J. (1994). Bullies and victims in school settings with reference to some Dublin schools. *Irish Journal of Psychology, 15*, 574–586.

Cairns, R. B., Cairns, B. D., Neckerman, H. J., Gest, S. D., Gariépy, J. L., (1988). Social networks and aggressive behaviour: Peer support or peer rejection? *Developmental Psychology, 24*, 815–823.

Camodeca, M., & Goossens, F. A. (2005). Aggression, social cognitions, anger and sadness in bullies and victims. *Journal of Child Psychology and Psychiatry, 46*, 186–197.

Carpenter, M. (2003, May 25). "R U There? Wt R U Doing Aftr Scl?": (Or how the young are taking over the world through instant messaging). *Pennsylvania Post Gazette*, p. A-1.

Carrington, P. M. (2006, June 6). Internet increases cyberbullying. Retrieved July 3, 2006, from http://timesdispatch.com/servlet/Satellite?pagename=Common% 2TMGArticle%2FPri.

Center for the Digital Future at the USC Annenberg School (2005). *The 2005 digital future report.* Available: http://www.digitalcenter.org

Chaker, A. M. (2007, January 24). Schools act to short-circuit spread of "cyberbullying". *The Wall Street Journal*, D1.

Charach, A., Pepler, D. J., & Zieler, S. (1995). Bullying at school: A Canadian perspective. *Education Canada, 35*, 12–18.

Charny, B. (2003, December 2). Gymgoers wary of camera phones. Retrieved July 3, 2006, from http://news.com.com/2102-1037_3-5112823.html.

Children's Internet Protection Act, 20 U.S.C. § 9134(f) (2007).

Civil Rights Act of 1964, 42 U.S.C. § 1983 (2006).

Cobb County School District Administrative Rules (2007). Retrieved February 4, 2007, from http://www.cobbk12.org/centraloffice/adminrules/J_Rules/Rule% 20JICDA-H.html.

Conn. Gen. Stat. § 10-222d (2006).

County of Sacramento v Lewis, 523 U.S. 833 (1998).

Coy v. Board of Education of the North Canton City Schools, 205F Supp. 2d 791 (2002).

Craig, W. M. (1998). The relationship among bullying, victimization, depression, anxiety, and aggression in elementary school children. *Personality & Individual Differences, 24*, 123–130.

Crisp, J. (2006, August 2). Fairytale ending for girl who defied yobs. *Macclesfield Express*. Retrieved August 2, 2006, from http://www.macclesfield-express.co. uk/news/s/215914.

C.R.S. 22-32-109.1 (2006).

Cunningham, P. B., Henggeler, S. W., Limber, S. P., Melton, G. B., & Nation, M. A. (2000). Patterns and correlates of gun ownership among nonmetropolitan and rural middle school students. *Journal of Clinical Child Psychology, 29*, 432–442.

Currie, C., Roberts, C., Morgan, A., Smith, R., Settertobulte, W., Sandal, O., & Barnekow Rasmussen, V. (Eds.) (2004). *Young people's health in context. Health behaviour in school-aged children (HBSC) study: International report from the 2001/2002 survey.* Retrieved February 20, 2007, from http://www.hbsc.org/downloads/IntReport04/HBSCFullReport0102.pdf.

Cyber bullies target girl (2006, July 5). *BBC News.* Retrieved July 5, 2006, from http://newsvote.bbc.Co.uk/mpapps/pagetools/print/news.bbc.co.uk/1/hi/England/nottinghams.

Cyber bullying (n.d.). Retrieved August 22, 2006, from http://www.loveourchildusa.org/parent_cyberbullying.php.

Davis v. Monroe County Bd. of Educ., 526 U.S. 629 (1999).

Dawkins, J. L. (1996). Bullying, physical disability, and the pediatric patient. *Developmental Medicine and Child Neurology, 38*, 603–612.

DeShaney v. Winnebago County Dep't of Soc. Servs., 489 U.S. 189, 197 (1989).

DeVoe, J.F., Peter, K., Noonan, M., Snyder, T.D., & Baum, K. (2005). *Indicators of school crime and safety: 2005* (NCES 2006–001/NCJ 210697). U.S. Departments of Education and Justice. Washington, DC: U.S. Government Printing Office.

Dreikurs, R., & Stoltz, V. (1991). *Children: The challenge.* New York: Plume.

Duncan, R. D. (1999). Peer and sibling aggression: An investigation of intra-and extra-familial bullying. *Journal of Interpersonal Violence, 14*, 871–886.

Duncan, R. D. (2004). The impact of family relationships on school bullies and victims. In D. L. Espelage, & S. M. Swearer (Eds.), *Bullying in American schools: A social-ecological perspective on prevention and intervention* (pp. 227–244). Mahwah, NJ: Lawrence Erlbaum.

Dybwad, B. (2005, April 26). Happy slapping increasingly slap-happy? Retrieved April 16, 2006, from http://www.engadget.com/2005/04/26/happy-slapping-increasingly-slap-happy/.

Dyrli, O. E. (2005, September). Cyber bullying: Online bullying affects every school district. Retrieved April 16, 2006, from http://www.DistrictAdministration.com.

Eagan, S. K., & Perry, D. G. (1998). Does low self-regard invite victimization? *Developmental Psychology, 34*, 299–309.

Education Amendments Act of 1972, Title IX, 20 U.S.C. § 1681(a) (2006).

Eisenberg, M. E., & Aalsma, M. C. (2005). Bullying and peer victimization: Position paper of the Society of Adolescent Medicine. *Journal of Adolescent Health, 36*, 88–91.

Eisenberg, M. E., Neumark-Sztainer, D., & Perry, C. (2003). Peer harassment, school connectedness, and academic achievement. *Journal of School Health, 73*, 311–316.

Espelage, D. L., & Swearer, S. M. (2003). Research on school bullying and victimization: What have we learned and where do we go from here? *School Psychology Review, 32*, 365–383.

FAQ-MySpace.com. (2006) Retrieved December 16, 2006, from http://www.myspace.com/Modules/Help/Pages/HelpCenter.aspx?

FBI: Blogging can be dangerous (2005, October 30). Retrieved April 16, 2006, from http://www.bloggersblog.com/familyblogs.

Fein, R., Vossekuil, B., Pollack, W., Borum, R., Modzeleski, W., & Reddy, M. (2002). *Threat assessment in schools: A guide to managing threatening situations and to creating safe school climates.* Washington, DC: U.S. Department of Education, Office of Elementary and Secondary Education, Safe and Drug-Free Schools Program and U.S. Secret Service, National Threat Assessment Center.

Fekkes, M., Pijpers, F. I. M., & Verloove-VanHorick, S. P. (2004). Bullying behavior and associations with psychosomatic complaints and depression in victims. *Journal of Pediatrics, 144,* 17–22.

Fekkes, M., Pijpers, F. I. M., Fredriks, A. M., Vogels, T., & Verloove-VanHorick, S. P. (2006). Do bullied children get ill, or do ill children get bullied? A prospective cohort study on the relationship between bullying and health-related symptoms. *Pediatrics, 117,* 1568–1574.

Fight Crime: Invest In Kids (2006, August 17). Communications. Retrieved August 17, 2006, from http://www.fightcrime.org/releases/php?id=231.

Fight crime sponsored studies: Opinion research corporation. (2006). *Cyber bully preteen.* Available: http://www.fightcrime.org/cyberbullying/cyberbullyingpreteen.pdf.

Fight crime sponsored studies: Opinion research corporation. (2006). *Cyber bully teen.* Available: http://www.fightcrime.org/cyberbullying/cyberbullyingteen.pdf.

Finkelhor, D., Mitchell, K., & Wolak, J. (2000). Online victimization: A report on the nation's youth. National Center for Missing & Exploited Children. Retrieved September 16, 2006, from http://www.unh.edu/ccrc/Youth_Internet_info_page.html.

Finkelhor, D., Ormrod, R., Turner, H., & Hamby, S. L. (2005). The victimization of children and youth: A comprehensive, national survey. *Child Maltreatment, 10,* 5–25.

Flores v. Morgan Hill Unified Sch. Dist., 324 F. 3d 1130, 1134 (9th Cir. 2003).

Focus: Brave new world (2006, July 9). Retrieved July 9, 2006, from: http://www.timesonline.co.uk/article/0,,2095-2261684,00.html.

Fonzi, A., Genta, M. L., Menesini, E., Bacchini, D., Bonino, S., & Costabile, A. (1999). Italy. In P. K. Smith, Y. Morita, J. Junger-Tasl, D. Olweus, R. Catalano, & P. Slee (Eds.), *The nature of school bullying: A cross-national perspective* (pp. 140–156). London: Routledge.

Franek, M. (2005/2006). Foiling cyber bullies in the new wild west. *Educational Leadership, 63,* 39–43.

Frederick v. Juneau School Board, No. 03-35701 (9th Cir, March 10, 2006).

Garofalo, R., Wolf, R. C., Kessel, S., Palfrey, S. J., & DuRant, R. H. (1998). The association between health risk behaviors and sexual orientation among a school-based sample of adolescents. *Pediatrics, 101,* 895–902.

Gehrke, R. (2006, August 19). Shurtleff joins child advocate group's campaign against cyber bullying. *The Salt Lake Tribune.* Retrieved August 22, 2006, from http://www.sltrib.com.

Girl tormented by phone bullies (2001, January 16). Retrieved July 5, 2006, from http://news.bbc.co.uk/1/ht/uk_news/education/1120597.stm.

Graham, S., & Juvonen, J. (2002). Ethnicity, peer harassment, and adjustment in middle school: An exploratory study. *Journal of Early Adolescence, 22,* 173–199.

Granneman, S. (2006, July 3). My space, a place without MyParents. Retrieved July 3, 2006, from http://www.securityfocus.com/print/columnists/408.

Gray, K. (2006, September 14). How mean can teens be? Retrieved January 4, 2007, from http://abclocal.go.com/kgo/story?section=bizarre&id=4560512&ft=print.

Gross, E. F., Juvonen, J., & Gable, S. L. (2002). Internet use and well-being in adolescence. *Journal of Social Issues, 58,* 75–90.

Grossman, L. (2006, December 13). *Time*'s person of the year: You [Electronic version]. *Time, 168.*

Harachi, T. W., Catalano, R. F., & Hawkins, D. (1999). Canada. In P. K. Smith, Y. Morita, J. Junger-Tasl, D. Olweus, R. Catalano, & P. Slee (Eds.), *The nature of school bullying: A cross-national perspective* (pp. 296–306). London: Routledge.

Harris Interactive and GLSEN (2005). *From teasing to torment: School climate in America, A survey of students and teachers.* New York: GLSEN.

Harris, S., Petrie, G., & Willoughby, W. (2002). Bullying among 9th graders: An exploratory study. *NASSP Bulletin, 86,* 630.

Hass, N. (2006, January 8). In your Facebook.com. *The New York Times,* Section 4-A, pp. 30–31.

Hawker, D. S. J., & Boulton, M. J. (2000). Twenty years' research on peer victimization and psychosocial maladjustment: A meta-analytic review of cross-sectional studies. *Journal of Child Psychology and Psychiatry, 41,* 441–455.

Haynie, D. L., Nansel, T., Eitel, P., Crump., A.D., Saylor, L., Yu, K., & Simons-Morton, B. (2001). Bullies, victims and bully/victims: Distinct groups of at-risk youth. *Journal of Early Adolescence, 21,* 29–49.

Hazelwood School District v. Kuhlmeier, 484 U. S. 269 (1988).

Health Resources and Services Administration (2006). Take a stand, lend a hand: Stop bullying now. Available: http://stopbullyingnow.hrsa.gov/adult/indexAdult.asp?Area=cyberbullying.

Hodges, E. V. E., & Perry, D. G. (1996). Victims of peer abuse: An overview. *Journal of Emotional and Behavioural Problems, 5,* 23–28.

Honigsbaum, M. (2005, April 26). Concern over rise of "happy slapping" craze. *The Guardian.* Retrieved April 26, 2006, from http://www.guardian.co.uk/mobile/article/0,2763,1470214,00.html.

Hoover, J. H., Oliver, R., & Hazler, R. J. (1992). Bullying: Perceptions of adolescent victims in the Midwestern USA. *School Psychology International, 13,* 5–16.

Idaho Code Ann. § 18-917A (2006).

Ind. Code Ann. § 20-33-8-0.2 (2006).

Internet bullies: The growing problem of internet bullying and "flaming." (2006, August). Retrieved August 22, 2006, from http://www.safesurfers.org/chat_room_flaming.htm.

i-SAFE (2004–2005). National assessment report: The effectiveness and measurable results of Internet safety education.

i-SAFE (2005–2006). At risk online: National assessment of youth on the Internet and the effectiveness of i-SAFE Internet safety education.

i-SAFE (2006–2007). National Assessment Center database: Query of pre-assessment questions for 5th through 8th grades nationwide for 06–07 academic year.

Janssen, I., Craig, W. M., Boyce, W. F., & Pickett, W. (2004). Associations between overweight and obesity within bullying behaviors in school-aged children. *Pediatrics, 113,* 1187–1194.

Jenkins, H. (2006). Discussion: MySpace and Deleting Online Predators Act (DOPA). Retrieved May 30, 2006, from http://www.digitaldivide.net/articles/view.php?ArticleID=592.html.

J.S. v. Bethlehem Area School District, 757 A. 2d 412 (Pa. Commw. 2000).

Juvonen, J. Graham, S., & Schuster, M. A. (2003). Bullying among young adolescents: The strong, the weak, and the troubled. *Pediatrics, 112*, 1231–1237.

Keith, S., & Martin, M. E. (2005). Cyber bullying: Creating a culture of respect in a cyber world. *Reclaiming Children and Youth, 13*, 224–228.

Kennedy, K. (2006, April 23) Not-so-MySpace anymore. *The Ledger.com*. Retrieved July 12, 2006, from http://www.theledger.com/apps/pbcs.dll/articleID=/20060423/News/.

Killion v. Franklin Regional School District, 136 F. Supp 2d 446 (W.D. Pa. 2001).

Kim, Y. S., Koh, Y., & Leventhal, B. (2005). School bullying and suicidal risk in Korean middle school students. *Pediatrics, 115*, 357–363.

King, L. (2006, August 15). No hiding from online bullies. Retrieved September 16, 2006, from http://www.news-leader.com/apps/pbcs.dll/article?Date=20060815.

K.M. v. Hyde Park Cent. Sch. Dist., 381 F. Supp. 2d 343 (S.D.N.Y. 2005).

Kochenderfer, B. J., & Ladd, G. W. (1996). Peer victimization: Cause or consequence of school maladjustment? *Child Development, 67*, 1305–1317.

Kohler, C. (2007, January 23). Teen tube terrors. Retrieved January 30, 2007, from http://www.cablevisioneditorials.com/content/LI/2007/LI_2007-01-23.html.

Kowalski, R. M. (2000). "I was only kidding!": Victims' and perpetrators' perceptions of teasing. *Personality and Social Psychology Bulletin, 26*, 231–241.

Kowalski, R. M., & Limber, S. P. (2006). Cyber bullying among middle school children. Manuscript under review.

Kowalski, R. M., & Witte, J. (2006). Youth Internet survey. Available: http://www.camss.clemson.edu/KowalskiSurvey/servelet/Page1.

Kraft, E. (2006). Cyber bullying: A worldwide trend of misusing technology to harass others, *The Internet Society II: Advances in Education, Commerce, & Governance, 36*, 155–166.

Kraut, R., Patterson, M., Lundmark, V., Kiesler, S., Mukopadhyay, T., & Scherlis. W. (1998). Internet paradox: A social technology that reduces social involvement and psychological well-being? *American Psychologist, 53*, 1017–1031.

Kruger, J., Epley, N., Parker, J., & Ng, Z. (2005). Egocentrism over e-mail: Can we communicate as well as we think? *Journal of Personality and Social Psychology, 89*, 925–936.

Kumpulainen, K., & Raasnen, E. (2000). Children involved in bullying at elementary school age: Their psychiatric symptoms and deviance in adolescence. *Child Abuse & Neglect, 24*, 1567–1577.

Kumpulainen, K., Raasnen, E., & Puura, K. (2001). Psychiatric disorders and the use of mental health services among children involved in bullying. *Aggressive Behavior, 27*, 102–110.

La. R. S. 17: 416.13 (2006).

Lackner, C. (2006, September 15). Blog reveals "poster boy" for school shooters. *Ottawa Citizen*. Retrieved September 15, 2006, from http://www.canada.com/ottawacitizen/news/story.html?id=341f18cd-af34-412c-91f6-7e87aa30382c.

Lagerspetz, K. M. J., Bjorkqvist, K., & Peltonen, T. (1988). Is indirect aggression typical of females? Gender differences in aggressiveness in 11- to 12-year-old children. *Aggressive Behavior, 14,* 403–414.

Lampert, A. (2006, April 8). Star wars kid settles lawsuit: Was victim of cyber bullying: Classmates ridiculed youth after video antics with mock lightsabre were spread across Internet. *The Gazette (Montreal),* p. A8.

Leary, M. R. (1983). Social anxiousness: The construct and its measurement. *Journal of Personality Assessment, 47,* 66–75.

Leary, M. R., Kowalski, R. M., Smith, L., & Phillips, S. (2003). Violence and rejection: Case studies of the school shootings. *Aggressive Behavior, 29,* 202–214.

Leith, S. (2006, December 18). Cingular hooks up with MySpace.com. *The Atlanta Journal-Constitution,* p. A14.

Lenhart, A., & Madden, M. (2007, January 7). Social networking websites and teens: An overview. Retrieved January 28, 2007, from http://www.pewinternet.org.

Lenhart, A., Madden, M., & Hitlin, P. (2005, July 27). Teens and technology: Youth are leading the transition to a fully wired and mobile nation. Retrieved July 3, 2006, from http://www.pewinternet.org.

Lenhart, A., Rainie, L., & Lewis, O. (2001). Teenage life online: Pew Internet & American Life Project. Retrieved July 3, 2006, from http://www.pewinternet.org.

Levine, B. (2006). Taking on the cyber bullies. Retrieved May 10, 2006, from http://www.newsfactor.com/story.xhtml?story_id=43130.

Li, Q. (2006). Cyber bullying in schools: A research of gender differences. *School Psychology International, 27,* 157–170.

Limber, S. P. (2003). Efforts to address bullying in U.S. Schools. *Journal of Health Education, 34,* S-23–S-29.

Limber, S. P. (2004). Implementation of the Olweus Bullying Prevention Program: Lessons learned from the field. In D. Espelage & S. Swearer (Eds.) *Bullying in American schools: A social-ecological perspective on prevention and intervention* (pp. 351–363). Mahwah, NJ: Lawrence Erlbaum.

Limber, S. P. (2006). The Olweus Bullying Prevention Program: An overview of its implementation and research basis. In S. Jimerson & M. Furlong (Eds.), *Handbook of school violence and school safety: From research to practice* (pp. 293–307). Mahwah, NJ: Erlbaum.

Limber, S. P., Nation, M., Tracy, A. J., Melton, G. B., & Flerx, V. (2004). Implementation of the Oweus Bullying Prevention Program in the Southeastern United States. In P. K. Smith, D. Pepler, & K. Rigby (Eds.), *Bullying in schools: How successful can interventions be?* (pp. 55–79). Cambridge, UK: Cambridge University Press.

Limber, S. P. (2006). Peer victimization: The nature and prevalence of bullying among children and youth. In N. E. Dowd, D. G. Singer, & R. F. Wilson (Eds.), *Handbook of children, culture, and violence* (pp. 331–332). Thousand Oaks, CA: Sage.

Magid, L., & Collier, A. (2007). *MySpace unraveled.* Berkeley, CA: Peachpit Press.

Maine School Management Association Sample Policy (2006). Retrieved February 17, 2007, from http://mainegov-images.informe.org/cabinet/Bullying_000.pdf.

Martlew, M., & Hodson, J. (1991). Children with mild learning difficulties in an integrated and in a special school: comparisons of behaviour, teasing and teachers' attitudes. *British Journal of Educational Psychology, 61,* 355–372.

Maryland State Department of Education (2005). Harassment or intimidation (bullying) reporting form. Retrieved May 3, 2007, from http://www.maryland-publicschools.org/nr/rdonlyres/0700b064-c2b3-41fc-a6cf-d3dae4969707/7243/harassmentorintimidationbullyingreportingform.pdf.

McKenna, K. Y. A., & Bargh, J. A. (2000). Plan 9 from cyberspace: The implications of the Internet for personality and social psychology. *Personality and Social Psychology Bulletin, 4,* 57–75.

Md. Education Code Ann. § 7-424 (2006).

Meadows, B., Bergal, J., Helling, S., Odell, J., Piligian, E., Howard, C., Lopez, M., Atlas, D., & Hochberg, L. (2005). The web: The bully's new playground. *People, 63*(10), 152–156.

Melton, G. B., Limber, S. P., Cunningham, P., Osgood, D., W., Chambers, J., Flerx, V., et al. (1998). Violence among rural youth. Final report. Washington, DC: U.S. Department of Justice, Office of Justice Programs, Office of Juvenile Justice and Delinquency Prevention.

Mikle, J. (2005, December 8). Harassed student's court win upheld. *Asbury Park Press.* § 160.775 R.S.Mo. (2007).

Nabuzoka, D., & Smith, P. K. (1993). Sociometric status and social behaviour of children with and without learning difficulties. *Journal of Child Psychology and Psychiatry, 34,* 1435–1448.

Nansel, T. R., Overpeck, M. D., Pilla, R. S., Ruan, W. J., Simmons-Morton, B., & Scheidt, P. (2001). Bullying behavior among U.S. youth: Prevalence and association with psychosocial adjustment. *Journal of the American Medical Association, 285,* 2094–2100.

National Children's Home (NCH; 2002). 1 in 4 children are victims of "on-line bullying." Available: http://www.nch.org.uk/information/index.php?i=77&r=125.

Naylor, P. Cowie, H., & del Rey, R. (2001). Coping strategies of secondary school children in response to being bullied. *Child Psychology and Psychiatry Review, 6,* 114–120. www.netlingo.com.

Nev. Rev. Stat. Ann. § 388.135 (2006).

New Jersey v. T.L.O., 469 U.S. 325 (1985).

New York State School Board Association (2006). *Sample policy on harassment, hazing, and bullying.* Latham, NY: Author.

N.J. Stat. § 18A:37-14 (2007).

O.C.G.A. § 20-2-751.4 (2006).

Ohio girls sentenced for MySpace threats (2006, June 28). Retrieved June 30, 2006, from http://mycrimespace.thetrenchcoat.com.

Ohio Resource Network for Safe and Drug Free Schools and Communities (n.d.) Retrieved February 17, 2007, from http://www.ebasedprevention.org/uploaded-Files/robbs/Sample_District_Policy2(1).doc.70 Okl. St. § 24-100.3 (2006).

Olsen, S. (2006a, April 11). MySpace reaching out to parents. Retrieved July 3, 2006, from http://news.com.com/MySpace+reaching+out+to+parents/2009-1041-3-6059679.html?tag=nl.

Olsen, S. (2006b).Wi-fi gives kids access to unchaperoned Net. Retrieved September 12, 2006, from http://news.com.com/Wi-i+gives+access+to+unchaperoned +Net/2009-1025_3-6114522.html.

Olweus, D. (1978). *Aggression in the schools: Bullies and whipping boys*. Washington, DC: Wiley.

Olweus, D. (1993a). *Bullying at school: What we know and what we can do*. New York: Blackwell.

Olweus, D. (1993b). Victimization by peers: Antecedents and long-term outcomes. In K. H. Rubin & J. H. B. Asendort (Eds.), *Social withdrawal, inhibition, and shyness* (pp. 315–341). Hillsdale, NJ: Erlbaum.

Olweus, D. (1994). Annotation: Bullying at school: Basic facts and effects of a school-based intervention program. *Journal of Child Psychology and Psychiatry, 35*, 1171–1190.

Olweus, D. (2001). *Olweus' core program against bullying and antisocial behavior: A teacher handbook*. Bergen, Norway: Author.

Olweus, D. (1996/2004). The Revised Olweus Bully/Victim Questionnaire. Bergen, Norway: Research Centre for Health Promotion (HEMIL), University of Bergen, N-5015 Bergen, Norway.

Olweus, D. (2004a). The Olweus Bullying Prevention Programme: Design and implementation issues and a new national initiative in Norway. In P. K. Smith, D. Pepler, & K. Rigby (Eds.), *Bullying in schools: How successful can interventions be?* (pp. 13–36). Cambridge, UK: Cambridge University Press.

Olweus, D. (2004b). Bullying at school: Prevalence estimation, a useful evaluation design, and a new national initiative in Norway. *Association for Child Psychology and Psychiatry Occasional Papers No. 23*, 5–17.

Olweus, D. Limber, S. P., Flerx, V. C., Mullin, N., Riese, J., & Snyder, M. (2007). *Olweus Bullying Prevention Program: Schoolwide guide*. Center City, MN: Hazelden.

Olweus, D., Limber, S. P., & Mihalic, S. (1999). *The bullying prevention program: Blueprints for violence prevention, Vol. 10*. Center for the Study and Prevention of Violence: Boulder, CO.

ORC Ann. 3313.666 (2006).

ORS § 339.351 (2006).

Ortega, R. & Mora-Merchan, J. A. (1999). Spain. In P. K. Smith, Y. Morita, J. Junger-Tas, D. Olweus, R. Catalano, & P. Slee (Eds.), The nature of school bullying: A cross-national perspective (pp. 157–173). London: Routledge.

Osmond, N. (2006, August 8). Cyber bullying is a faceless crime. *The Gulf News*. Retrieved August 8, 2006 from http://www.gulfnews.ca/index.cfm?iid= 1684&sid=12668.

Owens, L., Shute, R., & Slee, P. (2000). "I'm in and you're out . . .": Explanations for teenage girls' indirect aggression. *Psychology, Evolution, & Gender, 2.1*, 19–46.

Pardington, S. (2005, November 27). Is your little angel raising hell online? *The Sunday Oregonian*, p. A01.

Patchin, J. W., & Hinduja, S. (2006). Bullies move beyond the schoolyard: A preliminary look at cyber bullying. *Youth Violence and Juvenile Justice, 4,* 148–169.

Paulson, A. (2003, December 30). Internet bullying. *The Christian Science Monitor.* Retrieved September 25, 2006, from csmonitor.com/2003/1230/p11s01-legn. html.

Pellegrini, A. D. (2001). A longitudinal study of heterosexual relationships, aggression, and sexual harassment during the transition from primary school through middle school. *Journal of Applied Developmental Psychology, 22,* 1–15.

Pellegrini, A. D., & Bartini, M. (2000). An empirical comparison of methods of sampling aggression and victimization in school settings. *Journal of Educational Psychology, 92,* 360–366.

Pesznecker, K. (2004, July 1). District settled suit for millions. *Anchorage Daily News.*

Pham, A. (2002, September 9). Enter the "griefers." *Chicago Tribune.* Retrieved September 1, 2006, from http://www.gamegirladvance.com/archives/2002/09/09/ enter_the_griefers.html.

Poulsen, K. (2006, February 27). Scenes from the MySpace backlash. Retrieved July 3, 2006, from http://www.wired.com/news/politics/1,70254-0.html.

Prince William County Schools Code of Behavior (2006). Retrieved February 17, 2007, from http://pwcs.edu/studentservices/codeofbehavior.pdf.

Promoting civil rights and prohibiting harassment, bullying, discrimination, and hate crimes: Sample policy for Massachusetts School Districts (2005). Boston: Office of the Massachusetts Attorney General.

Pupils not the only victims of cyber bullies, says NAS/UWT (2006, July 28). *Education Parliamentary Monitor, 231,* 4.

Putting U in the picture – Mobile bullying survey 2005. Retrieved December 13, 2006, from http://www.stoptextbullying.com.

Redeker, B. (2006, September 15). Town tells white separatist singers "no hate here." Retrieved September 16, 2006, from http://articles.news.aol.com/news/ _a/town-tells-white-separatist-singers-no/.

Reese, T. (2006) Teens help teens stay safe online. Retrieved March 20, 2006, from http://www.connectforkids.org/node/4045.html.

Rehabilitation Act of 1973, Section 504, 29 U.S.C. § 794 (2006).

Rev. Code Wash. (ARCW) § 28A.300.285 (2007).

R.I. Gen. Laws § 16-21-26 (2007).

Rigby, K. (1993). School children's perceptions of their families and parents as a function of peer relations. *The Journal of Genetic Psychology, 154,* 501–513.

Rigby, K. (1994). Psychosocial functioning in families of Australian adolescent schoolchildren involved in bully/victim problems. *Journal of Family Therapy, 16,* 173–187.

Rigby, K. (1996). *Bullying in schools: And what to do about it.* Briston, PA: Jessica Kingsley Publishers.

Rigby, K. (2002). *New perspectives on bullying.* London: Jessica Kingsley.

Rigby, K., & Slee, P. T. (1993). Dimensions of interpersonal relations among Australian school children and their implications for psychological well-being. *Journal of Social Psychology, 133*, 33–42.

Rigby, K., & Slee, P. T. (1999). Australia. In P. K. Smith, Y. Morita, J. Junger-Tasl, D. Olweus, R. Catalano, & P. Slee (Eds.), *The nature of school bullying: A cross-national perspective* (pp. 324–339). London: Routledge.

Rivers, I., & Smith, P. K. (1994). Types of bullying behaviour and their correlates. *Aggressive Behavior, 20*, 359–368.

Roberts, L. D., Smith, L. M., & Pollock, C. M. (2000). "U r a lot bolder on the net": Shyness and Internet use. In W. R. Crozier (Ed.), *Shyness: Development, consolidation, and change* (pp. 121–138). New York: Routledge.

Rogers v. United States, 422 U.S. 35 (1975).

Rosenberg, M. (1965). *Society and the adolescent self-image.* Princeton, NJ: Princeton University Press.

Ross, S. (Executive Producer) (2006, September 12). *Primetime* [television broadcast]. New York: American Broadcasting Company.

Roth, D. A., Coles, M. E., & Heimberg, R. G. (2002). The relationship between memories for childhood teasing and anxiety and depression in adulthood. *Journal of Anxiety Disorders, 16*, 149–164.

Russell, D. W., Flom, E. K., Gardner, K. A., Cutrona, C. E., & Hessling, R. S. (2003). Who makes friends over the Internet?: Loneliness and the "virtual" community. *The International Scope Review, 10.*

www.ryanpatrickhalligan.org.

SB 5288, 60th Legislature (Wa. 2007).

S.C. Code Ann. § 59-63-120 (2006).

Schools face new cyber bullying menace (2006, May 28). *The New Zealand Herald.*

7-year-old's pic exploited on MySpace. (2006, June 29). Retrieved July 3, 2006, from http://mycrimespace.Thetrenchcoat.com/.

Seper, C. (2005, February 14). School bullies can land in court. *The Plain Dealer.*

SF 61, 82nd Gen. Assembly (Iowa, 2007).

Shariff, S., & Gouin, R. (2005). Cyber dilemmas: Gendered hierarchies, free expression, and cyber-safety in schools. Retrieved January 15, 2005, from http://www.oii.ox.ac.uk/research/cybersafety/extensions/pdfs/papers/shaheen_shariff.pdf.

Shields, A., & Cicchetti, D. (2001). Parental maltreatment and emotion dysregulation as risk factors for bullying and victimization in middle childhood. *Journal of Clinical Child Psychology, 30*, 349–363.

Slaby, R. G. (2002). Media violence: Effects and potential remedies. In J. Katzmann (Ed.), *Securing our children's future: New approaches to juvenile justice and youth violence* (pp. 305–337). Washington DC: The Brookings Institution.

Smith, A. (2007, January 19). Cyber bullying affecting 17% of teachers, poll finds. *The Guardian.* Retrieved January 20, 2007, from http://www.education.guardian.co.uk.

Smith, P., Mahdavi, J., Carvalho, M., & Tippett, N. (2006). An investigation into cyber bullying, its forms, awareness and impact, and the relationship between age and gender in cyber bullying. A report to the Anti-Bullying Alliance. Retrieved December 16, 2006, from http://www.dfes.gov.uk/research/data/uploadfiles/RBX03-06.pdf.

Smith, P. K., & Sharp, S. (1994). *Bullying at school.* London: Routledge.

Smith, P. K., Talamelli, L., Cowie, H., Naylor, P., & Chauhan, P. (2004). Profiles of non-victims, escaped victims, continuing victims and new victims of school bullying (2004). *British Journal of Educational Psychology, 74*, 565–581.

Social networking sites confound schools (2007, January). *E-School News, 10*(1), p. 1.

Social networking sites: Online friendships can mean offline peril (2006, April 3). Retrieved April 3, 2006, from www.fbi.gov/page2/april06/socialnetworking040306.htm.

Stevenson v. Martin County Bd. of Educ., 3 Fed. Appx. 25 (4th Cir. 2001).

Storch, E. A., Lewin, A. B., Silverstein, J. H., Heidgerken, A. D., Strawser, M. S., Baumeister, A., & Geffken, G. R. (2004a). Peer victimization and psychosocial adjustment in children with type 1 diabetes. *Clinical Pediatrics, 43*, 467–471.

Storch, E. A., Lewin, A. B., Silverstein, J. H., Heidgerken, A. D., Strawser, M. S., Baumeister, A., & Geffken, G. R. (2004b). Social-psychological correlates of peer victimization in children with endocrine disorders. *Journal of Pediatrics, 145*, 784–784.

Sudnow, D. (1967). *Passing on: The social organization of dying.* Englewood Cliffs, NJ: Prentice-Hall.

Sullivan, B. (2006, August 9). Cyber bullying newest threat to kids. Retrieved August 10, 2006, from http://www.msnbc.msn.com/id/14272228/.

Sutton, J. Smith, P. K., & Swettenham, J. (1999a). Bullying and "theory of mind": A critique of the "social skills deficit" view of anti-social behaviour. *Social Development, 8*, 117–127.

Sutton, J. Smith, P. K., & Swettenham, J. (1999b). Social cognition and bullying: Social inadequacy or skilled manipulation? *British Journal of Developmental Psychology, 17*, 435–450.

Swartz, J. (2005, March 7). Schoolyard bullies get nastier online. *USA Today*, p. 01a.

Swearer, S. M., Grills, A. E., Haye, K. M., & Cary, P. T. (2004). Internalizing problems in students involved in bullying and victimization: Implications for intervention. In D. L. Espelage & S. M. Swearer (Eds.), *Bullying in American schools: A social-ecological perspective on prevention and intervention* (pp. 63–83). Mahwah, NJ: Lawrence Erlbaum.

Swinford, S. (2006, June 4). Focus: The school bully is moving into cyberspace. Retrieved June 4, 2006, from http://www.timesonline.co.uk/article/o,,2087-2209828,00.html.

Take charge: Teen survey results. Retrieved August 9, 2006, from http://www.cox.com/takecharge/survey_results.asp.

Tenn. Code Ann. § 49-6-1015 (2006).

Tex. Educ. Code § 25.0341 (2006).

Thibaut, J. W., & Kelley, H. H. (1959). *The social psychology of groups.* Oxford, England: Wiley.

Thompson, D. Whitney, I., & Smith, P. (1993). Bullying of children with special needs in mainstream schools. *Support for Learning, 9,* 103–106.

Tinker v. Des Moines Independent Community School District, 383 U.S. 503 (1969).

United States Department of Justice (2006). Model acceptable use policy for information technology resources in the schools. Retrieved July 21, 2006, from http://www.usdoj.gov/criminal/cybercrime/rules/acceptableUsePolicy.htm.

Unnever, J. (2001). *Roanoke city project on bullying.* Final report of the Roanoke school-based partnership bullying study. Unpublished manuscript.

Unnever, J. D., & Cornell, D. G. (2003). The culture of bullying in middle school. *Journal of School Violence, 2*(2), 5–27.

U.S. Const., Amend. XIV.

Van der Wal, M. F., de Wit, C. A. M., & Hirasing, R. A. (2003). Psychosocial health among young victims and offenders of direct and indirect bullying. *Pediatrics, 111,* 1312–1317. http://video.google.com/videoplay?docid=1384277706451157121&q=white+and+nerdy (2006, September 19).

16 V.S.A. § 11 (2006).

W. Va. Code § 18-2C-2 (2006).

Walsh, D. (2004). *Why do they act that way?: A survival guide to the adolescent brain for you and your teen.* New York: Free Press.

Walsh, D., Gentile, D., Walsh, E., & Bennett, N. (2006).11th annual Mediawise video game report card. Retrieved December 4, 2006, from http://www.media-family.org/research/report_vgrc_2006.shtml.

Watt, N. (2006, May 17). "Happy slapping" spreads in London: Random victims get videotaped while being assaulted on streets. Retrieved May 17, 2006, from http://abcnews.go.com/Nightline/print?id=1972548.

Watts v. United States, 394 U.S. 705 (1969).

webopedia.com.

Whitney, I., Rivers, I., Smith, P., & Sharp, S. (1994). The Sheffield project: methodology and findings. In P. Smith & S. Sharp (Eds.), *School bullying: Insights and perspectives* (pp. 20–56). London: Routledge.

Whitney, I., & Smith, P. K. (1993). A survey of the nature and extent of bullying in junior/middle and secondary schools. *Educational Research, 35,* 3–25.

Willard, N. (2005a). *A parent's guide to cyberbullying and cyberthreats: Addressing online social cruelty.* Center for Responsible Internet Use. Retrieved August 3, 2006, from http://www.cyberbully.org/docs/cbct.parents.pdf.

Willard, N. (2005b). *An educator's guide to cyberbullying.* Center for Safe and Responsible Internet Use. Retrieved September 15, 2005, from http://www.cyberbully.org/docs/cpct.educators.pdf.

Willard, N. (2006). *Cyber bullying and cyberthreats: Responding to the challenge of online social cruelty, threats, and distress.* Eugene, OR: Center for Safe and Responsible Internet Use.

Williams, K., Cheung, C. K. T., & Choi, W. (2000). Cyberostracism: Effects of being ignored over the Internet. *Journal of Personality and Social Psychology, 79,* 748–762.

Williams, K., Harkins, S., & Latané, B. (1981). Identifiability as a deterrent to social loafing: Two cheering experiments. *Journal of Personality and Social Psychology, 40,* 303–311.

Williams, K. R., & Guerra, N. G. (2006). Prevalence and predictors of Internet bullying. Unpublished manuscript, University of California at Riverside.

Wing, C. (2005, November). Young Canadians in a wired world. Retrieved August 3, 2006, from http://www.media-awareness.ca.

Wolak, J., Mitchell, K., & Finkelhor, D. (2006). Online victimization of youth: Five years later. Retrieved August 3, 2006, from http://www.unh.edu/ccrc/pdf/CV138.pdf

word IQ (2006). Retrieved July 17, 2006, from: http//www.wordiq.com/definition/Restorative_justice.

Ybarra, M. L., & Mitchell, K. J. (2004). Online aggressor/targets, aggressors, and targets: A comparison of associated youth characteristics. *Journal of Child Psychology and Psychiatry, 45,* 1308–1316.

Ybarra, M. L., Mitchell, K. J., Wolak, J., & Finkelhor, D. (2006). Examining characteristics and associated distress related to Internet harassment: Findings from the second youth internet safety survey. *Pediatrics, 118,* 1169–1177.

YouTube (2006, August 30). In *Wikipedia, The Free Encyclopedia.* Retrieved August 30, 2006, from http://en.wikipedia.org/w/index.php?title=YouTube&oldid=72890340.

Yuan, L. (2006, April 30). Social networking goes mobile. *The Kansas City Star,* H16.

Yude, C., Goodman, R., & McConachie, H. (1998). Peer problems of children with hemiplegia in mainstream primary schools. *Journal of Child Psychology and Psychiatry, 39,* 533–541.

Žaborskis, A., Cirtautienè, L., & Žemaitienè, N. (2005). Bullying in Lituanian schools in 1994–2004. Medicina (Kaunas), *41*(7).

Zayas, A. (2006, August 28). Do online deaths prompt teens to suicide? *St. Petersburg Times.* Retrieved August 28, 2006, from http://www.sptimes.com/2006/08/28/Tampabay/Do_online_death_dialo_shtml.

Index